FORESHADOWING THE GREAT REBELLION

FORESHADOWING THE GREAT REBELLION

FORESHADOWING THE GREAT REBELLION
The Vellore Revolt, 1806

K. A. Manikumar

With a Foreword by
G. Viswanathan

Orient BlackSwan

FORESHADOWING THE GREAT REBELLION: THE VELLORE REVOLT, 1806

ORIENT BLACKSWAN PRIVATE LIMITED

Registered Office
3-6-752 Himayatnagar, Hyderabad 500 029, Telangana, India
e-mail: centraloffice@orientblackswan.com

Other Offices
Bengaluru, Chennai, Guwahati, Hyderabad, Kolkata,
Mumbai, New Delhi, Noida, Patna, Visakhapatnam

© Vellore Institute of Technology (VIT University), Vellore 2021
First published by Orient Blackswan Private Limited 2021

ISBN 978-93-5442-118-1

Typeset in
Minion Pro 11/13
by Le Studio Graphique, Gurgaon 122 007

033592

Printed in India at
Akash Press, New Delhi 110 020

Published by
Orient Blackswan Private Limited
3-6-752 Himayatnagar, Hyderabad 500 029, Telangana, India
e-mail: info@orientblackswan.com

CONTENTS

TABLES AND FIGURES

Tables

Figures

Glossary

ashoph	lord lieutenant
batta	allowance
chunam	limestone
Coast Army	the Madras Army, as it was known in England
daroga	an Indian police officer
Dheen, Dheen	war cry of Muslims; '*Dheen*' or '*Deen*' means faith
dhoot, dhoot	get lost, or 'away, away!'
dubash	a translator or interpreter, proficient in more than two languages of India
fakir	a religious mendicant of Islamic faith that wandered about the country and subsisted on alms
ferengi	the term used for a foreigner, specifically, a European
galloper gun	horse-drawn gun attached to cavalry regiments
Gentoo	the term used to distinguish a Hindu from a Muslim; from the Portuguese '*gentio*', meaning 'heathen'
ghurry	water clock
glacis	a slope originally designed to protect a fortification, as vertical walls could be easily smashed by artillery guns
harkara	informer

havildar	non-commissioned officer, corresponding to sergeant
jaghir	an assignment for the support of any public establishment, particularly of a military nature
jagirdar	holder of a *jaghir*
jamabandhi	settlement of the revenue amount assessed
jamedar	an Indian officer holding the title of the second in a company of sepoys, after subedar
kafer	turncoat
kalyana mandapam	marriage hall
killadar	commandant of a fort
lascar	equivalent to an artillery man (gun-lascar)
magazine	a room for keeping explosives and gunpowder in a fort
mahal	palace
maidan	field
mirasidar	landholder through inheritance; from '*mirazi*' meaning 'land'
mitta	a farm of several villages, smaller in size than a *mirazi*
mittadar	a person who possesses a *mitta*
munshi	writer, record keeper or language teacher in colonial India
musnud	throne
naik	head of a small body of soldiers in the British Indian army, equal to the rank of a corporal (non-commissioned officer)
nakhand	laughter
nattar	the ruling class with the power and authority to manage community resources in Tamil country
nawab	viceroy of the Mughal emperor

pagoda	gold coin in use during the pre-British period; Rs 3.50 equalled 1 pagoda
palayam	'little kingdom'; fiefdom of a Palayakkarar
parachery	living quarters of the Parayars
pettai	a suburb
Palayakkarar	a warrior chieftain of south India, who held authority over a *palayam*, but was feudatory to a greater sovereign
private	a soldier of the lowest military rank
ryotwari	the system under which land tax began to be collected directly from cultivators, eliminating all middlemen; first introduced by Thomas Munro
salam	the respectful way of greeting used by Muslims, by bowing with their right hand on their forehead
sardar	an Indian officer
subedar	the highest-ranking Indian officer in the Company's army
subha	a province
tapal	post or mail
thana	police circle
tindal	a petty officer, below the rank of corporal in the army
topee	hat or cap
topee-wallah	hat-wearer
urumaal	a headgear made of cloth
Valangai–Idangai	*valangai* (right hand) and *idangai* (left hand) are terms denoting two opposing and conflicting social groups in Tamil Nadu—right-hand groups comprised castes engaged in agriculture, while trading and artisan castes formed the left-hand division

vellam	jaggery
vibhuti	sacred ash
zamindar	a tax farmer for the state
zamindari	the estate of a *zamindar*
zenana	women's quarters

FOREWORD

The rebellion of 1857 has been studied from different angles and etched in the memory of the people of India as an important anti-imperial movement. The Vellore Rebellion of 1806, which has yet to be added as a glorious event in the early pages of the history of the Indian national movement, has not been studied from the Indian perspective and hence, has not been given its due place.

The Vellore region has the unique distinction of nurturing and preserving its pluralistic traditions. The solidarity and unity displayed by warriors of the Hindu and Muslim communities in 1806 have established this culture of people belonging to two different religious denominations living in amity and harmony in this part of the country. The Urdu-speaking Muslims have integrated into Tamil society to such an extent that many distinguished speakers and poets of Tamil are our Muslim brethren from the district.

Scholars and writers, while coining dubious sobriquets on Vellore, have conveniently forgotten to relate the other side of the story, that is, how the Vellore region was continuously ravaged by the invading armies of the Nayaks, the Sultans, the Mughals, the Marathas and, later, the British. These devastating invasions destabilised the region politically and impoverished the populace economically. Yet, when conditions, political and economic, stabilised, this battered region was put on the rails of development.

Schools and colleges established by European missionaries provided the base, but they were inadequate for the challenges faced, and disproportionate to the aspirations of the people. Thanks to the philanthropy and munificence of notable citizens of the district like C. Ayyadurai Mudaliyar (Sundathur) and C. Abdul Hakeem (Melvisharam), who vied with each other in dispensing charity, the Vellore region began to register relatively unprecedented growth and prosperity.

The Vellore Institute of Technology (VIT), an institute bearing the prefix of Vellore, founded in 1984 (then, Vellore Engineering College), spurned the donations of land offered in return for naming the institution after one individual or the other. The sole intention was to christen the institute after the historic town of Vellore and thereby cherish and perpetuate its name and fame. So, during the bicentenary year (2006) of the Vellore Rebellion (1806), we in VIT University brought out a commemorative volume to highlight this marvellous act of patriotism displayed by Indian soldiers at Vellore Fort that transcended barriers of caste, religion and region.

Since the publication of this book, the author, Professor K. A. Manikumar, has taken painstaking efforts to collect new data from the National Archives of Scotland, Edinburgh, and the British Library, London. Now, this enlarged and comprehensive volume is being published in association with Orient BlackSwan. I congratulate Professor Manikumar for establishing that all characteristics of the Great Rebellion of 1857 were foreshadowed in the Vellore Uprising.

This book is dedicated to those who, while bravely fighting the British in 1806, laid down their precious lives for the cause of the nation.

G. Viswanathan
Chancellor, VIT

PREFACE

By the early 1790s, it became clear to the British East India Company that it could never co-exist with vigorous Indian regimes like Tipu's. Tipu's secret correspondence with the French and the generals representing the Directory, promising friendship, alarmed the British. British secret agents intercepted some of these letters and handed them over to Governor General Richard Wellesley. Wellesley, who had already drawn up his plan to invade Tipu's territories, emphasised the possibility of Napoleon's forces heading towards India from Egypt and joining their ally in Mysore. Wellesley stormed Tipu's capital, Srirangapatnam, in 1799. Tipu was killed in battle, and the kingdom was handed over to the Wodeyar king of Mysore. After the fall of Tipu, his brother, Colonel Arthur Wellesley was given the responsibility of removing the family of the dead sultan to the fort of Vellore. Tipu's wives, sons, daughters-in-law, grandchildren and other close relatives, numbering forty-two, were sent to 'the swampy and largely uninhabited place', Vellore.[1]

Francis Buchanan, during the course of his journey through south India, visited the buildings being prepared for the families of Hyder and Tipu. He wrote,

> They are built with accommodations similar to those used by Mussulmans; and the architecture is more elegant, and the apartments are more commodious than those in the palace of Seringapatam. The building would have been still more elegant, had not the custom of those who were to occupy it

---

[1] Partha Chatterjee, *The Black Hole of Empire: History of a Global Practice of Power* (Princeton: Princeton University Press, 2012), 90–92.

required long dead walls, and narrow stair cases, with other
things that by us are considered as deformities.[2]

Starting with the first batch of people brought on 19 June 1799,
this 'retreat' from Mysore was led by Tipu's eldest son, Fateh Hyder
Bahadur, and was accomplished in various stages. By 1801, along
with them, their hangers-on and innumerable servants, forming
the 'Mysoreans in Exile', numbering about 3,000, had settled
around Vellore Fort.[3] For about five years, there was calm. Then,
suddenly erupted the armed insurgency.

I

At 2 a.m. on 10 July 1806, the Indian soldiers at Vellore Fort, where
the family of Tipu Sultan was interned, raised the standard of
revolt. About 500 native soldiers stormed the European quarters
in the fort and shot down white officers and soldiers. The rest
split themselves into several groups and, after killing the sentries,
took control of the pickets, magazines and ammunition. The
bayonets of native sepoys dripped the blood of English officers
and European troops onto Vellore's soil. They hoisted the Mysore
sultan's tiger standard and held the garrison under their control.
They were unchallenged until Colonel Robert Gillespie, stationed
at Arcot, 25 kilometres away, arrived at 9 a.m. with a squadron
of the Nineteenth Dragoons and the Seventh Madras Cavalry.
Gillespie's presence spurred the Englishmen to rally behind him,
relying solely on their bayonets. Soon, the galloper guns arrived
and the gate was blown open. The dragoons, supported by the
Madras Cavalry, then charged into the fort and wreaked vengeance
on the mutineers. Hundreds of fleeing soldiers were caught and

---

[2] Francis Buchanan, *A Journey from Madras Through the Countries of Mysore,
Canara and Malabar*, vol. 3 (1807; repr., New Delhi: Asian Educational Services,
1988), 464.
[3] Denys Forrest, *Tiger of Mysore: The Life and Death of Tipu Sultan* (Bombay:
Allied Publishers, 1970), 347–49.

butchered, while many were taken prisoner in different parts of the country over the next few days. It is probable that several hundred native soldiers (unfortunately, we do not have the precise number) were massacred after British authority was restored in the fort. This event, recorded in history, is variously described as the Vellore Massacre, the Vellore Insurgency, the Vellore Mutiny or the Vellore Revolt, according to one's ideological leanings.

The actual reasons behind the Vellore Uprising are not available to us—for no native soldier has left behind testimony, and we have to decipher their motives only from imperial sources. We may never know to what extent the rebellion was instigated by Tipu's descendants; but they were implicated in the 'conspiracy'. Even before the complicity of the princes was established by the British, they were exiled to Calcutta. Five of the princes' retainers, after a summary trial in Chittoor, were either sentenced to death or banished to Penang. The infamous order regarding the new headdress, which triggered the revolt in the first place, was rescinded. Both the governor of Madras and the commander-in-chief, with his adjutant-general, were removed by order of the Court of Directors. The 'ringleaders' in the native infantry were executed while the rest were, for tactical reasons, shown clemency and admonished. The Company government commended the bravery displayed by Gillespie and other European officials in quelling the rebellion, and awarded them promotions and pecuniary benefits. Even the turncoat, Mustapha Beg, was given a cash award. The First and the Twenty-Third Regiments, which indulged in mutiny, were struck off the army's rolls and replaced by two new regiments, the Twenty-Fourth and the Twenty-Fifth.

II

In the perception of British historians, the Vellore Revolt cast a slur on the Madras soldiers who were long considered unswerving in their loyalty. For E. G. Phythian-Adams, the 'Vellore Mutiny was the only stain which had sullied his [the Madras soldier's] loyalty during the Madras Army's 200 years of service'.[4] Even when the Bengal Army 'mutinied' in 1857, and revolts spread across the barracks of north India, the Madras Regiment was not affected. This would imply that the provocation for the uprising of 1806 was severe.[5] The new military regulations, forbidding Hindu sepoys wearing caste marks and earrings, and directing Muslim soldiers to shave their beards and trim their moustaches when in uniform, besides prescribing new leather headgear for native soldiers, were said to have led to the rebellion of the Madras Army. But, undoubtedly, they were only a trigger. A major uprising could not have been caused by such trifles, however provocative. The predisposing causes have to be sought elsewhere. Minor military outbursts in the form of disobedience at parade were not uncommon in the Madras Army, when there were arrears in pay for many months. But these never resulted in bloodshed and loss of life. The Vellore Revolt of 1806, by contrast, was a bloody affair resulting in massacres on both sides, the ruler and the ruled. When the Great Rebellion of 1857 broke out half a century later, Karl Marx called it a failure of the 'divide and rule' policy. He further observed, 'It is the first time that sepoy regiments have murdered their European officers, the Mussulmans and Hindus, renouncing their mutual antipathies, have combined against their common masters'.[6] Marx's observation is equally applicable to the Vellore Revolt, which had all the forebodings of the Great Rebellion.

In British imperial history, this revolt is recorded as the Vellore Massacre. Historians of British India incorporated it into history textbooks as early as 1811,[7] as a squalid episode, overplaying the killing of Europeans. The narrative of British historians depicted the slain European officials and sepoys as martyrs for the cause of Great Britain, while dubbing the rebel Indian soldiers as gangsters,

---

[4] E. G. Phythian-Adams, *The Madras Soldier, 1746–1946* (Madras: Government Press, 1948), 57.

[5] Phythian-Adams, *Madras Soldier*, 57.

[6] Quoted in Ainslee T. Embree, *1857 in India: Mutiny or War of Independence?*, Problems in Asian Civilisations Series (Boston: D. C. Heath, 1963), 20.

[7] John Malcolm, *The Political History of British India* (1811; repr., Delhi: Discovery Publishing House, 1986).

mutineers, betrayers and traitors.[8] John W. Kaye in *A History of the Sepoy War in India, 1857–1858* (1881) and William F. Butler in *A Narrative of the Historical Events Connected with the Sixty-Ninth Regiment* (1870) asserted that the behaviour of British soldiers in India was civilised and chivalrous. Butler, as we will see later, relished the reprisals which Gillespie unleashed at Vellore.

Military official-turned-historian W. J. Wilson's *History of the Madras Army* (1882) is rich in detail. The events before the outbreak of revolt and the restoration of British authority in Vellore Fort and other cantonments of south India have been narrated by Wilson. However, he chose not to deal with the causes of the uprising, but only to communicate the causes of disaffection as identified by the commission of enquiry and the Court of Directors. Scholars, writers and even history researchers in south India have generously used his data to narrate the eventful incident of 1806 in Vellore.

Kaye was fully convinced that the leadership of the princes was the decisive factor for the mutiny and added that the grievances of the Indian officers created the conditions for the Muslim conspiracy. S. S. Furnell, who documented the course of mutiny in his *The Mutiny of Vellore*, fragments of which are available at the Tamil Nadu Archives, attributed the cause of mutiny to the conspiracy by Tipu's descendants.[9]

The *Oxford History of India* (1923), in a passing reference, asserted that 'the childish regulations about the sepoys' dress and sectarian marks were more than enough to account for the tragedy, without seeking any further explanation'.[10] In the *Cambridge*

---

[8] James Mill and H. H. Wilson, *The History of British India, from 1805 to 1835*, vol. 7 (London: James Madden, 1840); John Clark Marshman, *The History of India: From Earliest Period to the Close of Lord Dalhousie's Administration*, vol. 2 (London: Longmans, Green, Reader & Dyer, 1867); H. G. Keene, *History of India: From the Earliest Times to the End of the Nineteenth Century*, vol. 1 (Edinburgh: John Grant, 1906).

[9] S. S. Furnell, *The Mutiny of Vellore*. Thirty pages of Furnell's analysis are available at the Tamil Nadu Archives, but there is no clue yet as to his identity and no details about the total number of pages. In A. D. Cameron's PhD thesis, submitted to the University of Edinburgh, the year and the place of publication of the book are given as 1840 and Madras, respectively.

[10] Quoted in A. D. Cameron, 'The Vellore Mutiny' (PhD thesis, University of Edinburgh, 1984), 330.

History of India (1929) there was hardly any discussion on the Vellore Revolt.[11]

In post-Independence India, Indian historians, concerned as they were with the north Indian regions, dealt with happenings in southern India in a dismissive manner. While 1857 was glorified, little mention was made of the early revolts against British rule in south India. Two articles on the Vellore Revolt by Indian authors C. S. Srinivasachari ('The Vellore Mutiny of 1806: A New Study of its Origin', 1948) and Haripado Chaudhuri ('The Vellore Mutiny: A Reappraisal', 1955), published in the *Proceedings of the Indian History Congress* and *Modern Review*, respectively, did not break any new ground. While the former was a brief survey of some previous interpretations of the causes of the revolt, the latter subscribed to the view that the European missionaries 'riding roughshod over the religious sentiments of the people had provoked the Revolt'.[12]

It is only in the second half of the twentieth century, particularly after the centenary celebrations of the Great Rebellion of 1857, that there was a movement to recognise the importance of the revolt at Vellore. Surendra Nath Sen in his *Eighteen Fifty-Seven* (1957) described the events at Vellore in the Preface as the first major offence to the religious prejudices of the sepoys. R. C. Majumdar in his *History and Culture of the Indian People* (1963) stated, 'One of the most serious expressions of discontent and disaffection, which bears a very close resemblance to the mutiny of 1857, so far as the genesis is concerned, was the mutiny at Vellore in 1806. It was caused by what the sepoys regarded as an affront to their religion.'[13]

In the southern Indian context, the princely rulers and Palayakkarars who revolted against the English in the initial phase of the East India Company's rule are portrayed passionately as heroes in textbooks and popular histories. The tenacity and heroism of chieftains like Puli Thevan, Kattabomman and the Marudhu brothers are celebrated in Tamil folk ballads. By contrast,

---

[11] Cameron, 'Vellore Mutiny', 330.

[12] Cameron, 'Vellore Mutiny', 335.

[13] R. C. Majumdar, *History and Culture of the Indian People*, vol. 9 (Bombay: Bharatiya Vidya Bhavan, 1963), 428.

incidents of collective resistance, involving a mass of people, but in which individuals do not have any decisive roles, are hardly found. In all probability, the Vellore Mutiny of 1806 has not been given a place in the annals of popular resistance in India as a result of this personality-oriented history.

K. K. Pillay presented a paper titled 'The Causes of the Vellore Mutiny' at the annual session of the Indian History Congress in 1957, the centenary year of the Great Rebellion. In his presentation, he concluded that the principal reason behind the mutiny was the political ambition of the members of Tipu's family. The intrigues of the aggrieved Palayakkarars strengthened it, while the dress regulation provided the pretext, he added.[14] Tamil scholar N. Sanjeevi's *Velur Puratchi* (1956), commemorating the 150th anniversary of the revolt, narrated the course of the mutiny and brought it to the knowledge of Tamil scholars. K. Rajayyan was the first Indian historian to explore the early resistance of the princes and the Palayakkarars. For Rajayyan, the Vellore Mutiny was probably not an event of the same magnitude as the revolt of the Marudhu brothers (1801) in Sivagangai. He did not, therefore, pursue an in-depth study of this event.[15] P. Chinnayan, building on his doctoral dissertation, provided an authoritative account in his book, *The Vellore Mutiny* (1983). But his history is descriptive, based on the accounts of military officials-turned-historians, and lacks a full-length analysis of the outbreak and suppression of the revolt.

III

There are two important PhD theses on the Vellore Mutiny; one, Samuelraj Pakkianathan's 'The Mutiny at Vellore and Related Agitations, 1806–1807' and the other, Alan Douglas Cameron's. Samuelraj's is the earliest well-researched work, a doctoral

---

[14] K. K. Pillay, 'The Causes of the Vellore Mutiny', *Proceedings of the Indian History Congress* 20 (1957), 311.

[15] K. Rajayyan, *South Indian Rebellion: The First War of Independence 1800–1801* (Mysore: Rao & Raghavan, 1971).

dissertation presented to the University of Saskatchewan, Canada, written as early as 1971. In this thesis, he is concerned more about the incidence of mutiny and other related agitations and hence does not analyse the mutiny itself. In his view, the new turbans and dress code were the decisive factors for the mutiny. He does not give any credence to the idea that the Mysore princes were responsible for the mutiny.[16]

Cameron's PhD thesis, titled 'The Vellore Mutiny', submitted to the University of Edinburgh (1984), is comprehensive and analytical.[17] Cameron, pointing out scholars' neglect of the Vellore Mutiny, attributes this to the perception of the whole event as an isolated incident occurring in the presidency, which according to him, was becoming a backwater, as the main activities of Company had begun to centre around Bengal.[18] He has argued that the Vellore Mutiny was a forerunner of the 'far more wide-spread events of 1857 and 1858'. According to him, the parallel between the events of 1806 and 1857 can be drawn if the phrase 'greased cartridge', the powder keg that resulted in 1857's Great Rebellion, is substituted with 'leather cockade' in the narrative, and the role of agent provocateurs, played by Bahadur Shah and Nana Sahib in 1857, is assigned to the Mysore princes.

R. E. Frykenberg, in an article titled 'New Light on the Vellore Mutiny' (1986), regretted that there was no comprehensive study yet on the Vellore Mutiny. As someone who had worked on Christianity in south India, Frykenberg pointed out how nearly 7,000 converted Christians were found in several new settlements that were coming up around Tirunelveli around this time.[19] Calling

---

[16] Samuelraj Pakkianathan, 'The Mutiny at Vellore and Related Agitations, 1806–1807' (PhD thesis, University of Saskatchewan, 1971). Despite my best efforts, this thesis could not be accessed. This review is based on the one done by Cameron.

[17] This thesis was accessed during a visit to the University of Edinburgh, as a part of visits to the British Library, London, and the National Archives of Scotland, Edinburgh, sponsored by the Indian Council of Historical Research, New Delhi.

[18] Cameron, 'Vellore Mutiny', 322.

[19] R. E. Frykenberg, 'New Light on the Vellore Mutiny', in *East India Company Studies: Papers Presented to Professor Sir Cyril Philips*, ed. Kenneth Ballhatchet and John Harrison (Hong Kong: Asian Research Service, 1986), 209.

upon scholars to study the subject afresh based on new sources, he observed that neither the local Muslims nor non-Muslims would have failed to notice the conversion movement that was progressing rapidly in Tirunelveli.[20]

Maya Gupta, in 'Vellore Mutiny, July 1806', and Devadas Moodley, in 'Vellore 1806: The Meanings of Mutiny', working with material available at the India Office Library, London, attempted to provide analytical accounts of the mutiny. Moodley, emphasising multiple causes in his article, added to these the prevailing agrarian distress, a result of continuous drought in the Madras Presidency, from 1805 leading to the terrible famine in 1807, as a cause for the escalation of discontent among the soldiers, many of whom had been drawn from land-owning and landless labouring agrarian households. Gupta bought the imperialist argument that the Indian soldiers' 'avarice for wealth overshadowed the higher objective and their leaders appeared to have little control over them',[21] forgetting for a moment that looting during a war has been a common practice of victorious armies throughout recorded history. Their accounts are wanting, in the contextualisation of the revolt as well as in the narration of the conflagration in its totality.

James W. Hoover, in his monograph, *Men Without Hats: Dialogue, Discipline and Discontent in the Madras Army, 1806–1807* (2007), provided a detailed chronological account of events that led to the revolt of the sepoys. He tried to show how the cultural arrogance of the British officers in the Madras Army precipitated the Vellore Mutiny. His argument that the Vellore Mutiny and related disturbances in several cantonments in south India were apolitical in nature is untenable. Hoover, like many others, failed to contextualise the revolt.

Recently, Sabyasachi Dasgupta's *In Defence of Honour and Justice: Sepoy Rebellions in the Nineteenth Century* (2015) and Ferdinand Mount's *The Tears of the Rajas: Mutiny, Money and*

---

[20] Mudalur, a Christian settlement with Nadar converts, came up as early as 1799.
[21] Maya Gupta, 'Vellore Mutiny, July 1806', in *Defying Death: Struggles Against Imperialism and Feudalism*, ed. Maya Gupta and Amit Kumar Gupta (New Delhi: Tulika, 2001), 24.

Marriage in India 1805–1905 (2015) have dealt with the Vellore Mutiny. Dasgupta summarises the essential facts of the mutiny in Vellore in seven pages. He has quoted the findings of the enquiry commission headed by Major General John Pater. But his inference that the mutiny proved that it was possible for the Madras Army to dissociate the Indian soldiers from their social moorings is not elaborated on. As for the book authored by Mount, it dwells on the Vellore Mutiny in forty-five pages. The author brings to light many new facts, putting the eyewitness accounts to best use. He argues that the fear of religious conversion, born out of people's past experiences, played a crucial role. Citing evidence in *Secret Department Sundries*, he points out how the Indian officers, not reconciling to Company rule, were in touch with both native officers in other garrisons as well as with the displaced chieftains' descendants in the south, with Maratha princes, deposed rulers of Hyderabad, and the French in Pondicherry.

Mount reminds us that as British rule was spreading across southern India, there was less and less chance of employment with native princes. Though the Company's service conditions were bad, the need of the hour was not to lose the only scope of earning a livelihood to protect one's family. The Company government was equally anxious not to lose the soldiers of south India, who, according to them, had been helpful in establishing the Company Raj. These aspects are examined in this book from the testimonies provided by the rebels while deposing before the enquiry commissions. The positive and negative roles of caste and religious factors are also dealt with in order to unravel the decisive causes that made Indian soldiers and officers, cutting across all boundaries—regional, caste, religious and linguistic— fight against the imperial British.

This book begins with an introduction to the Company Raj, the Madras Army and the garrison fort in Vellore (Chapter 1). Chapter 2, while dealing with the revolt, traces the course of the soldiers' insurrection up to its final suppression. The actions of the British administration in instituting enquiries, conducting proceedings and awarding punishments to the guilty and incentives to the loyalists based on their findings are discussed in

Chapter 3. Multiple causes, such as the grievances of the soldiers and the socioeconomic and political factors that provided the objective conditions for the outbreak of the uprising, are analysed in Chapter 4. Concluding remarks are made in Chapter 5.

Acknowledgements

D r G. Viswanathan, the chancellor of VIT, mooted the idea of bringing out a volume to commemorate the bicentenary of the Vellore Revolt (1806) and commissioned me for the task in 2006. The commemoration committee, comprising the venerable late parliamentarian Era Chezhian; former vice-chancellors M. Anandakrishnan of Anna University, Chennai, V. Shanmugasundaram of Manonmaniam Sundaranar University, Tirunelveli, P. Radhakrishnan of VIT, and V. P. Narayanan of M. G. R. Medical College and Research Institute (Deemed University); the late Thanjaivanan, former assistant director, Doordarshan Kendra, Chennai; and historian A. R. Venkatachalapathy, gave me a free hand in conducting research. In pursuing this task, the entire proceedings of the government of Madras, available in the Secret Department, which were later copied into twelve volumes and kept at the Tamil Nadu Archives,[1] were thoroughly consulted. All the published works were also consulted (see Bibliography). J. Shanmuga Raja, currently assistant professor of history at Madurai Kamaraj University, who was my research assistant for the project, did a thorough job of collecting data for the book at the Tamil Nadu Archives. I owe a debt of gratitude to David Ludden, New York University, USA, for arranging to send me an unpublished paper by Devadas Moodley and to Andrew Wyatt, University of Bristol, UK, for sending me photocopies of important material relevant to my book in the first instance. My thanks are due to K. Vijay Kumar, IPS, then additional

---

[1] H. H. Dodwell, *Report on the Madras Records, 1670–1856* (Madras: Government Press, 1934), 35.

director-general of police, government of Tamil Nadu, for putting in a word to I. S. Peter, then principal of the Police Training College, Vellore, to grant me permission to photograph the buildings inside the fort, to which the latter obliged, and to Puduvai Ilavenil for his professional photography.

The book, titled *Vellore Revolt, 1806*, was published by VIT in 2007. It was well received and there was a good review in the magazine, *Frontline*. The then chairman of the Indian Council of Historical Research, New Delhi, Sabyasachi Bhattacharya, sanctioned a foreign travel grant that facilitated my material collection at the British Library, London, and the National Archives of Scotland, Edinburgh. My visit to these places in 2009 gave me the privilege of accessing the Home Miscellaneous Series and the Madras Secret Proceedings, the Bentinck Papers, Agnew Papers, Minto Manuscripts and Munro Collections at the India Office Library, London. At the National Library of Scotland, I was able to consult diaries and private papers of discharged Scottish officials of the East India Company, and at the Edinburgh University Library, a number of books, including a memoir of Colonel Robert Gillespie, and a PhD thesis on the Vellore Mutiny by Professor Alan Cameron.

Since then, I have expanded the story of the 1806 uprising at Vellore using the material collected in London and Edinburgh. The chancellor of VIT, Dr G. Viswanathan, suggested that the publication of an expanded version of the book could be a collaborative venture between VIT and reputed publishers, so that the book could reach the target audience. Accordingly, this book has been brought out in English, in association with Orient BlackSwan. I am most thankful to the chancellor and to Orient BlackSwan for making this possible. I owe my special gratitude to A. R. Venkatachalapathy for graciously sparing his precious time to offer insightful comments on the preliminary draft of this book. I will be failing in my duty if I do not thank the anonymous referees whose suggestions helped to reorganise and rewrite it with a view to improving the content and readability of the book.

1

COMPANY, ARMY AND FORT

> The government of an exclusive company of merchants is, perhaps, the worst of all governments for any country whatever ... It is the interest of the East India Company, considered as sovereigns, that the European goods which are carried to their Indian dominions should be sold there as cheap as possible; and that the Indian goods which are brought from thence should bring there as good a price, or should be sold there as dear as possible. But the reverse of this is their interest as merchants. As sovereigns, their interest is exactly the same with that of the country which they govern. As merchants their interest is directly opposite to that interest.
>
> —Adam Smith (1852)[1]

Discrimination against natives in any colonial country provides stimulus to the growth of the feeling amongst the local people that they belong to one group, as their rulers despise them as such.[2] The emergence of such a solidarity is indicative of the true beginning of nationhood.[3] It is imperative that we understand the widespread armed revolts in large parts of early colonial south India, including that of Vellore (1806), from this perspective. For such an understanding, background knowledge is a *sine qua non*, which this introduction attempts. The first section

---

[1] Adam Smith, *An Inquiry into the Nature and Causes of the Wealth of Nations* (London: T. Nelson & Sons, 1852), 264.

[2] William L. Holland, ed., *Asian Nationalism and the West* (New York: Macmillan, 1952), 358.

[3] William Howard Russell, *My Indian Mutiny Diary*, ed. Michael Edwardes (London: Cassell, 1957), xxiii.

contains a brief account of the establishment of the English East India Company's rule in south India. The second section deals with the Madras Army and its early revolts. The history and the striking features of the Vellore Fort, in which rebellion broke out in 1806, form the third section.

I

Company

The East India Company was established in 1600 as a response to the Dutch-Portuguese monopoly on the spice trade. Queen Elizabeth I granted monopoly rights to the Company to trade with India and bring goods to England. William Hawkins, who was familiar with Eastern trade and could speak Turkish, was sent as an emissary to the Mughal court in 1609, where he was well received. However, because the Portuguese warned Surat's merchants that admitting the English would mean war with them, Jahangir turned down Hawkins' petition for exclusive trading privileges. Without losing hope, the East India Company deputed another emissary, Sir Thomas Roe, in 1615. Roe succeeded in obtaining permission from the Viceroy of Gujarat, Prince Khurram (Shajahan) in 1618. The Company's headquarters were established at Surat, from where its president and council controlled its factories at Ahmedabad, Broach and Agra. In the meantime, the Company managed to establish a factory at Masulipatnam (1611). The twin objectives of the Company were 'to sell "broadcloth" to the affluent class and to buy at first hand the spices and the piece goods woven in the neighbourhoods'.[4]

The Company obtained from the Nayak of Chandragiri a grant of the town of Madraspatnam, close to the ruined Portuguese settlement of San Thome. The Company was permitted to build a fortified factory and to exercise administrative authority over

---

[4] See K. N. Chaudhuri, *The English East India Company: The Study of an Early Joint-Stock Company, 1600–1640* (London: Frank Cass, 1965) for further details.

the town in return for the payment of a small annual quit-rent. The original trading station moved to the settlement of Madras (Fort St George) in 1641. In 1652, it was made into a presidency, an administrative unit governed by a president.[5]

The Charter of 1683, while confirming the privileges permitted earlier, authorised the establishment of a judicature to hear mercantile and maritime suits. Professional judges were sent from England to dispense justice. In 1687, the Company set up a corporation and a mayor's court at Madras.[6]

At the start of the eighteenth century, the Company's presence in India was confined only to trading outposts spread across the three presidencies of Bombay, Madras and Calcutta, along the coast. By the middle of the eighteenth century, the Company had become one of the greatest mercantilist enterprises in the world and the Indian agents in its growing network of operations gained enormous wealth. The personal fortunes of the Company's staff, arising from private trading, which was not prohibited until the time of Lord Charles Cornwallis, were left in the care of trusted Indian agents who took to lending money to Europeans for trading purposes.[7]

In the initial phase of the Company's existence, instructions came from London advising its officials not to get embroiled in Indian politics. However, for the East India Company based in Madras and Bombay, influence with the nizam was considered vital. Therefore, the Company involved itself in the disputed successions to the *subha* (province) of the Deccan and to the Nawabi of the Carnatic. The nizam, as *quid pro quo*, was obliged to hand over to the English the Northern Circars in 1766. The French army's debacle at the end of the Third Carnatic War (1763) emboldened

---

[5] In 1688, the island of Bombay, part of the dowry of Infanta Catherine of Braganza on her marriage to Charles II, was granted to the Company. Bengal was created as an independent presidency (Fort William) only in 1715.

[6] The Corporation was created by a royal charter issued on 30 December 1687 by King James II on the advice of the governor of the East India Company, Josiah Child, on the model of the Dutch government in the East Indies.

[7] Burton Stein, *A History of India* (New Delhi: Oxford University Press, 2004), 205–07.

Company officials to initiate more political involvement and greater territorial expansion.[8]

From the 1760s onwards, the government of Britain started controlling the authority of the Company under the pretext of rooting out corruption and abuse of power. The Regulating Act of 1773 raised the governor of Bengal to the rank of governor general, to govern the entire territorial jurisdiction of the Company, and whose nomination was to be approved by the Crown in the future. The Supreme Court of India was established, to which judges were appointed by the Crown. In 1765, in the aftermath of Robert Clive's victory at the Battles of Plassey and Buxar, the Diwani administration of the provinces of Bengal, Bihar and Orissa, with all their wealth, was placed at the disposal of the Company.[9]

The territories that formed the Madras Presidency, administered by the traders of Leadenhall Street, were acquired during the turbulent years between 1766 and 1801.[10] The failure of Indian rulers to share Hyder's insight and their fear of his growing strength brought to naught all attempts to jointly resist the rising power of the Company. Cornwallis's defeat of Tipu Sultan in the Third Mysore War in 1792–93 became possible, not because of British troops but because of soldiers drafted by the Company from the armies of the Marathas, Hyderabad's nizam and the maharaja of Travancore.[11] At the end of the war, the English acquired the districts of Salem (the Baramahal), Dindigul and Malabar. The tragic defeat and heroic death of Tipu in the Fourth Mysore War (1799) facilitated the expansion of English territory to include Canara and Coimbatore. In the same year, the English forced the

---

[8] Mark T. Berger, *From Commerce to Conquest: The Dynamics of Early British Imperial Expansion into Bengal* (Vancouver: University of British Colombia, 1983), 2–5.

[9] John William Kaye, *The Administration of the East India Company: A History of Indian Progress* (London: R. Bentley, 1853), 62–67.

[10] Except for a few trading settlements. Chengalpattu district, a *jaghir* (an assignment for the support of any public establishment), was made over to the East India Company by the nawab of Arcot in 1763, in a settlement of arrears of pay, for Company troops provided to the nawab.

[11] Stein, *History of India*, 210.

raja of Thanjavur to renounce and transfer his sovereign rights to the Company.[12]

Governor General Richard Wellesley epitomised this imperial interest and pursued a policy of subsidiary alliance, which paid rich dividends. In 1800, the area lying south of the Krishna and Tungabadra rivers, comprising the districts of Kadapa, Bellary, Anandapur and parts of Kurnool, was ceded by the nizam. Alleging a secret understanding between Nawab Umdat-ul-Umara and Tipu Sultan about his non-compliance with the instructions of the English to provision their forces during the Mysore wars, they deposed the nawab of Arcot in 1801. As a result, the districts of Nellore, North Arcot, South Arcot, Tiruchirappalli, Madurai and Tirunelveli were made over to the British.[13]

Thus, through treachery and deceit, the English brought the whole of south India under the direct rule of the John Company by 1801. The disdain with which the family of the nawab of Arcot had been treated was later recalled by the authors of an anonymous document found in the Secret Department files of the Madras Government. 'As soon as the Nabob acceded to the transfer, a set of native revenue servants were let loose upon the country who committed the most shameless depredations on the servants of the Nabob, depriving the women of their jewels and clothes under the pretext of securing arrears of revenue.'[14]

Simultaneously, the British took steps to suppress the powers of the Palayakkarars. The Palayakkarars of the 'southern *palayam*s ["little kingdom", or fiefdom]' in Tirunelveli and Madurai districts revolted against the encroachment on their status and power as 'little kings'. That the Palayakkarars of southern Tamil Nadu were looked upon as sovereigns by the local people was amply demonstrated

---

[12] S. Srinivasa Raghavaiyangar, *Memorandum on the Progress of the Madras Presidency during the Last Forty Years of British Administration* (Madras: Government Press, 1893). Serfoji only retained the fort and the capital city of Thanjavur.

[13] Raghavaiyangar, *Progress of the Madras Presidency*.

[14] Quoted in A. D. Cameron, 'The Vellore Mutiny' (PhD thesis, University of Edinburgh, 1984), 304.

by the people's support during the various Palayakkarar revolts: Kattabomman's (1799) and the Marudhu brothers' (1801).[15]

Similarly chieftains elsewhere, such as Velu Thambi of Travancore, later fought desperately for their independence, but were finally reduced to submission. By the turn of the century, the English no longer concealed their imperialistic tendencies. As George Barlow, then vice-president of the Calcutta Council (1803), echoing the views of English officials of the time, wrote, 'It is absolutely necessary ... that no native state should be left to exist in India which is not upheld by the British power or the political conduct of which is not under its absolute control.'[16]

II

Army

A strong army necessarily goes hand in hand with imperialism, and the John Company possessed it in each presidency. That the defence of the Company's interests became possible only with strong armed forces prompted the military historian John Kaye to remark: 'India had been won by the sword and must be retained by the sword.'[17] The growing militarism was evident from the numbers in the armed services. In 1763, troops in the Company's employ totalled approximately 18,000: Bengal, 6,580; Madras, 9,000; and Bombay, 2,550. By 1805, these figures had risen to: Bengal, 64,000; Madras, 64,000; and Bombay, 26,500.[18]

Three types of regiments made up the army: first were the European regiments (three in each presidency) consisting of

---

[15] C. A. Bayly, *The New Cambridge History of India: India's Society and the Making of the British Empire* (New Delhi: Orient Longman, 1988), 171–72.

[16] Quoted in Michael H. Fisher, *Indirect Rule in India: Residents and the Residency System, 1764–1857* (Delhi: Oxford University Press, 1991), 57.

[17] John Kaye, *A History of the Sepoy War in India, 1857–1858*, vol. 1 (London: W. H. Allen, 1881), 146.

[18] Philip Lawson, *The East India Company: A History* (London: Longman, 1993), 133–34.

European soldiers with European officers, followed by regiments of native infantry with native and European non-commissioned officers and European officers, and lastly, irregular cavalry of native troops with a small number of European officers. British regiments of the Queen's army, lent to the East India Company on hire charges, were also in India as Her Majesty's.[19] The army reforms introduced in 1796 led to the reorganisation of the native infantry into forty regiments of two battalions each, as well as provisions for pensions and promotions.[20] The European infantry was reformed into twelve companies of 100 rank and file each.[21]

Thirty to forty soldiers formed a platoon, while two or three platoons constituted one battalion. A regiment comprised two or three battalions. The establishment of a company, a part of a battalion, was fixed at one captain, one captain-lieutenant, two lieutenants, one lieutenant-fireworker, five sergeants, five corporals, ten gunners, two drummers and seventy matrosses. Each regiment of European infantry consisted of one colonel, two lieutenant colonels, two majors, seven captains, one captain-lieutenant, twenty-five lieutenants, ten ensigns, forty-eight sergeants, sixty corporals, twenty-six drummers and fifers, 1,140 privates and twenty-four *puckallies*.[22] The adjutant-general was the medium of communication between the commander-in-chief and those under his command on 'all subjects connected with the clothing and discipline of the army with military regulations and leave of absence'.[23]

As John Briggs of the Madras Infantry wrote:

> The Indian Army consisted of two classes, of which all armies to be effective must be and always have been composed: one

---

[19] Barbara English, *John Company's Last War* (London: Collins, 1971), 69.

[20] T. A. Heathcote, *The Military in British India: The Development of British Land Forces in South Asia, 1600–1947* (Manchester: Manchester University Press, 1995), 59.

[21] W. J. Wilson, *History of the Madras Army*, vol. 3 (Madras: Government Press, 1882), 71–73.

[22] Wilson, *History of the Madras Army*, vol. 3, 71–73

[23] P. A. Agnew, *Letter to the Honourable Court of Directors of the East India Company*, 1808, ref. W 2430(b), India Office Library, London.

class derived from the better order of society, accustomed
to command the services of domestics and underlings; and
the other class drawn from the lower grade, who are from
infancy habituated to obedience and taught to respect the
upper class.[24]

This kind of prejudice led the British to believe that the native
officers were devoid of any ability to maintain discipline and hence
they were never allowed to exercise independent command over
the sepoy battalions, ever since the battalions were raised in 1758–
59. In cases where they did hold such command, it was not over
regular troops, but over troops 'raised over levies by themselves
or over the local corps of little importance'.[25] The Indian officers
led the companies but only under the command of British officers.
This meant, in effect, that even when an Indian officer was in
charge of a battalion, the British officer appointed to the battalion
permanently had the real authority of commanding the corps as
well as the responsibility of training it. Each company was led by a
subedar, who was assisted by a *jamedar*, and both were invariably
natives. There were several non-commissioned officers, such as
havildars (corresponding to sergeant) and *naiks* (corresponding to
corporal), who provided the link between 'the indigenous Indian
sepoy and the professional British officer'.[26]

Trained and led by the European army personnel, the sepoys
had always behaved well. In the campaigns against Hyder Ali,
in the midst of hardships and temptations, they gave the most
remarkable proof of their faithfulness to the English. In the then
existing sociocultural context, two-thirds of the Madras sepoys
had married their relatives, old and young, who depended on them
for subsistence from their pay. From father to son, they looked
only to the same profession, entered the same regiment, made it
their home and recounted to future generations the actions of
their fathers and relatives who had served in it. There was no bar

---

[24] Philip Mason, *A Matter of Honour: An Account of the Indian Army, its Officers
and Men* (London: Ebenezer Baylis & Son), 173.
[25] Wilson, *History of the Madras Army*, vol. 3, 367–68.
[26] Wilson, *History of the Madras Army*, vol. 3, 367–68.

on members of the lower castes joining the army, but many upper caste native officers thought that those drawn from lower caste groups 'would be fit for the rough part of a soldier's life', so they were always preferred for employment in 'laborious occupations'.[27] We have a perspective from the Madras Army, in a letter addressed by Lieutenant Colonel Patrick A. Agnew to the Court of Directors of the East India Company:

> The Native Army of Madras from its composition, which admits all casts of men, and from constant association with European troops, on services of difficulty and distress, has, beyond all others in India become habituated to innovations of this nature. The Sepoys have long relinquished the practice of stripping to their meals when in the field; and they have frequently embarked to proceed by sea on distant foreign service. Men of the highest casts served in the ranks under Native Officers of the lowest; and the principle of military discipline and subordination, seemed, by gradual steps, to have triumphed over the distinctions of their civil and religious rank, *when engaged in the duties of their profession.* [emphasis as in original][28]

The uniform of an Indian sepoy consisted of knee-length 'short drawers', a white under-jacket, usually a loose white blouse with no collar and an open neck, and a red jacket-like coat, apart from cross-belts and pouches. Their European counterparts wore white breeches and stockings. The turbans worn by the sepoys in the early period of development of the Madras Army were *urumaal* (a headgear of cloth), similar to the one worn by the Telugu and Tamil men. Some of the sepoys put on stockings in blue or black colour. European-style neckcloth was added to the uniform, but this cravat was not resisted as a foreign innovation. Indian officers wore breeches, stockings and boots, appearing like Europeans, the only difference being that the former wore a turban.[29]

---

[27] Charles F. Kirby, *The Adventures of an Arcot Rupee*, vol. 2 (London: Saunders, Otley, 1867), 290–96.

[28] Agnew, *Letter to the Honourable Court of Directors*, 10.

[29] James W. Hoover, *Men Without Hats: Dialogue, Discipline and Discontent in the Madras Army, 1806–1807* (New Delhi: Manohar, 2007), 268–70.

In Madras, the native foot soldiers in the service of the East India Company were known as peons. As their salary was poor (Rs 5), there were frequent desertions and mutinies.[30] Peons were originally employed to watch and guard the suburbs. Later, they were given military training by the Portuguese army and engaged in warfare.[31] The first recorded mutiny in the Madras Army was in 1780, when personnel of the native infantry at Vizagapatnam, provoked by their being shipped to Madras against their wishes, fired at Europeans from the ships, killing three. They contended that they were only 'armed peons', enrolled for local service, and were not meant to fight Hyder Ali. In 1784, infantry and artillery men of the Madras Army revolted in Arcot, followed by the rebellion of a cavalry unit in Arni, fighting against the non-payment of salary. In both cases, the two leaders were subjected to court martial and blown from a gun. Similar uprisings took place at Poovirunthavalli (Poonamallie) in January 1785, by a Crown unit and by three battalions in Tiruchirappalli, against the stoppage of *batta* (allowance). While no one was punished in these two incidents, in an incident in 1798 concerning the Twenty-Seventh Madras Infantry in Guntur, the leader was blown from a gun.[32]

The word 'mutiny' originally referred to the collective action of the soldiery against their military authority. As we have discussed, earlier mutinies were triggered by grievances relating to their service conditions. But what distinguished the armed revolt of the soldiery in Vellore Fort in 1806 from earlier ones was not only the magnitude of the mutiny but also its ideological impulses, involving widespread defiance of authority with a political objective. The rebels of Vellore had a political aim, as they attempted to dislodge the ruling British. Further, it had interesting parallels with the events of 1857. The primary difference from

---

[30] H. S. Bhatia, ed., *Military History of British India, 1607–1947* (New Delhi: Deep & Deep Publications, 1977), 34.

[31] Manas Dutta, 'The Army as a Tool for Social Uplift: The Experience of the Paraiyans in the Madras Presidency Army, 1770–1895', *Social Scientist* 44, no. 3/4 (March–April 2016): 59.

[32] S. L. Menezes, *Fidelity and Honour: The Indian Army from the Seventeenth to the Twenty First Century* (New Delhi: Oxford University Press, 1999), 94–97.

1857, apart from its geographical extent, was the absence of civil rebellion reinforcing the mutiny. Before unfolding the story of the 1806 Rebellion, let us turn our attention to the Vellore Fort.

III

Fort

> Situated in a beautiful and most fertile valley, nearly surrounded by hills, and in some degree commanded by one called Sazarow, the Fort of Vellore is one of the prettiest and most perfect specimens of native masonry to be met with in the East.[33]

Lingama Nayaka, the son and successor of Chinna Bomma Nayaka, built the Vellore Fort. He was a feudatory of Krishnadeva Raya, the king of Vijayanagar and a contemporary of Krishnappa Nayaka, a ruler at Senji. Lingama Nayaka raised the standard of revolt against Vijayanagar in 1603. In the ensuing battle, Lingama Nayaka had to surrender and relinquish his fiefdom. Venkata Raya and his queen took up residence 'in the marble palace of Lingama Nayaka adorned with gold and precious stones'. Vellore thus became the second royal residence of Venkata II, from around 1606. Hence the sobriquet, *Raya Veluru* (the Vellore Raja).[34]

Concern for regional interests led to mutual antagonism and a civil war broke out amongst the three Nayak kingdoms of Senji, Thanjavur and Madurai between 1614 and 1617, ravaging the Tamil country and providing the sultans of Bijapur and Golconda the scope to expand their territories in south Carnatic. Legend has it that the reigning Hindu king, fearing danger from invaders, hid the idol of the presiding deity of the temple in Vellore Fort and it was never recovered. Thus the epithet, 'temple without God'.[35]

---

[33] James Welsh, *Military Reminiscences*, vol. 2 (London: Smith, Elder, 1830), 7.
[34] C. S. Srinivasachari, *A History of Gingee and its Rulers* (Annamalainagar: Annamalai University, 1943), 103–07.
[35] *Memorandum of the Fort of Vellore and Others in its Neighbourhood as Recorded in 1815.*

The descendants of Krishnadeva Raya managed to retain the fort until 1677, when it passed into the hands of the Marathas. Shivaji held sway over it until his death in 1680 and the Marathas controlled the region up to 1686. Thereafter, a Mughal army led by Aurangzeb's envoy Zulfikar Khan succeeded in capturing the fort. After devastating and plundering the region, he left behind his general, Daud Khan, as the nawab of Carnatic. Daud Khan, who founded the modern Arcot, transferred the headquarters of the Carnatic subha from Senji to Arcot.[36] Nawab Sadatulla Khan, on his nomination to the nawabi, gave the Vellore jaghir to his brother Murtaza Ali. Murtaza Ali successfully retained the fort against the continuous onslaughts of the East India Company's army until 1756. That year, the nawab of Arcot, Mohammed Ali, in view of his personal animosity with the *jagirdar* (holder of a jaghir) or *killadar* (fort commandant) of Vellore, Murtaza Ali's son, stormed the fort accompanied by Clive and took possession of it. An English garrison, with the consent of the nawab, occupied the fort in 1761.[37] Major John Call, who ably conducted the war against the killadar of Vellore thought that Vellore, with its three hill forts, formed the strongest fortifications he had seen in India.[38]

In 1768, Hyder attempted to storm the fort, but in vain. Therefore, to the English, Vellore was an impregnable fortress. In 1791, Cornwallis used it as the base for his military operation and marched on Bangalore.[39] After the fall of Srirangapatnam and the death of Tipu Sultan, Vellore Fort was considered the safest place to keep his children, wives, relatives, servants and 'adherents' in internment. They were all accommodated in special quarters built exclusively for them.

The Vellore Fort lay south of the Palar river and was almost 25 kilometres away from Arcot. To the north and east of the fort, lay two adjacent *pettai*s (village), one newly developed at the time,

---

[36] *Memorandum of the Fort of Vellore and Others in its Neighbourhood as Recorded in 1815.*
[37] W. Francis, *Gazetteer of South India* (New Delhi: Mittal Publications, 1988), 37.
[38] Henry Meredith Vibart, *The Military History of the Madras Engineers and Pioneers from 1743 up to the Present Time*, vol.1 (London: W. H. Allen), 1881, 60.
[39] Vibart, *Madras Engineers and Pioneers*, vol. 1, 60.

and the other well-established. A system of three forts, Sazarow, Guzarow and Mortaz Agur, built atop the surrounding hills, bordered the main pettai. The first of these was large, strongly built and able to withstand assault. The second was slightly smaller, but harder to access, and the third had hardly any features of strategic importance. Together, they provided protection to the north, east and south sides of Vellore Fort with canon-fire. There were also ramparts and towers, a ditch and a hedge around each that offered further defence.[40]

The fort of Vellore was a 'curious specimen of ancient Indian fortification with much foliage about the battlements', so wrote the major of the Madras Army and the author of *Adventures of an Arcot Rupee*, Charles F. Kirby. To him, 'it looked as if constructed for a thousand years and been employed upon it under the prevailing rule of forced labour in the service of the sovereign'. The outer wall was crowned with a row of upright stone slabs, uniformly rounded at the top. It was at a height of about 9 metres, built with small protruding watch towers at regular intervals. The space between this wall and a second line of bastions served as a wide defensive wall. The fort was approximately 1.5 kilometres in circumference, and entirely of stone, cemented with *chunam* (limestone). Blocks of granite, 3–4 feet thick and 18–20 feet in length, were first cut and then blasted by fire out of the solid rock and removed by hard labour (see Figures 1.1 and 1.2).[41]

The parapets of the fort were inclined and also rich in stonework. There were openings, 1 metre wide inside and 3 metres wide outside, in these towers to turn the cannons to any direction to fire at enemies outside the fort. It is believed that a modification to this arrangement was made by the English on their occupation of the fort. The walls of the fort were made up of cyclopean stones with each stone having three holes facing three different directions. The holes had been made in such a way that the person firing from

---

[40] *Description of Vellore Fort, the Pettahs, the Hills and the Attack Carried on by the English Army under the Command of John Caillaud*, 1761, India Office Library, London.

[41] Kirby, *Adventures of an Arcot Rupee*, vol. 2, 152–53.

within could target the enemy on the glacis without the latter noticing them.[42]

The width of walking space at the ground level was 6.3 metres and this was maintained all around the fort. About thirty-four sentry rooms, not noticeable from the outside, were part of the defence mechanism of the fort.[43] The floor of the verandah and rooms were barely raised above the ground so that they could not be viewed from the outside.[44] A moat, 191 feet wide and 29 feet deep, running to a length of about 3 kilometres, protected the fort. Across the moat, on the southern side, was the exit point for troops to make sudden and surprise attacks on the surrounding enemy. This is called 'sally port' in military language. A stone pathway served as an approach road to its gate.

An important part of the fort of Vellore was the ditch full of large alligators. Some were said to be 18 feet long, and were reared in the moat as the first line of defence. As observed by Kirby,

> These amphibious reptiles had originally, from the unfinished state of the counter-scarp, been in the habit of rowing all about the neighbourhood, and had been known to travel as far as Arnee during the night; but their principal resort after the ditch of Vellore, was a very fine lake, Chitterbury tank, about four miles to the westward, which, however they frequented during the rains only.[45]

The ditch was impassable in those days, except on a raft or by the causeways. A drawbridge connected the main entrance of the fort.[46] There were four strong, massive gates for entry. Initially the entrance was through a winding roadway. Later, a straight road was cut through the rampart.[47]

---

[42] A. K. Seshadri, *Vellore Fort and the Temple through the Ages* (Vellore: Sri Jalakandeswarar Dharma Sthapanam, 2006), 49–51.

[43] Seshadri, *Vellore Fort and the Temple through the Ages*, 50.

[44] Seshadri, *Vellore Fort and the Temple through the Ages*, 156–60.

[45] Seshadri, *Vellore Fort and the Temple through the Ages*, 160.

[46] R. Mani, *History of Vellore Fort* (Vellore: Poongavanam Ramasamy Illam, 2004). Also see the note issued by the Department of Museums at Vellore Fort, dated 14 November 2005.

[47] P. Chinnayan, *The Vellore Mutiny, 1806: The First Uprising Against the British* (Madras, 1982), 2.

Caillaud, the commander of the Madras Army, summarised the strength of the fort thus:

> In short, the Fort of Vellore had always been esteemed very strong by the several reports we had of it, and by the convenience of its situation was sure sanctuary to the people of the country during the incursion of the Marattas, for no country-power could attempt to molest them while protected by Mortaz Ally Cawn. Besides this strength and propriety of situation, Vellore was moreover respectable by its size, and goodness of the Walls and Ditch, which surrounded it; for they were much superior to those which ordinarily surround the places built by the country government.[48]

The Jalagandeswara Temple, dedicated to Lord Siva (Figure 1.3), situated north-east of the fort had been turned into an arsenal since the British occupied it. This temple, believed to have been built before the fort was completed, was adorned with Hindu religious figures all around the ramparts, a beautiful *kalyana mandapam* (marriage hall) adjoining it, and a pond in front,[49] in which the celebrations for the boat festival took place in the halcyon days of Hindu kingdoms.[50] There was also a mosque. The mosque (Jumma Masjid) in the fort would have been established between 1687 and 1700 (Figure 1.4). It is not known when it was closed. Curiously, there was not one chaplain or missionary either at or near Vellore in 1806.[51] The government of Madras established a church inside the fort only in 1846 with a seating capacity of 280 people (see Figures 1.5 and 1.6). Major C. G. Ottley, the fort's adjutant at the time, designed and built it.[52]

---

[48] *Description of Vellore Fort, the Pettahs, the Hills and the Attack Carried on by the English Army under the Command of John Caillaud*, 1761, India Office Library.
[49] The pond was an excavated tank that was levelled by the British and the space turned into a parade ground.
[50] Seshadri, *Vellore Fort and the Temple through the Ages*, 16–18.
[51] Ferdinand Mount, *The Tears of the Rajas: Mutiny, Money and Marriage in India, 1805–1905* (London: Simon & Schuster, 2015), 35.
[52] Eugene P. Heideman, *From Mission to Church: The Reformed Church in America Mission to India* (Michigan: Wim. B. Eerdman Publishing, 2001), 74.

Originally, the interior of the fort had housed a large number
of native houses. They were all pulled down after the British took
over and a great number of European houses were built in their
place. Located in the north-west of the fort, the European barracks
could accommodate about 800 men. Surrounded by European
bungalows and sepoy barracks (Figure 1.7), the open ground at the
centre was large enough to permit the entire battalion to assemble
for roll call. The pond was levelled and made a parade ground.
The palace complex was separated from the parade ground by the
garrison hospital and by several residential quarters for British
officers.[53] The commandant's quarters (Figure 1.8), situated to the
left of the main gate, was occupied by the commanding officer.
It was a large 'up-stair' building, with a flat terraced roof, which
had a panoramic view of the scenery. A few yards away, beyond
this building, was the main guard, the security centre of the fort.
The other officers and soldiers of the garrison lived in barracks
and public quarters within the fort and outside. Outside the fort,
around 1 kilometre south, besides the line of buildings where the
sepoys of the garrison lived with their families when not on duty,
there existed a few garden bungalows for British officers.[54]

Vellore looked different in the 1810s, during the visit of Major
James Welsh, the erstwhile commandant of the Palayamkottai
garrison, soon after the armed uprising. As he wrote in his *Military
Reminiscences*,

> This place [Vellore], now completely modernized, is greatly
> improved in the interior, having got rid of many crowded
> patches of native houses, and every kind of rubbish. There is
> a capital parade in the centre, wide streets in every direction,
> and all the bastions have got the original heavy stone
> battlements replaced by regular parapets, with embrasures
> for cannon; while those of the fosse-bray still standing

---

[53] Arthur F. Cox, *A Manual of the North Arcot District in the Presidency of Madras*
(Madras: Government Press, 1881), 191–93.
[54] Kirby, *Adventures of an Arcot Rupee*, vol. 2, 154–56. Also see Cox, *A Manual of
the North Arcot District*, 187–88.

entire, present an extraordinary and agreeable admixture of Oriental and European architecture.[55]

The hill forts that had been repaired were occupied by 'small guards'. The princes and their attendants had been removed to Bengal, but the women still resided in their originally allotted apartments in the palaces built exclusively for use by the family of Tipu Sultan (Figure 1.9). The erstwhile ruler of Kandy (Ceylon), Sri Vikramaraja Singha, continued to languish as a state prisoner there. Lieutenant Colonel Augustus Andrews, the paymaster of stipends, was in charge of the fort.[56]

Welsh, during an earlier visit, noticed the alligators inhabiting the moat, which had been cleaned up along with other repair work after the mutiny. The alligators in the moat were protected by orders of the government until 1822. However, in that year, the son of a subedar fell into the ditch and was tragically killed, and many of the alligators were hunted and killed as a result. During his short stay, Welsh himself killed six or eight of them.[57]

After the 1806 rebellion, Walter Hamilton in his *The East India Gazetteer* described the Vellore Fort thus:

Vellore fortress is of such extent that it contains within a square of handsome buildings, besides spacious barracks, every necessary accommodation for a garrison. The great pagoda on one side of the square is used for a magazine. From the attributes of the statues, sculptured of blue stone, which still ornament its front, and the frequent images of the bull Nandi, recumbent on the ledges of the walls, it may be inferred that Siva was the deity worshipped. The pettah of Vellore lies to the south of the fort close under the hills, and joined by connecting battlements with the old castellated works on the triple peaks above. It is a large and populous town, with an exceedingly busy bazaar, containing many good houses, interspersed with large proportion of Mussulman tombs, thickly wooded with coconut trees, but without any public buildings of note, the white-washed mosque of Chundah

[55] Welsh, *Military Reminiscences*, vol. 2, 180.
[56] Welsh, *Military Reminiscences*, vol. 2, 180–84.
[57] Welsh, *Military Reminiscences*, vol. 2, 180–84.

Saheb being the most remarkable edifice. Connected with the fortified rocks above the town is a barrier wall and fosse, stretching across from their base to the margin of the Palaur, with a gateway that commands the high road to Arcot.[58]

In the context of the Fourth Mysore War ending in the death of Tipu (1799), and the resultant decision of the Company government to keep Tipu's family members confined in the specially built palaces, Hyder Mahal and Tipu Mahal, certain extra security arrangements were made. It was found to be extremely difficult to keep a watch over the day-to-day affairs of the palaces, so the government of Madras appointed a paymaster of stipends to be entirely responsible for the supervision of the princes. Lieutenant Colonel Thomas Marriott became the first officer to hold the new post.[59] The fort's commandant who had done the job previously was divested of this responsibility. According to Marriott, the princes brought with them all their dependents, servants, horses and baggage, and was convinced that no less than 3,000 Mysoreans had settled there. Vellore also registered an increase in population by 5,000–6,000.[60]

In the Madras Presidency, there were about 8,283 British and 56,550 Indian militia men, including the European personnel and native forces in Vellore Fort.[61] The English garrison of Vellore, at the time of the uprising, consisted of four companies of the Sixty-Ninth Regiment, six companies of the First Battalion, First Regiment of the Native Infantry, and the Second Battalion, Twenty-Third Regiment. The Europeans were about 370 in number,[62] and the natives, 1,500. Most of the sepoys (soldiers) lived in the pettai

---

[58] Walter Hamilton, *The East-India Gazetteer*, vol. 2 (London: W. H. Allen, 1828), 695.

[59] Hoover, *Men Without Hats*, 50. Thomas Marriott was born and brought up in India. He spoke Urdu and Persian fluently.

[60] *Home Miscellaneous Series*, file 116, vol. 508, India Office Library, London.

[61] Mount, *Tears of the Rajas*, 32; Devadas Moodley, 'Vellore 1806: The Meanings of Mutiny', in *Rebellion, Repression, Reinvention: Mutiny in Comparative Perspective*, ed. Jane Hathaway (Westport: Praeger, 2001), 3.

[62] In some sources, the number given is 383. See Mount, *Tears of the Rajas*, 32.

adjoining the fort, while their arms were lodged in the fort.[63] On the day before 10 July 1806, the day of the mutiny, the men on night duty had been taken from the Sixty-Ninth and the First Regiments. The Sixty-Ninth Regiment consisted of three sergeants, four corporals, two drummers and forty-four privates under Lieutenants Eley and Popham. One sergeant, two corporals and twelve privates of the Sixty-Ninth were on duty at the barracks. There were three sentries, namely one at the gate of the barrack yard, one immediately outside the barracks, and one over the regimental magazine close to the ramparts. Captain Isaac Miller of the First Regiment was captain on the day. From the First Regiment, the number of men on duty amounted to four native officers, nine havildars and 251 rank and file under Lieutenant O'Reilly. The men were divided between the main guard, the general magazine and the gate. The main guard furnished five sentries, namely one at the guard, and four at different points separated by a small distance, from which it was reckoned that there were about twenty rank and file with one or two sergeants and a subaltern.[64]

The First Battalion of the First Regiment was the oldest in the service and had earned the appreciation of the British for its loyalty. It comprised Muslims from Mysore, many of whom had been in the service of Tipu. The Twenty-Third Regiment had been raised in the district of Tirunelveli, and contained in its ranks a number of followers of the chiefs of the southern palayams, whose possessions had been confiscated after the suppression of Veerapandya Kattabomman of Panchalamkurichy (1799) and the Marudhu brothers of Sivagangai Palayam (1801).[65]

The sepoys of the First Battalion, First Regiment and the First Battalion, Twenty-Third Regiment lived in huts outside the fort. But as was customary, the whole of the Second Battalion, Twenty-Third Regiment had permission to sleep in the fort on the night of 9 July in order to be ready for target practice early in

---

[63] *Secret Department Sundries*, vol. 2A, 822.

[64] Wilson, *History of the Madras Army*, vol. 3, 177.

[65] James Mill and H. H. Wilson, *The History of British India, from 1805 to 1835*, vol. 7 (London: James Madden, 1840), 84; *Secret Department Sundries*, vol. 2A, 822.

the morning on 10 July. Curiously, all the guards in the fort had been furnished by the First Regiment. Later, it was noted that the native adjutant, whose responsibility it was to choose the men for the guards, 'had contrived to put as many of his own faith who were sworn mutineers'.[66]

Thus, the English East India Company, with only a handful of trading posts in the seventeenth century, succeeded in eliminating their rival European powers, starting with the French. They thereupon embarked on a policy of territorial conquest. Their local rivals, the regional rulers or Palayakkarars, were easily overpowered because their mutual hostilities deterred them from putting up a united front. Besides, the English had better weapons and better organisation. By 1801, the Company had acquired the sovereign rights to all 'little kingdoms' and established their seat of power at Madras. The vanquished south Indian dynasties and their descendants remained unreconciled and conspired against the Company government. The fallout was the Vellore Revolt of 1806, to which we turn our attention now.

---

[66] Kirby, *Adventures of an Arcot Rupee*, vol. 2, 252.

FIGURE 1.1 Vellore Fort

Source: Puduvai Ilavenil.

FIGURE 1.2 Vellore Fort with three hills detached from each other

Source: Puduvai Ilavenil.

FIGURE 1.3 **Fort temple**

Source: Puduvai Ilavenil.

FIGURE 1.4 Jumma Masjid

Source: Puduvai Ilavenil.

FIGURE 1.5 St John's Church

Source: Puduvai Ilavenil.

FIGURE 1.6 St John's Church: inner view

Source: Puduvai Ilavenil.

FIGURE 1.7 Sepoy quarters

Source: Puduvai Ilavenil.

FIGURE 1.8 Commandant barracks

Source: Puduvai Ilavenil.

FIGURE 1.9 Tipu's family cemetery at Vellore

Source: Puduvai Ilavenil.

FIGURE 2.1 European barracks

Source: Puduvai Ilavenil.

FIGURE 2.2 Magazine

Source: Puduvai Ilavenil.

FIGURE 2.3 Magazine: inside view

Source: Puduvai Ilavenil.

FIGURE 2.4 Tombstone of Lieutenant Colonel Fancourt

Source: Puduvai Ilavenil.

FIGURE 2.5 Tombstone in memory of Lieutenants Popham and Eley, and five sergeants, four corporals, one drummer and seventy privates of Her Majesty's Sixty-Ninth Regiment

Source: Puduvai Ilavenil.

Fateh Hyder   **Mohi-Ud-Din**   **Moiz-Ud-Din**

FIGURE 2.6 Tipu's sons implicated in the uprising

Source: Francis Bucanan, *A Journey from Madras through the Countries of Mysore, Canara, and Malabar*, vol. 3 (London: W. Bulmer and Co., 1807).

FIGURE 2.7 Robert Gillespie

Source: William Thorn, *A Memoir of Major-General Sir R. R. Gillespie* (London: T. Egerton, 1816).

FIGURE 2.8 Sally port: a closer view

Source: Puduvai Ilavenil.

FIGURE 2.9 Sally port

Source: Puduvai Ilavenil.

FIGURE 4.1 Basha Mahal: front view

Source: Puduvai Ilavenil.

FIGURE 4.2 Rani Mahal

Source: Puduvai Ilavenil.

FIGURE 4.3 Hyder Mahal

Source: Puduvai Ilavenil.

FIGURE 4.4 Tipu Mahal: front view

Source: Puduvai Ilavenil.

FIGURE 5.1 Tombstone of Solomon Frost

Source: Puduvai Ilavenil.

2

THE REVOLT

Courage resides in the breast and not in the dress.

—Mir Alam (1806)[1]

S oon after Sir John Cradock assumed office as the new commander-in-chief of the Madras Army, he found that there was no general code of military regulations for the army of the presidency.[2] He submitted a proposal to the governor and obtained his permission on 12 March 1805 to codify the voluminous regulations of the military department, on the condition that 'no rules should be added to those in force without the express sanction of the Government'.[3] In November 1805, Major Paul Bose, who commanded the Second Battalion, Fourteenth Regiment of the Native Infantry, then stationed at Wallajahbad, requested permission to change the turbans of the corps, and forwarded to Major Frederick Pierce, deputy adjutant-general, the pattern of the turban he proposed. According to him, this pattern was extremely convenient, light, cheap and perfectly agreeable to the men of his corps. The commander-in-chief inspected the pattern and instructed the adjutant-general, Colonel Patrick A. Agnew, to ascertain what the opinions of three men,

---

[1] Quoted in Sarojini Regani, *Nizam-British Relations, 1724–1857* (repr., New Delhi: Concept Publishing, 1988), 198. Mir Alam was the diwan of Hyderabad during the revolt in 1806.

[2] Cradock, though appointed on 21 November 1803, assumed office on 17 October 1804.

[3] Mount, *Tears of the Rajas*, 34. Cradock, the son of the archbishop of Dublin, was a stickler for discipline and authority. He spent most of his earlier military career suppressing native dissent in Ireland, the West Indies and Egypt.

a Muslim, a Hindu and a Rajput, were after wearing the turban.[4] Bose also prepared the regulations which the commander-in-chief approved and submitted for approval to the government in January 1806, but without drawing attention to the changes that had been introduced. Particularly, no intimation was given to the governor about the alterations proposed in dress and other related matters.[5] The outcome of this hasty move was resentment and ill-feeling among native sepoys and officers, both Hindu and Muslim, in different cantonments, leading to mutinies. This chapter describes the fallout of the enforcement of the code of military regulations and the new turban by the Company administration.

I

The code of military regulations was notified to the army by the commander-in-chief on 13 March 1806. The new regulations prohibited the use of *vibhuti* (sacred ash) or any other caste marks on the foreheads of sepoys while on military duty. The controversial part of the regulation was in paragraph 10, section 11 of the order. It read,

> It is ordered by the regulations that a native soldier shall not mark his face to denote his caste or wear earrings when dressed in his uniform; and it is further directed, that at all parades, and upon all duties, every soldier of the battalion shall be clean-shaved on the chin. It is directed also that uniformity shall, as far as is practicable, be preserved, in regard to the quantity and shape of the hair upon the upper lip.[6]

The chief secretary, George Buchan commended the deputy adjutant-general, Pierce, for compiling the code. In his minutes, dated 11 March 1806, the chief secretary remarked that the

---

[4] Agnew was in command of the forces in Tirunelveli and led the war on Panchalamkurichy Palayam.

[5] Marshman, *History of India*, vol. 2, 209–10; Wilson, *History of the Madras Army*, vol. 3, 169–71.

[6] *Secret Consultations*, vol. 19, 1032–35.

principle on which the code was prepared was 'in all aspects calculated to promote the efficiency of the military service' of this government. He also recorded the board's appreciation for the compilation, as testimony to the talents and great efforts of the deputy adjutant-general.[7]

So, the new regulations were enforced with the object of increasing the smartness of the sepoy regiments on parade. But in making these alterations, it was later alleged that 'too much consideration was given to the pipe-clay traditions of European armies', while too little attention was paid to the customs and sentiments of the Indian soldiers.[8] The order on military regulations infringed the customary practices of both Hindu and Muslim soldiers. Yet they were defended saying that notwithstanding any formal order prohibiting these customs, no soldier in any well-regulated corps appeared with caste marks and ornaments on parade. Letters from Major General Archibald Campbell, Lieutenant Colonel John Chalmers and Bose were quoted in support of this assertion.[9]

The notorious order introducing a new pattern of turban 'for the native commissioned officers, non-commissioned officers, and rank and file of regiments of native infantry, of companies of golandauze [fresh corps without professional training], and of gun lascars attached to battalions of artillery belonging to the Army on the establishment of Fort St. George',[10] added fuel to the fire when it was issued on 14 November 1805. The following is an extract from the order:

> The turband so established shall be considered to be the uniform of the abovementioned corps, and shall be worn as such, to the exclusion of every other that may heretofore have been authorised ... Sealed patterns of the turban will be furnished to corps; and the Commander-in-Chief forbids

[7] *Documents Connected with the Case of Colonel P. A. Agnew*, 1808, British Library, London, 21–22.

[8] Demetrius C. Boulger, *Lord William Bentinck*, Rulers of India, ed. W. W. Hunter (Oxford: Clarendon Press, 1897), 31.

[9] Wilson, *History of the Madras Army*, vol. 3, 169–201.

[10] Wilson, *History of the Madras Army*, vol. 3, 169.

any deviation, whatever from those patterns, as established, for Grenadiers, Light infantry, and battalion companies, either in their fashion or trimmings, or in their dimensions or weight.[11]

On 20 June, the commander-in-chief noted, 'I highly approve that every exertion should be made in the completion of the turbans "in Order" as a refractory spirit has been shewn *which must be put down*' [emphasis as in original].[12]

The most obnoxious innovation in the new turban, from the native perspective, was the leather cockade. To make matters worse, the front part of the uniform had been converted into a cross, a symbol of Christian faith. Usually, the turban was formed of materials such as iron frames, blue braid cloth and a plume, or cotton tufts, with the exception of the leather cockade.[13] The cockade of the new turban was made of animal skin.[14] Pig skin was anathema to Muslims, while upper caste Hindus shunned anything to do with cow hide. As John William Kaye writes, 'The new hat was not merely an emblem of Christianity, and therefore possessed of a grave moral significance, but materially also, it was discovered to be an abomination.'[15] In south India, the hat was always identified with Europeans and Christians. Therefore, while substituting a hat for the national characteristic headdress, the turban, utmost care ought to have been taken. But without realising the implication, a change of significant importance was effected incautiously.

II

The first incident of protest occurred in May 1806. On the grounds of caste, the men in the Second Battalion of the Fourth Regiment

---

[11] Wilson, *History of the Madras Army*, vol. 3, 193.

[12] Agnew, *Letter to the Honourable Court of Directors*, 6–7.

[13] *Secret Department Sundries*, vol. 2A, 850–51.

[14] Hoover, *Men Without Hats*, 57. It was later found that the leather cockades were crafted by Chakliyars who worked for military contractors attached to the garrison.

[15] Kaye, *Sepoy Army in India*, vol. 2, 218–19.

at Vellore refused to wear the new turban. Their objection was that it bore an offensive resemblance to the hat, or cap, worn by the East Indian Drummers, who were invariably drawn from the Parayar caste. This battalion, Lieutenant Thomas Maclean later disclosed, was principally composed of 'high caste men, Moormen, Rajputs and Gentoos [Hindus].'[16] On the evening of 6 May, the battalion commander, Lieutenant Colonel John Darley, ordered the adjutant to have a roll call in the barracks at six o' clock. The adjutant reported that the men refused to don their sidearms. When Darley enquired about it, the native officers replied that they had directed their men to put their sidearms on, but the men refused to obey them. Darley snatched the swords and reported the matter to the officer commanding at Vellore, Colonel John Fancourt, who directed Darley to return the swords to the soldiers saying that he saw no reason to deprive the men of their arms. Anguished by Fancourt's decision, Darley reported the incident to the adjutant-general of the army: 'I have now been 26 years in Native Corps and never known an instance during that period, sepoys refusing to obey an order of their superiors ... and it was from so many years of experience of the character that I acted and I do sincerely regret that their swords were restored to them.'[17]

Darley paraded the corps on the morning of 7 May and marched them into the barracks. He made them remove their turbans and carry them into the stores. In the evening, when the corps was about to disperse after the parade, somebody from the sepoy crowd jeered, 'dhoot, dhoot', meaning 'get out', as interpreted later by the government lawyer, Gulam Ali. An enraged Darley ordered the corps to fall in again.[18] This time Fancourt reported the matter to the commander-in-chief. Acting on the advice of his staff, the commander-in-chief informed Fancourt that there was no real basis for the sepoys' objection to the turban and ordered that the ringleaders be arrested and sent to Madras for trial. Darley remonstrated and prevailed upon Fancourt to postpone

---

[16] *Secret Department Sundries*, vol. 2B, 912.
[17] *Secret Department Sundries*, vol. 1, 22.
[18] *Secret Department Sundries*, vol. 1A, 79–80.

the execution of the order until they heard from the government. Fancourt too pleaded for a delay, but there was no response to this suggestion from the governor.[19] A detachment of the Nineteenth Dragoons (cavalry) was ordered to escort the rebels, twenty-one privates, against whom charges had been framed, to Madras for a trial.[20]

The Second Battalion of the Fourth Regiment was removed from Vellore, and the Second Battalion of the Twenty-Third Regiment was directed from Wallajahbad to relieve it. The prisoners were marched to Madras with handkerchiefs tied about their heads. Jamedar Sheik Kasim (Shaik Cossim), along with a guard of the First Battalion of the First Regiment, was ordered to accompany them. In Fort St George, Imam (Emam) of the Light Company met him at the gate and advised him to be cautious or he might be killed, telling him that 600–700 men of the Fourth Regiment had been in the barracks through the night and were prepared to mutiny, while 200 had gathered outside with the intention of attacking the cavalry and rescuing the prisoners.[21]

Havildars and naiks of the Grenadier Company stationed in Vellore, who, in the first instance, refused to wear the new turban, were reduced to the ranks. Subsequently, two havildars and four naiks were discharged from the corps for the same reason.[22] The demoted havildars and naiks accused the koat havildar of the Grenadier Company, Sheik Imam (Shaik Emam), of inciting them to disobey.[23]

The commander-in-chief set up a court to examine and report the causes which led to insubordination by the men in the Second Battalion, Fourth Regiment of the Native Infantry. Lieutenant Colonel James McKerras, commanding the Second Battalion, Twenty-Third Regiment, was appointed president, and Lieutenant

---

[19] Wilson, *History of the Madras Army*, vol. 3, 170.

[20] P. A. Agnew to John Fancourt, 7 May 1806, quoted in Wilson, *History of the Madras Army*, vol. 3, 171. Also see Mount, *Tears of the Rajas*, 34.

[21] *Secret Department Sundries*, vol. 2A, 696–97; Secret Consultations on 2 February 1807, cited in *Secret Department Sundries*, vol. 8B, 400–08.

[22] *Secret Department Sundries*, vol. 2A, 853–54.

[23] *Secret Department Sundries*, vol. 1A, 35–36.

Colonels Nathaniel Forbes, commanding the First Battalion, First Regiment, and Thomas Marriott, commanding the First Battalion, Fifth Regiment, were made members of this court of enquiry.

This military court sought the opinion of two native officers of high rank and caste. The opinion of Havildar Major Karuppan, a Malabar (Tamil), was that 'there is no objection at all to the turban, nor will the wearing of it, to the best of my opinion, degrade a man of the highest cast [caste], nor will it affect the prejudice of cast'.[24] Jamedar Mir Gulam Ali (Meer Gholaum Ally), native adjutant, responded, 'I think that any cast man might wear it without degradation and that there is nothing about it to prejudice the cast of any one.' Subedar Sheik Imam (Shaik Emaum), during interrogation, declared that there was nothing in the turban to affect the strictest prejudices of religion and Jamedar Chaing Singh, who was Brahmin by caste, in a reply to the question, 'Whether in his opinion, there was anything about the new turban either in shape or materials, that could affect the prejudices of the highest and most tenacious caste?', answered, 'No; any cast might wear it.'[25]

The court martial, after investigation, tried twenty-one privates (ten Muslims and eleven Hindus) for defiance.[26] Governor William Bentinck communicated the result of the trial to the adjutant-general for action. In response to that order, two soldiers Sheik Abdul Rymen and Anantaraman, a Muslim and a Hindu respectively, refused to apologise and were sentenced to receive 900 lashes each and to be discharged from service as 'turbulent and unworthy subjects'.[27] The remaining nineteen who complied with the orders of the court and apologised were sentenced to 500 lashes each, but were pardoned 'in consequence of their full acknowledgement of error, deep contrition, and solemn promises of future good conduct'.[28]

---

[24] William Bentinck, *Memorial Addressed to the Honourable Court of Directors*, 7 February 1809, ref. 9055 h5 in V8872, India Office Library, 16.

[25] Bentinck, *Memorial*, 16.

[26] During the trial held on 14 May, none of the native officers had objected to the new turban or opined that it was an offence to their religious principles.

[27] Boulger, 'Lord William Bentinck', 29–39.

[28] Wilson, *History of the Madras Army*, vol. 3, 172–73.

The governor, while dealing with the case and in awarding punishment, showed undue haste and was seized of the subject in the same uncritical spirit as the commander-in-chief. He disclosed his determination to employ all possible means to suppress dissent and enforce the order. This convinced native troops that they could expect no justice from their European superiors, no consideration for their sentiments from the commander-in-chief and no hope of redressing grievances through dignified representation to the government.[29] Neither the severity shown to those punished, nor clemency to those admonished helped allay the misgivings of the natives in the Madras Army. The stringent measures accorded in the case of the Second Battalion, Fourth Regiment, made them more determined to oppose the new turban.

At secret meetings held frequently in the military lines of the native battalions at Vellore, the men vowed to resist all innovations and evolved a plan to attack and kill all white officers and men. These meetings were attended by a majority of the native officers and allegedly by several retainers of the sons of Tipu in the fort.[30] However, when Forbes later heard about the intended mutiny on 17 June, he spoke with the sepoys about their grievances, with a view to redressing them. Specifically, he conversed with the native adjutant, Sheik Ali, the following morning to ascertain what he had heard about the turban. The native adjutant denied that there were any grievances with regard to the turban.[31]

III

The commander-in-chief, Cradock, was on an inspection tour and was camping at Nandydurg late in June 1806 when he received a letter from Lieutenant Colonel James Brunton, the military's auditor general. In it, Brunton pointed out the discontent prevailing in the Madras Army following the introduction of the new turban and pleaded earnestly for the withdrawal of the order. Forwarding

---

[29] Mill and Wilson, *History of British India*, vol. 7, 93.
[30] Wilson, *History of the Madras Army*, vol. 3, 175.
[31] Bentinck, *Memorial*, 150.

this letter to the government on 29 June 1806, the commander-in-chief said that he had 'at last come to the conclusion that the objections to the turband were almost universal, and that it was commonly believed that the next attempt would be to force the sepoys to become Christians'.[32] Cradock added that if it was a military issue, he would have felt no embarrassment, but being one of caste, he was desirous to have the advice of his 'coadjutors' in the government.[33] Brunton's letter warned that 'many things of serious movement have originated in trifles', and the introduction of the drummers' hat was 'widely feared to be only a prelude to forcible conversion en masse to Christianity in India'.[34] Bentinck scoffed at this caution and remarked that 'the health of that officer had long been so bad that his nerves were gone, and that he suffered from great despondency'.[35]

Yet, the government, after a great deal of deliberation, took a tactful decision, which was communicated to the governor officially on 4 July:

> If there had been reason to suppose that the late change of dress was liable to the objection of militating against the religious principles of the inhabitants of this country, we should have had no hesitation in immediately recommending to your Excellency the relinquishment of the intention to establish the proposed change, but as it appears from the evidence taken in the late enquiry at Vellore, that no objection of this nature exists, we certainly deem it advisable that the alternative of yielding to the clamour arising from an unfounded prejudice should, if possible, be avoided.[36]

The government also sent the draft order, intended to be published by the commander-in-chief with the object of reassuring the sepoys. But the notification of the order was deferred at the instance of the governor, who believed that the 'disinclination to wear the turband was becoming more feeble'. The idea of assuaging the feelings of

---

[32] Cameron, 'The Vellore Mutiny', 59; also see Mount, *Tears of the Rajas*, 34.
[33] Wilson, *History of the Madras Army*, vol. 3, 173–74.
[34] Mount, *Tears of the Rajas*, 34.
[35] Mount, *Tears of the Rajas*, 175.
[36] Wilson, *History of the Madras Army*, vol. 3, 173–74.

the agitated sepoys was thus dropped. Bentinck was in favour of adopting a firmer attitude, stating, 'To recede from a lofty position, is at all times a dangerous compromise of authority; and no principle can be clearer than this, that a concession extorted by the mutinous efforts of an armed soldiery is generally fatal to military discipline,' and that whatever might have been the objection to the passing of the regulations in question, 'yielding in the face of force was to be avoided'.[37] As events proved, this was a costly mistake.

The possibility of mutiny was thus in the air for about a month before 10 July. This is corroborated by the disclosure of Havildar Yusuf Khan (Esoph Cawn), of the Second Battalion, Twenty-Third Regiment, that all the native officers had at different times spoken to him about it.[38] The intention of the sepoys was known to some of the people of the palace for some time before it took place, and in particular, to Prince Moiz-ud-Din. As we know from the testimonies of several witnesses, discussed in Chapter 3, an oath not to wear the new turban was taken by a great number of sepoys in both battalions.

But the intentions of the mutineers were divulged to Forbes by Mustapha Beg from the First Battalion, First Regiment on the night of 17 June. Forbes, instead of making serious enquiries, sent for his native officers, who, on being questioned, feigned innocence. Professing their readiness to wear the turban, the native officers said Mustapha Beg was a well-known madman, previously imprisoned for drunkenness, and persuaded Forbes to confine Mustapha as being 'insane'.[39] Mustapha was put behind bars 'for scandalizing the corps', and remained in lock-up till the day of the hostile outbursts, when some of his friends set him free.[40]

W. Jones, the leather manufacturer in Vellore who had received the contract to supply ornaments for the turbans, complained that he was being threatened with death if he made them.[41] A European woman, Mrs Burke, attempted to apprise Fancourt of

[37] Bentinck, *Memorial*, 9; Boulger, *Lord William Bentinck*, 33.
[38] *Secret Department Sundries*, vol. 2B, 1173–83.
[39] Wilson, *History of the Madras Army*, vol. 3, 175.
[40] *Secret Department Sundries*, vol. 2A, 894.
[41] *Secret Department Sundries*, vol. 2, 867.

what she had heard about the plan to murder the European officers in the fort, when she went to him to apply for the posthumous reward announced for her husband. But Fancourt damned her as a woman of easy virtue and sent her away.[42] All the warnings were ignored as 'bazaar gossip' and nothing was done either to reinforce European troops at Vellore or to take extra precautions inside the fort.[43] Ironically, on 10 July, when the 'assurance of the re-establishment of discipline' was transmitted from Vellore Fort to the commander-in-chief, and through him to the government at Fort St George, 'the smouldering embers of sedition and mutiny burst into a flame'.[44]

Though it was maintained that absolute tranquillity prevailed in the fort on the eve of the mutiny, it was remembered later that on the previous afternoon, there was a flurry of activity in the fort. As Kaye wrote, 'Some mounted and some on foot, seemingly on no especial business; all with an insolent, braggart air, laughing and rollicking, making mimic battle among themselves, and otherwise expressing a general expectancy of something coming.'[45] Jamedar Rangappa later recalled, while being deposed before the enquiry commission, that 'he has been 15 months doing duty in this garrison and never before saw so many horsemen or crowd of people in the palace, when he was on guard that afternoon.' Another recollection was from that evening; the adjutant of a sepoy regiment had been abused 'by the vilest term of reproach in the local language'.[46]

Also, 9 July was the wedding day of one of Tipu's daughters, Princess Noor-ul-Nissum. The guests who were invited, thronging the main entrance gate, were full of excitement and bonhomie. This, the British officers thought, was owing to the prospect of seeing their confined royal relatives once again. Little did they realise that the wedding guests were, in reality, the rebel reinforcements in disguise.[47] Assistant Surgeon John Dean, who had dinner with

---

[42] Wilson, *History of the Madras Army*, vol. 3, 175–76.
[43] Mount, *Tears of the Rajas*, 39.
[44] Furnell, *Mutiny of Vellore*, 6–7.
[45] Kaye, *Sepoy Army in India*, vol. 2, 227.
[46] *Secret Department Sundries*, vol. 1B, 241–48.
[47] Quoted in Mount, *Tears of the Rajas*, 39–40.

his commanding officer that night, 'crossing the parade ground to [his] house, found more than usual gaiety in the palace'. As he later recollected, 'The Mahal was lighted up, and the sound of music gave every appearance of mirth and gaiety and I little dreamt that the hand I had so recently shaken, warm with friendship, would in a few short hours be cold as death, near the spot where I then stood.'[48]

Similarly, it was initially claimed that the officers on duty observed nothing unusual during the night. But it was later found, based on evidence given by an Indian sepoy who was in the main guard, that the European officer on duty that night, Captain Isaac Miller of the First Battalion of the Twenty-Third Regiment, did not go on his rounds and asked one of the native officers, the subedar, to take up the duty. The subedar too feigned indisposition, and Jamedar Sheik Kasim of the First Battalion, First Regiment, later one of the principal accused, volunteered to do it and left the guard ostensibly for that purpose.

As the Twenty-Third Regiment was scheduled to have a field day on the morning of 10 July, the leaders of the regiment used it as a pretext to sleep in the fort on the night of 9 July. The night guards on that day were drawn from a battalion of the First Regiment and the Muslim native adjutant posted many of his loyalists on duty in the fort. Some key personnel of the First Regiment also slept with them inside the fort under various pretexts.[49]

The native officers who were seen in the fort on the night of 9 July and the morning of 10 July and were later implicated in the mutiny were Subedars Sheik Adam and Sheik Hameed, and Jamedar Sheik Hussein, of the Second Battalion, Twenty-Third Regiment, and two subedars and Jamedar Sheik Kasim of the First Battalion, First Regiment.[50] Sheik Kasim was later charged for holding secret parleys in which participants, after taking an oath of secrecy, deliberated plans of operation proposed by him. Jamal-ud-Din,[51]

---

[48] Quoted in Mount, *Tears of the Rajas*, 40.
[49] Cox, *Manual of North Arcot District*, 83.
[50] *Secret Department Sundries*, vol. 3A, 1223–24.
[51] Jamal-ud-Din, a foster brother of Moiz-ud-Deen, is sometimes confused with Alla-ud-Deen, who was an agent of the Mysore princes.

a foster brother of Prince Moiz-ud-Din, was assigned the task of reporting the proceedings to his master, the prince. As was disclosed to the commission of enquiry, Jamal-ud-Din, one of the twelve princes of Tipu's family who played a key role in the revolt, kept telling the assemblage that the prince only required them to keep the fort for eight days before which time 10,000 men from Gurram Gondah, and several other Palayakkarars, would arrive to support them. He disclosed to them that letters had been written to those Palayakkarars soliciting their assistance. He also informed them that there were several *sardars* (Indian officers) in the service of Purniah (Tipu's minister) who were formerly in the sultan's service and would undoubtedly join the standard.[52]

IV

At 2 a.m. on 10 July, as trees cast dappled shadows on the moonlit parade ground of Vellore Fort, the guns boomed. The sentry at the main guard informed Corporal Piercy that guns had been fired near the European barracks. Before Piercy could respond, the sepoys attacked, firing simultaneously at the British guards, the European barracks, and the officers' quarters. In the process, Piercy himself was severely wounded. In the European quarters (see Figure 2.1), the windows were open, because of the sweltering heat. So the Europeans, 'lying naked and unprotected in their beds', would have been easily targeted 'through the barred windows.'[53] Bawah Sahib, lance naik of the Seventh Company, set fire to the European quarters.[54] This was to force the Europeans to leave their homes. Soldiers were deployed to watch the dwellings of the European officers, ready to shoot anyone who came out. A part of the First Regiment took possession of the magazines (firearm storehouses) and supplied ball cartridges to the soldiers (see Figures 2.2 and 2.3). A select band of First Regiment soldiers, led

---

[52] *Secret Department Sundries*, vol. 7B, 3654–55.

[53] Kirby, *Adventures of an Arcot Rupee*, 254.

[54] Kirby, *Adventures of an Arcot Rupee*, 122–24.

by Ismail Khan, made their rounds, massacring European officers in their quarters.[55]

Fancourt, commandant of the garrison, alerted by the firing at the main guard which was close to his house, rushed out in his dressing gown.[56] His wife, Amelia Fancourt, relates what happened on that fateful night:

> Colonel Fancourt and I retired to rest at ten o'clock. About the hour of two on Thursday morning, we were awakened at the same instant by a loud firing. We both got out of bed and Col. Fancourt went to the window of his writing-room; which he opened and called aloud and repeatedly, to know the cause of the disturbance, to which he received no reply but by a rapid continuation of the firing by numberless sepoys assembled at the main guard ... I looked at my husband. I saw him pale as ashes. I said, "Good God, what is the matter, Sir John?" To which he replied, "Go into your room, Amelia." I did so for I saw his minds agitated. I did not think it right to repeat my question at that moment. I heard him two minutes after leaving the writing room and go out of the house.[57]

Fancourt had gone straight down in his dressing gown to the front door. 'Don't go out, sir, for your dear life's sake,' the guard pleaded. 'Never mind,' Fancourt replied, and walked out to the parade ground shouting, 'Fall in!' He was shot down a few yards from his front door.[58] He lay in his dressing gown, dying slowly (see Figure 2.4).

The second victim, McKerras, the commanding officer of the Twenty-Third Regiment, had not communicated the new military regulations officially as he was informed that it would be a great cause of dissatisfaction. The sepoys had found out through unofficial channels. He was shot while haranguing his men on the parade ground. After they shot him, the sepoys stuck his corpse with the butt-end of their firelocks and kicked and spat

---

[55] Kirby, *Adventures of an Arcot Rupee*, 255.
[56] Cox, *Manual of North Arcot District*, 83–84.
[57] Quoted in Mount, *Tears of the Rajas*, 41.
[58] John Kaye, *History of the Indian Mutiny of 1857–8*, ed. G. B. Malleson, vol. 1 (London: Longmans, Green, 1914), 166.

upon it, and abused him for ordering they wear the new turbans. Yusuf Khan claimed that he had wanted to kill only the adjutant, Lieutenant John Coombs, but when McKerras came out of his house and proceeded towards the main guard, he shot him near the *tapal* (post) office.[59] Coombs, the unpopular adjutant of the Second Battalion, Twenty-Third Regiment, managed to flee from his back verandah to Marriott's house, where he hid himself and escaped.[60]

Lieutenant John Eley of the Sixty-Ninth Regiment, who was wounded and had a handkerchief tied round his head, was brought from the ramparts. He, with his young daughter in his arms, begged the sepoys for mercy. A Muslim, reportedly from the palace, struck him but the door behind him bore the brunt of it. Afterwards, he was chased into the guard room and slain in the presence of his wife.[61] Later it was found out that this appalling act, inspired by a motive of revenge, was a case of mistaken identity.

It was the consequence of the decision of a court of enquiry, held on 3 March 1806, into the shooting of a four-year-old Indian child by Lieutenant Baby at Vellore on 12 February 1806. No action was taken against the officer. The rejoinder of Lady Gwillim, wife of a Madras judge, throws more light on this incident. As she describes it, while the young Baby was carelessly practising his shooting, he shot an infant by mistake. He was arrested but was court martialled instead of being tried publicly. He was not charged, because the court believed he did not intend to kill the child, to the dissatisfaction of the child's parents. In the midst of the mutiny at the fort, mistaking Eley for Baby, the child's father killed him and his young child out of revenge.

The death of Lieutenant O'Reilly, who was in charge of the troops of the First Regiment, who were on night duty, is known from the account of Amelia Fancourt. During the revolt, she had brought her two children—one boy, aged two, and a baby girl—into her room and bolted the doors. She stood at the lower end of

---

[59] *Secret Department Sundries*, vol. 2B, 1173–83.

[60] Hoover, *Men Without Hats*, 112.

[61] *Secret Department Sundries*, vol. 1, 77. Also see William Thorn, *A Memoir of Major-General Sir R. R. Gillespie* (London: T. Egerton, 1816), 100–01.

the hall, which opened into the verandah, to look where the firing was taking place. Then, she recalls,

> a figure approached me. It was so dark I could only see the Red Coat by the light of the firing at the Barracks. I was dreadfully frightened expecting to be murdered and having left the children in my bed room, I had, however, the courage to ask who was this and the answer I received was "Madam, I am an officer of the Main Guard." I enquired what was the matter— he said it was a mutiny—that *every* European had already been murdered on Guard *but* himself and that we should *all* be murdered. I made no reply but walked away to the room where my babes and female servant were. The officer then went out of the opposite door of the hall where we had spoken together and never got downstairs for he was butchered most cruelly in Col. F's dressing room. I have since heard his name: Lt. O'Reilly of the 1st. [emphasis as in original][62]

Havildar Abdul Qadir, who was charged with assassinating Lieutenant Popham, killed O'Reilly too (see Figure 2.5).[63]

Surrounding the barracks, scores of native soldiers stormed the houses of the Europeans and put to death all those they could find. The house where Miller and Lieutenants John Tichbourne and Charles Smart lived together was also broken open. Perumal, an orderly boy in the Miller household, tried to persuade them to turn away, saying the officers had fled. The soldiers ignored him and searched the house. Tichbourne and Smart had been hiding in a small room for some time. Smart, on seeing a man from his own company, stood up to identify himself believing that they would now be safe. The response was a gunshot that killed him instantly. His companions, Miller and Tichbourne, fled into the bath, where they were killed. Lieutenant John Blakiston recorded this incident in his memoir: 'I saw their bodies just as they lay after the fatal deed—all huddled together in the bath, with their clothes half burnt from the fire of the muskets.'[64]

---

[62] Mount, *Tears of the Rajas*, 44.

[63] Hoover, *Men Without Hats*, 111.

[64] John Blakiston, *Twelve Years' Military Adventure*, vol. 1 (London: Henry Colburn, 1829), 298.

Major Charles Armstrong of the Sixteenth Native Infantry was passing outside the fort when he heard the sound of firing. He alighted from the palanquin he was travelling in and advanced to the glacis to ask about the firing. He was answered with a volley of bullets from the ramparts, which killed him instantly. It is believed that Armstrong was killed by Grenadier Mohammad Ali.[65]

Sepoys dragged Captain David Willison from his house and killed him for making them wear *topees* (hats). Sergeant Solomon Frost was shot down in his house, near the main guard. But his Indian wife was protected by the orders of one of the prince's servants. Sergeant James Watters's wife, Charlotte Watters, was also rescued from the gun-toting soldiers by the intervention of a palace servant.[66] In the barracks, eighty-two privates died, and ninety-one were wounded. One officer concealed himself under his bed, hidden by a pillow from the rebels who were searching the room. Others had sufficient time and warning to hide in a house near the European barracks. They came out only after the sepoys had begun to disperse for plunder.[67]

Contemporary British historians give a hyperbolic account of the attack on the European barracks, calling it the Vellore Massacre. The depiction of unarmed officers, their wives and children murdered in their bedrooms, some even in their hospital beds, evoked such a deep hatred in the minds of Englishmen that even a generation later, social reformer Raja Rammohan Roy was pelted with stones on the streets of Bristol by youths who shouted, 'Tipu! Tipu!'[68]

While examining a mass of material—official, semi-official and private—Kaye had to reject personal observations of some writers that hitherto had formed part of the narrative of the 'Massacre of Vellore':

> However serviceable they may be for purpose of effective historical writing, they are, I am sorry to say, at best apocryphal.

[65] *Secret Department Sundries*, vol. 1, 77.
[66] *Secret Department Sundries*, vol. 1, 77.
[67] Mill and Wilson, *History of British India*, vol. 7, 85–86.
[68] C. A. Bayly, *Imperial Meridian: The British Empire and the World, 1780–1830* (London: Longman, 1989), 114.

It has been said that the officer who carried the tidings to Arcot escaped through a sally-port, and swam the ditch of the Fort so famous for the number and size of its alligators. Sober official correspondence states that Major Coats, who was the bearer of the news, was outside the Fort at the time of the outbreak. It is very generally stated, too, that when Gillespie wished to enter the Fort in advance of his men, as there were no ladders and no ropes, the survivors of the 69th fastened their belts together, and thus drew him up the walls. But I have before me two letters, signed "R. Gillespie", which state that he was drawn up by a rope. Among the fictitious incidents of the mutiny may be mentioned the whole of the foul stories which tell of the murder of English women, and the burning of little children before their mothers' eyes.[69]

But even Kaye was not objective in his observations, as is known from the following spiteful comment he made while writing about the fate of English women. It is a travesty of truth when he says, 'The tender mercies of the wicked, with a refined cruelty, preserved them [the Englishwomen] for a worse fate than death. The people from the Palace told the sepoys not to kill them, as all the English would be destroyed, and the Moormen might then take them for wives.'[70] The fact of the matter was that Marriott, the officer in charge of the Mysore princes, refused to permit soldiers under Colonel Robert Gillespie's command to enter the palace, stating that the stipendiary princes were under his care, and hence he was accountable to the government in any eventuality.

One version of events stated that leaders of the mutiny, after the killing spree in the European barracks, had proclaimed Fateh Hyder, the second son of Tipu, as king in the open square. This claim was rejected even by the commission of enquiry. Muniappa (Mooniapah), a sepoy of the First Battalion, First Regiment, acting as the naik guarding the arsenal, deposed before the commission that while he was on his way to the sally port, he heard Grenadier Sheik Jaffer calling to somebody who lived in the palace close to Marriott's quarters, 'Come out Sir, Come out Sir, we have 300 men

[69] Kaye, *Sepoy Army in India*, vol. 2, 232.
[70] Kaye, *Sepoy Army in India*, vol. 2, 227–29.

ready for you.' A short fat man, whose name he did not know, but presumably Fateh Hyder, the eldest of the Mysore Princes (Figure 2.6), looked out of the window, but seeing the party, said, 'Go, Go, you fools there is not enough, do you think I will accompany such a party as that.'[71] This made the sepoys desperate, and we now know that, later, three or four sepoys of the First Battalion of the First Regiment, standing on the rampart near the gateway, made a signal with a piece of cloth, calling and abusing the sepoys in the pettai for not coming into the fort.[72]

During the period that the events unfolded, as is seen in official records, active communication was kept up between the mutineers and the palace, and many of the servants and followers of the princes were conspicuously active in the scenes of murder and plunder. Jamal-ud-Din seems to have acted as a liaison between the sepoys and the palace.[73] A flag, which had once belonged to Tipu and bore his insignia—a sun in the centre and green tiger stripes on a red field—was brought out of the palace and hoisted on the flagstaff amidst thunderous acclamation from the assemblage.

As was the wont of any victorious army, the soldiery resorted to looting. This prompted H. H. Wilson to write,

> Subordination was speedily at an end; the Sipahis and followers of the palace dispersed in quest of plunder; and many who had been reluctant participators in the mutiny, who began to fear its consequences, or who sought to secure the booty they had obtained, availed themselves of the confusion to leave the fort.[74]

It was officially reported that 'property to the amount of star pagodas [gold coin issued by the Company in Madras] 2,908,733.39 was plundered from the cash chest of the payment at Vellore.'[75]

---

[71] *Secret Department Sundries*, vol. 1B, 241–48.

[72] *Secret Department Sundries*, vol. 3A, 1223–24.

[73] Maya Gupta, 'Vellore Mutiny, July 1806', in *Defying Death: Struggles Against Imperialism and Feudalism*, ed. Maya Gupta and Amit Kumar Gupta (New Delhi: Tulika, 2001), 22. Note that it is not Alaudin. See Special Commission Report in *Secret Department Sundries*, vol. 2A, 821–40.

[74] Mill and Wilson, *History of British India*, vol. 7, 84–86.

[75] *Military Department Despatches to England* (641), vol. 38, 21 October 1806.

V

There is no official account of the subsequent course of events. We have to weave the story from reports of incidents sent by military officers at different levels to the commander-in-chief and the governor. In this list of military officials are Lieutenant Colonel Marriott, Captains Marriott and Maclachlan, Corporal Piercy, Major Coates, Sergeants Cosgrave and Brady, Lieutenants Mitchell, Baby, Cutcliffe, Ewing and Jenour, Surgeon Jones and Assistant Surgeon Dean.

Cosgrave, the barracks guard on the day, hearing the trampling of feet, called the sentry at the guard house door at about 2:30 a.m., expressing astonishment that the patrol should pass that way. He had scarcely spoken when a party of sepoys formed in front of the gate and discharged a volley of musketry on the guard, because of which several men of the Sixty-Ninth Regiment fell into the barracks. The barracks of the Sixty-Ninth was the first target of attack, 'the result of which has been so fatal to so many brave officers and soldiers'.[76]

At about 3 a.m., Lance Naik Mohammed Yakub of the First Battalion, First Regiment, went to the house of Captain Charles Marriott, of the same battalion, to warn him not to go near the European barracks as the men of the Twenty-Third Regiment were firing upon them. Captain Marriott immediately went to the Ambur gate, where he found a guard of his own regiment under arms. The naik of this guard, Syed Ahmed, also advised him not to approach the barracks. Thereupon, he returned to his quarters, where he was joined by Lieutenant Bissett of the Sixty-Ninth. They resolved to go to the main guard. Venkatram, the naik in command of the main guard, told Captain Marriott not to venture near the parade. The two officers returned to the other side of the palace by the magazine, and succeeded in entering a house behind the main guard. After waiting there for a while, they jumped over the wall and landed in the main guard, which looked deserted. They hid there until the arrival of the Arcot cavalry at 9 a.m.[77]

---

[76] *Military Department Despatches to England* (641), vol. 38, 21 October 1806.

[77] Mill and Wilson, *History of British India*, vol. 7, 84–86.

Lieutenant Colonel Marriott, who lived in the fort with his brother, Captain Marriott, the assistant paymaster of stipends, was awakened by the firing. He was informed by the naik of his guard, who belonged to the First Battalion of the First Regiment that the men of the Twenty-Third Regiment were mutinying. The lieutenant colonel went to his guard, where he learnt that the adjutant, Coombs, of the Twenty-Third, who was very unpopular with his sepoys, had slipped out of his quarters. Marriott wanted the guard not to venture out from his house, and as he was leaving, a band of mutineers of the Twenty-Third came up and ordered his guard to join them. They did not attempt to harass the lieutenant colonel and so he returned to his house, where he found Lieutenant Gunning of the Sixty-Ninth, who had come there after an abortive attempt to reach the barracks. At dawn, the house was surrounded by sepoys, who took possession of the lower rooms, and fired a volley of bullets upstairs; Captain Marriott was wounded. Thereafter, they set fire to Coombs's house. At about 7 a.m., the sepoys fired another volley and went upstairs, calling for the adjutant of the Twenty-Third. After some anxious moments, Lieutenant Colonel Marriott and his friends returned to the basement of the house unobserved.[78]

Surgeon John Jones and his assistant Dean, of the Twenty-Third Regiment, along with Maclachlan, Mitchell, Baby, Jenour, and Brady, of the Sixty-Ninth Regiment, and Cutcliffe (badly wounded) assembled at the house of the adjutant, Lieutenant John Ewing, of the First Battalion, First Regiment, at about 3:30 a.m. As expected, in a quarter of an hour, a mob of sepoys attacked the front of the house. Ewing had arms and ammunition, seized from one naik and three sepoys, and hence could return fire and force the rebel soldiers to retreat. Thereafter, Ewing and his surviving colleagues retired to the adjoining house, Jones's.[79]

[78] Wilson, *History of the Madras Army*, vol. 3, 179–83.

[79] Wilson, *History of the Madras Army*, vol. 3, 179–80; Vibart, *Madras Engineers and Pioneers*, vol. 1, 402–04. Surgeon Jones and his assistant, Dean, the only white officers who survived death and disability, later sent a detailed report to the commander-in-chief describing the events, from which we know their whereabouts.

At the time of leaving Ewing's house, Brady was asked to collect information on what was going on. After an hour, he returned with news of the murder of every European in the different guards, the murder of European officers, including the commandant of the garrison, and the hoisting of the Mysore flag.

Mitchell left for the barracks at 7 a.m. Thereafter, they heard nothing but cries and constant heavy firing of guns and musketry in different parts of the fort. They remained in this state of anxious suspense until about eight in the morning, after which they moved out of Jones's house to reach the barracks, still under fire from the insurgents.[80] On entering the barracks they found every man shielding himself as best as he could from the incessant gunshots. Many lay killed or wounded. There they found Mitchell. Maclachlan, as the senior-most officer, took command, and it was determined that they would sally out from the windows opposite to the *parachery* (living quarters of Parayars; which had huts occupied by civilians attached to the army), and reach the adjoining ramparts. Having exhausted all six rounds of the ball cartridges they possessed, they went to the magazine at the bottom of the ramparts. All the ball cartridges had been taken by the insurgents, and only a few blank ones were left.[81]

Climbing the ramparts, braving a heavy fire of muskets, they picked up soldiers who had assembled in a nearby bastion and proceeded to fight the Indian horsemen in arms there. They succeeded, but 'with the loss of further services of Captain Maclachlan', who sustained a severe wound in the thigh. Several others also suffered injuries.[82]

While advancing further, they were joined by Captain Barrow, of the Sixty-Ninth, who took command and they continued along the ramparts. Despite being under a constant fire of musketry, they succeeded in taking possession of the gateway. But the gate remained locked. The fire from the palace at this time was heavy. A six-pounder remained opposite the gate for its defence,

---

[80] Vibart, *Madras Engineers and Pioneers*, vol. 1, 404.
[81] Wilson, *History of the Madras Army*, vol. 3, 180–81.
[82] Vibart, *Madras Engineers and Pioneers*, vol. 1, 404.

but since there was no ammunition for it, it was left to the care of the Europeans across the gateway. At this stage, the European detachment's attempt to take possession of the grand magazine proved impossible.[83]

The detachment then proceeded with Barrow to attempt, unsuccessfully, take over the bastion at the south-east face of the fort, which was being defended by a committed band of Indian soldiers. In the shootout, Barrow fell by a musket shot through his leg. Thereafter, no officer except Jones and Dean in the fort remained to lead the Europeans. They managed to retain the bastion but with the loss of several European lives. The rebel Indian soldiers retreated into the central part of the fort and deployed themselves in the gateway of the granary. In the meantime, a small group of Europeans left from the rampart to the site of the flagstaff. Sergeant McManus and Private Philip Bottom of the Sixty-Ninth Regiment pulled down the Mysore flag.

Heavy fire was kept up from the pettai and the fort, and men fell fast. They proceeded to the magazine and burst it open, only to find some loose combustible powder.[84] Jones and Dean, therefore, had to depend on pieces of gravel for firing.[85] The men wanted to proceed to attack the sepoy barracks, but the idea was instantly opposed as the strength of the party was very much reduced. In the absence of ammunition, they decided to return and keep possession of the gateway and cavaliers until the arrival of relief.

Ewing, separated from the other officers after leaving Jones's house, assembled several European stragglers. Making his way out of the fort, he joined Forbes, who was one of the few officers who managed to escape, as he was staying outside the main fort. Accompanied by a number of unarmed men belonging to the First Battalion of the First Regiment, these two officers took possession of the principal hill fort, where they remained until the authority of the British was restored in the main fort.[86]

---

[83] Vibart, *Madras Engineers and Pioneers*, vol. 1, 404.

[84] Vibart, *Madras Engineers and Pioneers*, vol. 1, 404.

[85] Mount, *Tears of the Rajas*, 47–48.

[86] Mill and Wilson, *History of British India*, vol. 7, 84–86.

Ferdinand Mount, the author of *The Tears of the Rajas*, describes Dean's account, about the melancholic condition that prevailed: 'Some of the non-commissioned officers came to him and said that they were now without any officers, their numbers were greatly reduced, they had no ammunition left and no provisions, and the sepoys also had possession of the hill fort ... They considered their case hopeless and saw no chance of relief.'[87] However, as relayed by Mount, Dean was able to convince the non-commissioned officers that several officers living outside the fort would have passed information to the cantonment at Arcot and soon reinforcements would arrive. The emotionally charged Dean is said to have pulled off the mattress he had laid over the corpse of his friend Willison, of the Second Battalion, Twenty-Third Regiment, and asked the non-commissioned officers, 'What could be expected but similar treatment from men who had committed such dreadful excesses?'[88] Thus, the remainder of Europeans who survived the massacre were convinced against thinking of surrendering and were prevailed upon to wait until Gillespie arrived from Arcot.

VI

Coates, an officer of the English regiment who was on duty outside the fort, on hearing of the mutiny, sent an officer, Captain Stevenson of the Twenty-Third, to Arcot with a letter addressed to Gillespie, who commanded the cavalry cantonment there. Upon receiving it, Gillespie set out immediately, taking with him a squadron of the Nineteenth Dragoons under Captain Young, supported by a strong troop of the Seventh Native Cavalry under Lieutenant John Woodhouse. He instructed Colonel James Kennedy to follow him with the rest of the cavalry. A small detachment was left behind to protect the cantonment and to keep up communications.

Gillespie was an old colleague of Fancourt from St Domingo (Figure 2.7). He was scheduled to dine with the family of his old

---

[87] Mount, *Tears of the Rajas*, 48.
[88] Mount, *Tears of the Rajas*, 48–49.

friend, Fancourt, the day before, on 9 July; but as he mounted his horse for that purpose, letters arrived from the government warranting immediate reply. Thereupon, Gillespie cancelled his visit and sent an apology to Fancourt 'for his unavoidable absence'. 'There is visible interposition of Divine Providence in this disappointment; since, had it not been for the imperative circumstance of duty which detained him at Arcot, Colonel Gillespie would, in all probability, have shared the melancholy catastrophe of his brave and unfortunate acquaintance,' writes William Thorn, Gillespie's biographer.[89] Gillespie was unaware of the insurgency in Vellore on the morning of 10 July. When he mounted his horse the next morning at six o' clock to set out, with the intention of joining Fancourt for breakfast, 'the dismal tidings came of the tragic fate of his friends and of the horrors that were still prevailing'.[90]

When Gillespie arrived at Vellore Fort at 9 a.m., the drawbridge was down and the two outer gates were open. The third gate had been opened by some of the surviving men of the Sixty-Ninth. But when the reinforcements arrived in front of the fourth gate (the inner one), they found that it was completely under the control of the Indian soldiers. Gillespie wanted to wait for the arrival of the guns, since there was continuous firing. The cavalry, under Kennedy, came from Arcot at about ten o' clock. The gate was blown open with the galloper guns of the Nineteenth Regiment, under the direction of Blakiston. The troops entered the fort, headed by a squadron of the cavalry under Captain Skelton and ably supported by the native cavalry.[91]

The Sixty-Ninth were met with severe crossfire. But the dragoons, with a strength of 450 men, galloped with swords in hand and charged.[92] In the ensuing pitched battle, Gillespie himself suffered bruises. The sepoys retreated. Hundreds escaped over the walls of the fort, or threw down their arms and pleaded for mercy. Then, the cavalry regiment resolved to pursue the fleeing soldiers

---

[89] Thorn, *Memoir of Major-General Gillespie*, 98.
[90] Thorn, *Memoir of Major-General Gillespie*, 101.
[91] Wilson, *History of the Madras Army*, vol. 3, 169–201.
[92] Furnell, *Mutiny of Vellore*, 8.

who were trying to escape through the narrow passage afforded by the sally port (Figures 2.8 and 2.9). What happened thereafter is graphically described in *Manual of the North Arcot District*:

> Numbers were cut down while thus in retreat, and many others despatched upon the glacis by a troop of dragoons and some native horsemen sent round to intercept the fugitives ... All the buildings in the Fort were explored, and mutineers found in them pitilessly slaughtered. A considerable number had taken possession of the deserted European barracks, from whence they fired on all who passed. A party of dragoons and Governor's body guard dismounted, entered the building, and attacked those within. The sickening sight of the mutilated bodies of the Europeans, and of the sick of the 69th, who had been dragged from the regimental hospital and butchered in front of the mahal gates, excited ... resentment, and the men clamoured to be allowed to enter the building and revenge themselves on the princely instigators of the plot; but Colonel Gillespie held them back.[93]

But the fact of the matter was that Gillespie was bent on finishing off the wards of Tipu. It was Lieutenant Colonel Marriott and not Gillespie who resisted the dragoon's attempt to kill the princes.[94]

However, Gillespie is said to have brought the fort under the control of the English in about fifteen minutes (see Appendix 14, for Gillespie's report to the commander-in-chief after restoring normalcy in the fort). Colonel George Harcourt, commanding officer at Wallajahbad, was appointed to the temporary command of Vellore on 11 July.[95] Harcourt assumed command of the garrison on 13 July 1806 and clamped martial law.[96] Captain Wilson of the Nineteenth Dragoons was appointed to the temporary charge of pay office.[97] It was believed that the prompt and decisive actions of Gillespie put an end to 'the dangerous confederacy' and had the fort

---

[93] Cox, *Manual of North Arcot District*, 86. The discovery of the body of Lieutenant George Jolly is said to have enraged them into thinking of this revenge.

[94] Read Marriott's deposition to the enquiry commission in Chapter 3.

[95] *Secret Consultations*, vol. 19, 823–25.

[96] Hoover, *Men Without Hats*, 126–27.

[97] *Military Department Despatches to England* (642), vol. 38, 21 October 1806.

remained in the possession of the insurgents for a few more days, they would have been joined by 50,000 from Mysore. Cradock, who was so convinced of the immense value of the service performed by Gillespie, called it, in his dispatch, 'a military wonder'.[98] According to W. J. Wilson, the troops from Arcot sustained minimum loss of life, with one European trooper killed and three wounded.[99] S. S. Furnell's estimate of the number of Europeans massacred by the insurgents is 113. Among them were Fancourt and thirteen other officers.[100] Kaye thought that 'the massacre included fourteen officers and ninety-nine soldiers killed. There were, moreover, several officers and men wounded, some of them later mortally'.[101] 'Volley after volley through the venetians, till eighty-two had been killed and ninety-one wounded ... Then the sepoys proceeded to the residences of the officers, and killed thirteen of them', was the information from John Clark Marshman.[102] Thomas Munro's estimate was sixteen officers and about a hundred Europeans of the Sixty-Ninth Regiment.[103]

The officers killed were: Colonel Fancourt, Thirty-Fourth Regiment, commandant of the garrison, Lieutenant Colonel McKerras, Captain Willison and Lieutenants Winchip and Jolly of the Twenty-Third, Captain Miller, Lieutenants O'Reilly, Smart, and Tichbourne of the First, and Lieutenants Eley and Popham of the Sixty-Ninth, deputy commissary of stores, William Mann, conductor of ordnance, Samuel Gill, military paymaster, S. S. Smith, and Major Armstrong, First Battalion of the Sixteenth Regiment. Captains Barrow and Maclachlan and Lieutenant Mitchell of the Sixty-Ninth and Lieutenant Cutcliffe of the First were severely wounded, while Captain Marriott, assistant paymaster of stipends, was wounded slightly.[104]

[98] Thorn, *Memoir of Major-General Gillespie*, 104.
[99] Wilson, *History of the Madras Army*, vol. 3, 186.
[100] Furnell, *Mutiny of Vellore*, 8–9.
[101] Kaye, *Sepoy Army in India*, vol. 2, 230.
[102] Marshman, *History of India*, vol. 2, 208–09.
[103] G. R. Gleig, *The Life of Major-General Sir Thomas Munro*, vol. 1 (London: Henry Colburn, 1830), 365.
[104] *Secret Department Sundries*, vol. 1A, 204–205.

On the other hand, a large number of sepoys were killed in the counter-violence unleashed by Gillespie and his storm troops. According to one source, about 350 of the mutineers fell in the attack of the dragoons, and about 500 were imprisoned in Vellore and in other places to which they had fled. This is only to underplay the cause for which the sepoys laid down their lives. In Arthur Cox's estimate, a great number of mutineers were killed; 800 were found dead in the fort alone.[105] In W. J. Wilson's reckoning, of the 1,700 native troops stationed at Vellore on the night of 9 July, 879 were dead or missing, 378 were confined for mutiny and 516 were considered implicated but not imprisoned.[106] Those who had taken asylum in neighbouring villages were captured by the police, and no less than 600 were in irons at Vellore and Tiruchirappalli for their role in the revolt.[107] As reported by the town major at Fort St George, the prisoners in the St Thome Lunettes numbered 172 and the Madras-domiciled, detained for trial in Madras, were thirty-nine in number.[108]

We have the letter of the commanding officer of the fort that helps ascertain the number of prisoners in Vellore. Harcourt, in a statement sent to the government on 13 November 1806, stated that the prisoners in Vellore Fort totalled 466. According to him, a further number of soldiers of the two battalions that formed the garrison of Vellore on 10 July, and who took part in the revolt, were still at large. Including that number, the total figure worked out to 787. He suggested that these persons escaped confinement as the fort was already overcrowded with prisoners. He further made it known that of the 466 prisoners at Vellore, the granary contained 319 prisoners, a further thirty-seven were in a part of the arrack godown, and the remaining 110 were in the main guard.[109]

Commander-in-chief Cradock reported that including the twenty-nine persons tried and sentenced, there were still twenty-one native officers and 891 persons of inferior rank either charged

[105] Cox, *Manual of North Arcot District*, 85–86.
[106] Wilson, *History of the Madras Army*, vol. 3, 186.
[107] Cox, *Manual of North Arcot District*, 86.
[108] *Secret Department Sundries*, vol. 11, 1628–1705; vol. 12, 32–39.
[109] *Military Department Dispatches*, vol. 359, 8425–27.

with or strongly suspected of participation in the mutiny. Those who had fled at the first appearance of the cavalry from Arcot had since been imprisoned in different places in the Carnatic. The commander-in-chief observed that according to Forbes, of those present at Vellore, only four officers were exempted from suspicion. The official account, albeit incomplete, is provided in Appendix 1. Only twelve native officers and 409 non-commissioned rank and file were initially declared innocent. The remaining 1,801 persons were imprisoned and summarily dismissed from service. But later, all of them were condoned and ordered to report for duty, indicating the conciliatory attitude of the Company government.[110]

VII

Vellore had its echoes in Hyderabad, Wallajahbad, Bangalore, Nandydurg, Palayamkottai and Bellary.

Hyderabad

In the immediate aftermath of the Vellore outbreak, there was 'strange behaviour' reported in the Second Battalion of the Eleventh Regiment at Hyderabad, where the British Resident Thomas G. Montresor of the Twenty-Second Dragoons commanded a subsidiary force numbering about 10,000. In a letter addressed to Captain Thomas Sydenham, Montresor explained the alarming situation in Hyderabad thus:

> The idea circulated among the troops was by forcing them to give up everything that distinguished one caste from another, the government was trying to gradually convert them to Christianity. They also suspected that the Europeans would massacre the native soldiers. There were also several other alarms like Europeans were about to make a human sacrifice.

---

[110] *Secret Department Sundries*, vol. 3B, 1569–70.

However ridiculous these reports might have been, they patently worked on the minds of the natives.[111]

Sydenham, based on information he obtained in Hyderabad, reported that 'the native troops had been invited to desert their colours, to break out in open mutiny, and to murder their officers'. Planning to make use of the commotion in the city at the time of the insurrection in the cantonments, Mir Alam (Meer Allum), and all those in the interests of the English, were to be killed, the nizam was to be imprisoned, and Fariddun Jah (Feridoom Jah) was to be made diwan or placed on the *musnud* (throne).[112]

It was the considered opinion of the men of the Second Battalion of the Fifteenth Infantry Regiment that the military regulations on dress and hat were part of the English ploy to annihilate caste, destroy the religion of the natives, and forcibly convert them to Christianity. Besides, the officers of the Second Battalion of the Eleventh Regiment reported that their men had served under difficult conditions for many years and furthermore had suffered a significant loss of pay due to the need to exchange star pagodas for Hyderabadi rupees.[113]

Rumours were rife. One of the rumours that caused excitement was that an oracle had predicted there was treasure at the bottom of the well in the European barracks, and that this treasure could not be discovered until a certain number of human heads had been offered to the tutelary deity of the well. It was thought that the heads were going to be provided by Europeans troops, who would be employed at night to waylay the natives. The discovery of a headless corpse near the Residency gave new wing to the rumours.[114]

On 12 July, the Second Battalion of the Fifteenth Regiment refused to wear the turban, and the other battalions were also reportedly in a defiant mood. Lieutenant Colonel Gabriel Doveton

---

[111] *Home Miscellaneous Series*, vol. 509, India Office Library, 45–60.

[112] Mir Alam was the incumbent diwan of Hyderabad in 1806.

[113] *Home Miscellaneous Series*, vol. 507, 540–43; Quoted in Hoover, *Men Without Hats*, 152–53.

[114] Wilson, *History of the Madras Army*, vol. 3, 194–95.

informed Montresor that the cavalry would not draw their swords to put down any riot that might erupt in the event of an attempt to force the new turban on the infantry.[115]

As the feeling of resentment among the native troops was so strong, some senior native officers exhorted Montresor not to enforce the new army regulations. But he replied that he had been selected for the task and hence could not shirk his duty. But when news of Vellore reached Hyderabad, he saw at once the logic behind the plea of the senior officers and withdrew the regulations in anticipation of instructions from the Madras government. Yet, the troops remained discontented. Having triumphed over the 'hat issue', they were determined to redress their grievances over their leather stockings as well. Sepoys of the First Battalion of the Twenty-Second Regiment, at the instigation of their native officers, pulled out their stockings and cast them contemptuously on the ground during the parade. This defiance was dealt with sternly.

On 14 August, the troops in Hyderabad were ordered under arms, flanked by the English regiment. Then, the four Indian officers of the Native Infantry, Subedars Sidi Hussein, Qadir Beg and Umar Ali and Jamedar Sheik Hussein, who were believed to be the ringleaders in the incident, were called to the front and marched off to Masulipatnam under a guard of thirty Europeans and a company of sepoys. Kaye wrote on the effect of this show of strength:

> Mutiny was awe-struck; sedition was paralysed; conciliatory explanations and addresses, which had before failed, were now crowned with success, and early in the following month Sydenham wrote from Hyderabad that everything was "perfectly tranquil, both in the city and the cantonments." "The Sepoys," he added, "appear cheerful and contented, and the Government goes on with considerable vigour and regularity."[116]

Of the four ringleaders identified, the three subedars of the Fifteenth Regiment in Hyderabad were transported to Penang

---

[115] Wilson, *History of the Madras Army*, vol. 3, 194–95.
[116] Kaye, *Sepoy Army in India*, vol. 2, 236–37.

for life, and the jamedar of the Second Battalion of the Eleventh Regiment was sentenced to be shot. This sentence was later commuted to transportation for life.[117]

Wallajahbad

The Native Infantry at Wallajahbad, in the wake of Vellore revolt, held memorials in honour of the soldiers killed at Vellore Fort. As disclosed by Sepoy Muhammed Syed Khan, the discontented sepoys were meeting in secret at the residence of a *fakir* (religious mendicant of Islamic faith) and planning something prejudicial to the interests of the Company government.[118] Lieutenant Colonel Ross Lang, who was in command of the cantonment, realising that his troops had plans of massacring the European officers, took immediate measures of defence. Three companies of European troops marched from Poovirunthavalli under Gillespie's command to restore order at Wallajahbad on 27 July. Subedar Venkata Naik, previously in Tipu's army, was dismissed for inciting soldiers on the issue of the hat (turban), which had led to the unruly behaviour of the native soldiery.[119] The First Battalion of the Twenty-Third Regiment at Wallajahbad was subsequently disarmed. Criminal cases were registered against several persons at Wallajahbad, leading to their dismissal.[120]

On this occasion, Cradock himself proceeded to Wallajahbad and conducted an investigation. Later, he informed the governor that the idea of anything like 'a concerted plan of disaffection and evil design was totally unsupported by evidence'. He pointed out the striking fact that 'the suspected Battalion marched out of camp and returned with the most exact obedience and alacrity, though in possession of their ball cartridges ... Nothing, has appeared

---

[117] Kaye, *Sepoy Army in India*, vol. 2, 236–37. Sheik Hussein, Second Battalion, Eleventh Regiment, was probably exonerated of the charges.
[118] Sabyasachi Dasgupta, *In Defence of Honour and Justice: Sepoy Rebellions in the Nineteenth Century* (Delhi: Primus Books, 2015), 21.
[119] Gupta, 'Vellore Mutiny, July 1806', 20.
[120] Bentinck, *Memorial*, 29–30.

against them beyond the irregular tumults at the Barracks and the loose expressions of individuals, and something of a general mysterious conduct.'[121]

The governor's council resolved that a discreet officer, in the confidence of the government, should be sent to Wallajahbad to enquire and report on the state of affairs. Colonel Munro, the quartermaster-general, was chosen for the assignment.[122] Munro's investigation showed that the 'disaffection' was limited to a few native officers. The other conclusion that emerged from the probe was the 'extreme indifference' of native officers in the discharge of their duty, and the lack of effort on their part to check 'inflammatory expressions' articulated by some of the sepoys at Wallajahbad.[123] The government accepted Munro's report and the concurring opinion of the commander-in-chief that 'there were not sufficient grounds for the adoption of measures of severity towards any of the corps stationed at the cantonment of Wallajahbad.'[124]

Nandydurg

Nandydurg, situated in the heart of the Mysore region, was 50 kilometres away from the military station at Bangalore. The fortress, which was built on a high, scarped rock, was one of uncommon strength and had assumed strategic importance because of its location. At the time of the Vellore Revolt, the Nandydurg garrison consisted of companies detached from Bangalore, which was under the command of Major Alexander Muirhead. The native troops were few, since the First Battalion, Eighteenth Regiment, had been moved to Vellore in the wake of the mutiny. The remaining men of the Second Battalion of the

---

[121] Bentinck, *Memorial*, 29–30.
[122] Furnell, *Mutiny of Vellore*, 6; Kaye, *Sepoy Army in India*, vol. 2, 243. Colonel Munro is not Thomas Munro.
[123] Wilson, *History of the Madras Army*, vol. 3, 196.
[124] *Secret Department Sundries*, vol. 2A, 778–79.

Eighteenth Regiment at Nandydurg were therefore well aware and upset over the slaughter that ended the Vellore Mutiny.[125]

Subedar Kasturi, of the Second Battalion, Eighteenth Regiment, noted that since the Company's defeat at the hands of the Holkars in 1804–05, there was a rumour that Tipu Sultan's nephew, the son of his brother Karim Sahib, would arrive via Hyderabad with a detachment of the Holkar army. In his testimony, Kasturi stated that when the signal came from Tipu's nephew, a revolt was to take place, and if successful, Indian officers would hold all positions in the new military service, from general downwards, with their corresponding pay.[126]

The influence of fakirs, conjurors, puppet-showmen and propagators of strange prophecies ran deep in Nandydurg. Subedar Kasturi was of the view that the puppet shows corrupted most of the non-commissioned officers—Subedar Muhammad Reza in particular. Jamedar Sheikh Dawood vowed not to wear the new turban and his companions, Subedar Venkatachellam and Havildar Sheikh Nattar, endorsed his view. Subedars Muhammad Reza and Venkatachellam, and Jamedar Tika Ram held the view that the Company Raj was built on treachery, draining away the wealth of the country and giving its sepoys only a 'trifling allowance'.[127] Subedar Kasturi conveyed this to Muirhead, who, based on the report received, arrested both Muhammad Reza and Venkatachellam. This action enraged the entire soldiery in the garrison.

Since then, Muslims and Hindus bound themselves by oath to act together in the common cause of fighting the British. The programme of action was planned and even the day and time were fixed. However, on 28 October, an English officer informed the commandant, Major Cuppage, that the sepoys were about to revolt. Hardly had the news been conveyed than an old and distinguished native officer came panting with the same intelligence. This timely intelligence pre-empted the soldiers' mutiny. There was no time to be lost and a letter requesting reinforcements was dispatched to

[125] Hoover, *Men Without Hats*, 188.
[126] Hoover, *Men Without Hats*, 170, 189.
[127] Hoover, *Men Without Hats*, 190–191.

Bangalore. The officers took position in one of their houses in the temple square, which seemed best suited for the situation, and waited anxiously. The night passed without an attack and by three o' clock the following afternoon, a squadron of dragoons from Bangalore, led by Lieutenant Colonel Henry Davis, arrived.[128] But contrary to his expectations, there was calm. The officers were found missing and the soldiers remained in their barracks, 'dismally quiet'.[129]

Davis ordered a court of enquiry, that showed that offensive slurs had been uttered against English officers and various attempts had been made to instigate insubordination. Major General Archibald MacDowall monitored and reviewed the court of enquiry proceedings, as directed by the commander-in-chief. MacDowall relied on the testimony of Jamedar Sheikh Dawood and concluded that 'the most daring and atrocious acts had been averted at Nandidurg by prompt, vigorous action'.[130] Seventeen persons were dismissed from service.

The existence of a spirit of rebellion at Nandydurg, similar to other places, was beyond doubt.[131] A circular from the government stated that 'from evidence examined at Nandydrug and Bangalore it had been ascertained that agents were suspected to be at work in different parts under the guise of fakirs poisoning the minds of native troops.'[132] Writing about the Nandydurg enquiry, Lieutenant Colonel Alexander Dyce, in a letter addressed to Welsh, remarked that the plan originated in the Holkar camp, involving the nizam's brothers, Tipu's sons and some others.[133]

Bangalore

Lieutenant Colonel Samuel William Ogg, the officer commanding at Bangalore, on hearing about the incident at Nandydurg, took the

---

[128] Kaye, *Sepoy Army in India*, vol. 2, 239–40.
[129] Hoover, *Men Without Hats*, 194.
[130] Hoover, *Men Without Hats*, 196–97.
[131] Furnell, *Mutiny of Vellore*, 29–30.
[132] *Secret Department Sundries*, vol. 9A, 638–42
[133] Quoted in Hoover, *Men Without Hats*, 201.

initiative of pre-empting any secret plot in his regiment. In a bid to expose conspirators, Ogg ordered the house of a *munshi* (writer, record keeper or language teacher) to be searched for seditious materials. Ogg, from the papers he collected, was able to prove the existence of a plot to free the Mysore prisoners at Vellore. Ogg also searched the residence of a travelling fakir, Syed Muhammad, and again claimed to find evidence of sedition. Impressed by Ogg's actions, MacDowall instructed him to expand the scope of investigation. One of the deponents, Sepoy Ramaswamy, informed the court of enquiry what Jamedar Syed Hussein had told him twenty days before the outbreak at Nandydurg. At that time, Jamedar Syed Hussein had told Ramaswamy that 'he would see, in ten days, a scene of confusion in this place, and ... all the Europeans put to death'. After a few days, Sepoy Syed Ibrahim told the court of enquiry that if Muhammad Reza, arrested at Nandydurg, was executed, his brother, Naik Muhammad Usman, would kill 'some person of consequence' in revenge. The court of enquiry however, having decided not to give any credence to this theory of conspiracy, did not pursue the matter further. The court, after hearing such depositions for about three weeks, arrived at the conclusion that 'there was no evidence, whatsoever, to suggest that the sepoys of the Second Battalion of the Eighteenth Native Infantry were mutinous'. Lieutenant Colonel (later, Sir) John Malcolm, who succeeded Mark Wilks as resident, wrote to his friend, Colonel Arthur Wellesley, that the 'weakness, distractions and, and incompetence of the government were to blame for the Vellore crisis'.[134]

Bellary

At Bellary, Lieutenant Colonel George Martin who commanded the Second Battalion of the Fifth Regiment and the Second Battalion of the Seventh Regiment, brought to the notice of Campbell the activities of certain native officers and sepoys that

---

[134] Hoover, *Men Without Hats*, 198–201.

posed serious threat to the 'public tranquillity of Bellary'. In his report to Campbell, Martin pointed out that two fakirs, Alam Ali Sha and Nur Khalil Shah, had come to Bellary before the Vellore Mutiny and that both men, receiving the patronage of Sepoy Abdul Nabi and Subedar Mir Bakr, had begun to propagate their 'evil doctrines'. Abdul Nabi's attitude towards orthodox Islam alienated him from the Muslim community in Bellary. Therefore, the court of enquiry that was set up comprised local notables with the *qazi* of Bellary presiding.[135] Abdul Nabi denied all the charges against him in the court of enquiry. Subedar Mir Bakr, who had close contact with Abdul Nabi and another sepoy, Abdul Ghurry, refused to admit that he had done anything wrong. However, the subedar was convicted, for having, 'in collusion with two sepoys, aided two fakirs to preach sedition against the British', and consequently, he was dismissed.[136]

Palayamkottai

After anxious moments at Nandydurg and Bangalore, it was believed that the uneasiness had passed. But towards the end of the third week of November 1806, the Company government believed that the Muslim sepoys in Palayamkottai were about to rise and massacre all the Europeans. According to the plan, some buildings were to be fired at in the cantonment to draw the English officers from their homes, and in the melee, all the English officers were to be slain, the fort was to be seized, and the rebel flag hoisted on the ramparts. Sensing the plot, a Malabari went to the mosque in disguise, collected information and transmitted it to the English commandant.[137]

Welsh, with six European officers under him, commanded the First Battalion of the Third Regiment at Palayamkottai, in which there were many relatives of mutineers 'cut up' at Vellore, and were brooding over the loss of their dear ones. The suspicious behaviour

---

[135] Hoover, *Men Without Hats*, 229–33.
[136] Furnell, *Mutiny of Vellore*, 29–30.
[137] *Secret Department Sundries*, vol. 9A, 638–42.

of two sentries belonging to the Maravar caste at Palayamkottai prompted Welsh to interpret it as the beginning of a mutiny. On being told by a sepoy that Maravars were a 'treacherous race', Welsh sought and obtained permission to disarm and retrench 161 Maravar sepoys from military service. Welsh's actions were approved by the governor-in-council because of the reports of unrest at Wallajahbad and Hyderabad, following the Vellore Revolt in July.[138]

Despite Welsh's pre-emptive measures, elaborate stories and rumours continued to spread in the Palayamkottai garrison portending trouble. On the morning of Sunday, 16 November, the attention of Reverend Ringletube was drawn to blood stains on the church door at Palayamkottai Fort. On examination, he found two large stains on each side of the threshold and drops of blood leading through the railings, up one grave and completely round another. He also learnt next morning that the minds of the sepoys had for some nights been exercised by a ghost, which demanded bread and water, informing those it met that it was the spirit of a Muslim commandant who had been blown from a gun by the English.[139]

Major Welsh consulted the district magistrate, George Stratton, who showed him the circular from the Company government ordering the investigation of all religious mendicants. As fakirs had gained access to Palayamkottai cantonment, Welsh felt panicky. He discussed the situation with his senior military and civil officers and suggested that the entire European population leave Palayamkottai at once. Stratton and the collector, James Hapburn, preferred to disarm the troops. Welsh accepted the suggestion and on his return to the fort, wanted to ascertain whether his officers had any malicious intentions. So he ordered two prominent native officers to go on an errand to Tirunelveli town. One of the officers objected to going and his open defiance confirmed Welsh's suspicions. Welsh and his colleagues armed themselves and paraded the battalion. After ordering the sepoys to keep their

---

[138] *Secret Department Sundries*, vol. 9A, 139–140.
[139] *Secret Department Sundries*, vol. 9A, 638–42.

muskets in a corner, they took them to the central *maidan* (field). There, all of the non-Muslims were ordered to form a separate division. Welsh provided the 150 Hindu sepoys with muskets and informed the 450 Muslim soldiers that they were being deprived of their arms, pending investigation into the alleged plot to murder the European officers.[140]

Meanwhile, Welsh dispatched a letter to Thomas Maitland, governor of Ceylon, asking for European troops. Describing the situation 'as tantamount to a full-scale revolt', Welsh asked for three companies of European infantry.[141] The call was promptly heeded. But the Company government restrained Welsh from utilising the services of the Ceylon contingent, as adequate force had been sent from Tiruchirappalli.[142] On 19 November, Welsh, after disarming Muslim troops, claimed that they 'have now quiet possession of the arms of the battalion having turned out 450 moormen and confined 20 native officers'.[143] Welsh, a staunch Christian, had an intense dislike for Muslims. In his *Military Reminiscences*, while commenting on his Muslim sepoys visiting a fakir near Chitradurg hills while returning from the Second Anglo-Maratha War in January 1806, he writes, 'This imposter certainly gulled them completely, and was likely to have done us serious injury, had not Providence watched over our safety, and proved him, like his Arabian master, a false prophet.'[144]

Welsh and his colleague Dyce decided to play the communal card to manage the tricky situation. They tried to take the Hindu sepoys into confidence and isolate the Muslim men. Dyce, who commanded the district of Tirunelveli, dropped in at Palayamkottai and summoned the Hindu sepoys. Dyce came

> to maintain the authority of the Company, or to die in the defence of the colours which he had sworn to protect. He then called upon those who were of the same mind to approach the British flag for the same purpose, but if not, to depart in

---

[140] Hoover, *Men Without Hats*, 242–43.
[141] Hoover, *Men Without Hats*, 243.
[142] Kaye, *Sepoy Army in India*, vol. 2, 237–40.
[143] *Secret Department Sundries*, vol. 6A, 3032–33.
[144] Quoted in Hoover, *Men Without Hats*, 243, 260.

peace. They went up and took the oath to a man, presented arms to the colours, gave three unbidden cheers in earnest of their unshaken loyalty, and fell in as on a muster-parade.[145]

Besides, Hindu sepoys were given pay raises and promotions. With the Muslim officers in confinement, orders were instantly issued promoting five of the Hindu sepoys to the rank of subedar, another five to jamedar, twenty-five to havildar, and twenty-five to naik, with the attendant monetary benefits.[146]

The government, however, held the view that the precipitate actions of Welsh brought discredit upon them and condemned him as an alarmist.[147] Apprehension of this kind, they ruled, was 'disgraceful and groundless panic'.[148] The Muslim troops at Palayamkottai were allowed to enter the fort and take up their arms again.[149] Welsh was tried by court martial at Fort St George in February 1807, for 'having taken such extreme steps without justifiable cause, adequate necessity, or sufficient investigation; such conduct being calculated to produce disunion, and distrust'.[150]

The court martial was composed of Archibald Scott of the civil service, Lieutenant Colonels John Munro and John Malcolm, who were appointed to enquire and report their opinion on the alleged Mohammedan conspiracy for the subversion of British rule in India, a view which had been forcefully conveyed in a letter addressed to the government by Major Joseph Haslewood, of the Second Battalion, Twenty-Fourth Regiment. The proceedings were wound up on 19 March 1807. The officers came to the conclusion that 'the inferences drawn by Major Hazlewood were not supported on any sufficient grounds'. The government, on 2 April, concurred

---

[145] Hoover, *Men Without Hats*, 243, 260.

[146] Hoover, *Men Without Hats*, 244.

[147] Hoover, *Men Without Hats*, 245–46. The panic and apprehension he shared with Lieutenant Colonel Grant, who commanded two battalions of the garrison in Ceylon, prompted him to disarm the Travancore Subsidiary Force for which he was reprimanded by the Company government, which had to tender a formal apology to the sepoys.

[148] Kaye, *Sepoy Army in India*, vol. 2, 238–40.

[149] Hoover, *Men Without Hats*, 244.

[150] Wilson, *History of the Madras Army*, vol. 3, 196–98.

with the conclusion of the investigation. Subedar Sheik Hyder was proclaimed the principal conspirator in Palayamkottai. The other two accused were Sikander Khan and Sheik Nuttar. They were dismissed from service.[151] Welsh was acquitted, and the proceedings were approved by the government. Nevertheless, the government, while giving these officers credit for their good intentions and zeal for public service, condemned them for their precipitate action and errors of judgement.

Even after containing the Palayamkottai unrest, there was no let up for Company administrators, as evidenced from the report sent by Bentinck to the Court of Directors. Bentinck wrote:

> Four months had now elapsed since the Mutiny of Vellore. During the interval every lenitive had been applied by Government to the irritated feelings of the troops, and of the public in general. All these efforts seemed as yet ineffectual. The irritation not only continued, but gained ground. Every day made the aspect of affairs more ominous. The most injurious reports received universal credit; prophesies denouncing the fall of the British power were eagerly circulated; and religious mendicants were represented as traversing the country, in order to sow the seeds of disaffection. The position of the Army was critical; a panic prevailed among the European Officers and the Sepoys, according to many private opinions, conditions were ripe for a revolt.[152]

Summary

Sir Cradock, on assumption of office as commander-in-chief of the Madras Army, issued an order in March 1806 detailing a new military dress code. The new code was commended by the chief secretary and the military board and approved by the commander-in-chief of the army. However, the regulation that a native soldier should not denote his caste on his forehead or wear earrings when dressed in his uniform, and should have his chin clean-shaven at

---

[151] *Secret Department Sundries*, vol. 9A, 638–42.
[152] Bentinck, *Memorial*, 37.

parades, caused resentment in the Native Infantry as it was viewed as an attempt to coerce them into Christianity. The news that the cockade in the new turban was made of animal skin added fuel to fire.

The Second Battalion of the Fourth Regiment at Vellore was the first to refuse to wear the new turban. The commandant of the Vellore Fort, Colonel Fancourt, when informed of the discontent of the Indian military contingents by Lieutenant Colonel Darley, conveyed it to the commander-in-chief who, instead of examining the points at issue, ordered that the protestors be arrested and tried in Madras. Of the twenty-one privates on trial—ten Muslims and eleven Hindus—Sheik Abdul Rymen and Anantaraman refused to apologise and were hence given 900 lashes and dismissed from military service. The remaining nineteen apologised for their actions and so were sentenced to 500 lashes each, but were reinstated with a reprimand. The measures adopted in the case of the Second Battalion, Fourth Regiment did not deter others from opposing the new turban. Cradock and the governor were briefed on the brewing discontent. Yet they chose to push through the reform.

The plan to mutiny had been in the air for some time. Mustapha Beg, of the First Battalion, First Regiment, disclosed this plan to Lieutenant Colonel Forbes. When Forbes enquired about it with the native officers, they misled him into believing that Beg was a madman notorious for his drunkenness. Consequently, he was ordered to be chained and kept in confinement. Mrs Burke, a European woman, also attempted to apprise Fancourt of what she had heard in the parachery about a pending revolt, but he was dismissive of her version.

It seems the Indian soldiery put some thought into fixing the date for revolt. The day before the revolt, 9 July, was the wedding day of one of Tipu's daughters. So, under the pretext of attending the wedding celebrations, a crowd of people had gained access to both the inside and the outside of the palace. Additionally, the Twenty-Third Regiment was to have field day on the morning of 10 July, and claiming that they would have to wake up early, the sepoys and prominent leaders of that regiment slept in the fort. The

English officer who was to go round the palace at night on guard duty deputed a subedar for the purpose. But the subedar asked Jamedar Sheik Kasim to do the job. Kasim used this opportunity to ensure that all the necessary preparations had been made to wage war the next day.

In the early hours of 10 July, every step of the plan was assiduously carried out. Subedar Sheik Adam took upon himself the responsibility of overseeing the distribution of cartridges and firearms. Lance Naik Bawah Sahib set fire to European barracks so that European officers could be shot down while leaving their homes. In total, fourteen officers, including Fancourt, were shot dead. Two prominent figures identified for killing European officers were Yusuf Khan and Abdul Qadir. (For the British, the event was known as the Vellore Massacre. Most British historians of the nineteenth century, including Kaye, provided an imperialistic account of the mutiny.)

After killing all resident British officers, except those who had fled or hid themselves within the fort, the insurgents allegedly proclaimed the eldest living son of Tipu, Fateh Hyder, as the sultan. But available evidence suggests that Fateh Hyder did not succumb to such a tempting offer. Thereafter, the victorious native armed men resorted to plundering. But British reinforcements from Arcot led by Colonel Gillespie changed the whole picture dramatically.

In view of the tactical blunder committed by the native troops of not checking how many European privates were hiding and how many had left the fort, Surgeon Jones of the First Regiment and Assistant Surgeon Dean of the Twenty-Third Regiment collected all those who had survived the native troops' firing and succeeded in bringing under their control a nearby bastion and cavalier at the north-east face of the fort, notwithstanding the enormous loss of life suffered by them.

The adjutant, Lieutenant Ewing, who managed to slip out of the fort, assembled several Europeans and joined Forbes. Accompanied by a number of unarmed men belonging to the First Battalion, First Regiment, these two officers took possession of a hill fort and waited there till British authority was re-established in the main fort.

Meanwhile, informed about the revolt by Major Coates, Gillespie arrived with dragoons from Arcot. The insurgents kept firing, due to which, by Gillespie's own admission, many from the Sixty-Ninth Regiment suffered heavy loss of life. However, with the help of the cavalry under Lieutenant Colonels Kennedy and Doveton, and Captain Mason, soon the spirit of the native troops was shattered. The fleeing sepoys were pursued and killed. British authority was restored in the fort. Colonel Harcourt, commanding officer at Wallajahbad, was appointed as commandant to the Vellore garrison on 13 July 1806.

There is no consensus amongst historians on the death toll. The estimated loss of life on the side of the English almost tallies in their accounts. As for the number of native sepoys and officers killed and executed, there is wide variance in accounts. We may not know the exact number of those 'cut up' by Gillespie's Nineteenth Dragoons. Yet W. J. Wilson's estimate of 879 out of 1,700 native soldiers fallen in the fort is plausible. Harcourt's official figures help us to know the number of prisoners; there were 466 prisoners in Vellore, while 321 were still at large. Apart from these 787 prisoners, there were also persons kept in confinement in different parts of the country.

The revolts in 1806 were not confined to Vellore alone. It had echoes in Hyderabad, Wallajahbad, Bangalore, Nandydurg, Bellary, and Palayamkottai. In Hyderabad, the British resident who commanded the Subsidiary Force, Colonel Montresor, decided not to force the new turban on the infantry, yet the sepoys brought up grievances about their leather stockings. Umar Ali, Qadir Beg, Sidi Hussain and Sheik Hussain were identified as ringleaders and transported to the prison at Penang for life.

On learning of the Indian soldiers' intended uprising in Wallajahbad, three companies of European troops marched from Poovirunthavalli under Gillespie's command to restore order. Subedar Venkata Naik was held responsible for the mutinous behaviour of the soldiers and dismissed from service. The battalion of the Twenty-Third Regiment at Wallajahbad was subsequently disarmed.

In Nandydurg, the rebels identified were Subedars Muhammad Reza and Venkatachellam, Jamedars Sheik Dawood and Tika Ram, and Havildar Sheik Nuttar. The arrests of Muhammad Reza and Venkatachellam by Major Alexander Muirhead enraged the entire soldiery. The report of the court of enquiry confirmed that the plan originated in the Holkar camp.

Informed about incidents at Nandydurg, Lieutenant Colonel Ogg, the officer commanding at Bangalore, in a bid to forestall any violent eruption, ordered the search of the houses of two suspects, one a munshi and another a travelling fakir. However, the court of enquiry set up for the purpose determined the information to be false.

In Bellary, discontent, when noticed, was immediately probed. It was found out that two fakirs, Alam Ali Sha and Nur Khalil, with the backing of Sepoy Abdul Nabi and Subedar Mir Bakr, were instigating the sepoys to revolt. The court of enquiry constituted with the local notables held Mir Bakr guilty and dismissed him from service.

Palayamkottai began to experience tumult in November 1806. There, the relatives of those killed and executed in Vellore Fort were in Company military service. In anticipation of trouble, Major Welsh, the commandant of the First Battalion, Third Regiment, sacked 165 Maravars from service. He also asked for European troops from the governor of Ceylon, Thomas Maitland, but the Company government rushing additional troops from Tiruchirappalli restrained Welsh from utilising the services of troops from Ceylon.

Welsh adopted a *divide et impera* (divide-and-rule) policy. He disarmed the Muslim soldiery, and favoured Hindu sepoys with promotions and salary hikes. Welsh appeared before a court martial for this nefarious decision, but he was acquitted. Subedar Sikander Khan and Havildar Sheik Nuttar were fixed as conspirators and retrenched.

Once the unrest in Palayamkottai was contained, the Madras government heaved a sigh of relief. Yet panic continued to prevail among the European officers and the sepoys. The government could no longer attribute the uprising to the dress code. It set up a special commission superseding the one constituted by Gillespie and ordered a probe. Forbes and the adjutant, Lieutenant Combs, also investigated and presented their findings to the court martial that conducted its proceedings in Vellore. The government rewarded those who were instrumental in putting down the revolt in Vellore Fort, starting with Gillespie. At the same time, it identified some as ringleaders and dealt with them cruelly. These aspects are discussed in Chapter 3.

3

THE AFTERMATH

What is come over the Army at Fort St George? What are we
to believe? ... Surely the brave fellows who went through the
difficulties and dangers of the Maharatta campaign cannot
have broken their allegiance. I can never believe it till I shall
see that proved in the clearest possible manner.

—Arthur Wellesley to Sir John Malcolm[1]

Immediately after the suppression of the rebellion, Colonel
Robert Gillespie constituted a court of enquiry, presided over
by Lieutenant Colonel James Kennedy of the Nineteenth
Dragoons. The members were Lieutenant Colonels Forbes and
Floyer, Majors Trotter and Henry, and Captain Mason. Attaching
importance to the conduct of a thorough enquiry, the Madras
government appointed a special commission to do the job on
12 July 1806, with Major General John Pater as president and
Lieutenant Colonel G. Dodsworth, of the Thirty-Fourth Regiment,
Nathaniel Webb and J. H. D. Ogilvie of the judiciary, Major W.
Dowse of the Eighth Regiment of the Native Infantry, and Major
James Leith, judge advocate general, as members.[2]

Gillespie's court of enquiry, presenting its report before
the commencement of the special commission's proceedings,
identified active participants in the mutiny and held the Mysore
princes responsible. The court concluded, 'The Vellore mutiny was
not a spontaneous rebellion, but a well-planned coup attempt, the
ultimate goal of which was the overthrow of British power in south
India', and added that the Muslims domiciled in the pettai and a

---

[1] Quoted in Cameron, 'Vellore Mutiny', 42.
[2] Wilson, *History of the Madras Army*, vol. 3, 190.

band of disgruntled native officers had hoped to establish 'a new Mysoran sultanate'.[3] The special commission began its proceedings on 27 July, interrogating deponents, both native and English. The depositions of a select number of sepoys and native officers made under oath,[4] and the views of surviving English officers recorded by the commission, are detailed in the first section.[5] The measures adopted by the government of Madras in punishing the rebels and rewarding turncoats are dealt with in the section following that. In the third section, the recall of the governor and commander-in-chief, leading to the former's rebuttal of all charges levelled against him, is discussed. The final conclusions of the Court of Directors is provided in the last section of this chapter.

I

Depositions of English Officers

Major Charles Trotter

Major Trotter, an officer in the Second Battalion, Twenty-Third Regiment, when asked to state what he knew about the causes of the mutiny, pleaded ignorance. When asked for a description of castes in his battalion, said, 'It is composed of the worst and lowest caste of men he has ever known in the service.' He further added that 'the corps was chiefly raised in the Polygar [Palayakkarar] country at Shankrancoil [Sankaran Kovil], near Shevegury [Sivagiri]'. Though he could not confirm it with certainty, he could assert that a great many of them were recruited from the Palayakkarars'

---

[3] Hoover, *Men Without Hats*, 127.

[4] Sheik Ahmed, sepoy of the First Battalion, First Regiment, presented the military court with a list of names of persons who bound themselves by an oath to stand by each other in refusing to wear the new turban (see Appendix 2 for the names).

[5] Depositions before the special commission and testimonies taken by the military court of enquiry happened simultaneously and are mixed up in government records, making the task of researchers arduous. Therefore, without mentioning the place of deposition, the substance of evidence given by Indian soldiers and officers, as well as the explanations offered by the English officials are furnished.

army.[6] Lieutenant John Coombs, adjutant, Second Battalion, Twenty-Third Regiment, who had been adjutant to the corps from the time it was first regimented in November 1805, noted too that the corps was raised at Sankaran Kovil, and formed the seventh extra battalion. The evidence, according to him, suggested that the corps was chiefly composed of the lower castes like 'Parriahs and Chucklies.'[7] On further being asked whether there were many Palayakkarar people amongst the sepoys in the battalion, Coombs said, 'There are a great many people in it from that part of the country—Tinnevelly.'[8]

Lieutenant Colonel Thomas Marriott

Lieutenant Colonel Marriott, the officer in charge of the family of the late Hyder Ali and Tipu Sultan, and paymaster of stipends, was one of the key witnesses grilled by the commission. Marriott testified that the only grievance of a general nature, which he had heard of, was regarding the turban that the sepoys had been ordered to wear. Marriott disclosed that he had occasion to notice the general discontent amongst the sepoys, for the first time at Captain Moore's quarters, on the morning of 6 May 1806. When the sepoys of the Grenadier Company, Second Battalion, Fourth Regiment, had positively refused to wear the new turban, he said he had gone down to Moore's quarters 'to hear their reasons and to endeavour to argue them out of their objections.'[9]

Marriott later recalled the opportunity he had of serving as one of the members of a committee, appointed by the commander-in-chief, to investigate the causes of this and other acts of insubordination that had taken place in the Second Battalion of the Fourth Regiment. The committee, according to him, in its report, 'imputed the cause of the insubordination to have originated

---

[6] *Secret Department Sundries*, vol. 2A, 884–86.
[7] It was probably the stereotype used contemptuously to refer to the lower castes. In Company records of the time, names of Pallars are prominent, but not those of the Chakliyars (Chucklies).
[8] *Secret Department Sundries*, vol. 2A, 884–86.
[9] *Secret Department Sundries*, vol. 2A, 884–86.

in the jealous and lively prejudices of the natives in any matter respecting dress, which in this country is so intimately connected with caste and religion, acting upon the weak minds of illiterate and uniformed men.' Marriott also told the commission about information conveyed by a horse-keeper named Mahomed Ashroff that two of Moiz-ud-Din's servants, Munavar and Rustom, had met with a native commissioned officer and about twenty sepoys of the First Battalion, First Regiment, at the prince's stables at night between fifteen and twenty days before the mutiny broke out.

After registering these details, Marriott narrated what he had seen and experienced on the eventful day of 10 July.[10] He had woken up on hearing the firing of muskets. Soon, he learnt from the naik of his guard that the sepoys of the Twenty-Third Regiment were firing in every direction. He went down with the guard to find out more about the cause of the firing. There, he met Coombs, and learnt from him about the heavy firing targeting his house. Marriott advised him to go upstairs and hide. Soon, he was confronted by a crowd of soldiers of the Twenty-Third, numbering forty to fifty, but they did not harass him. Marriott went upstairs where he noticed the presence of Lieutenant Gunning, acting adjutant of the European Regiment (the Sixty-Ninth). They both made attempts to negotiate with the sepoys, but they continued to fire. Eventually, the sepoys succeeded in taking possession of the ground floor of Marriott's residence. This prevented the European officers hiding in the bathroom upstairs from escaping to the European barracks. The sepoys, in the meantime, had set Coombs's house on fire.

A jamedar of the Twenty-Third, who led this group of soldiers, caught hold of a Portuguese boy on the steps, and threatened to put him to death if he did not tell him Coombs's whereabouts. However, the sepoys soon left, to the great relief of Marriott and his colleagues. Marriott relates what happened after that:

> At this time I was entirely ignorant of their having put many of the officers to death, consequently apprehended no danger to myself … After this time the sepoys quitted house, and did

[10] *Secret Department Sundries*, vol. 2A, 863–68.

not return shortly after I heard them call out Futtee Hyder
"come out Nabob, come out Nabob and don't be afraid" …
I saw several sepoys of the 1st come into the fort with their
jackets on and go towards the Barracks to get their arms—
about eight o'clock I heard the sepoys say the Europeans had
got out of the Barracks, and about half an hour afterwards
they passed the word, that the Regiment of Cavalry from
Ranepet [Ranipettai] had arrived … [At] 10 o'clock, when
the guns arrived, and the gate was blown open. I came out
to meet the Cavalry on the parade, and to show them the
way into the palace, being apprehensive that the iron gate
had been fastened and that … the railings of the palace were
lined with sepoys of two *Harrcarrahs* [informers], at Moiuz-
Ud-Deen's and Mouih-Ud-Deen's, one had been shot by the
sepoys, and the other gave me information that the Mysore
flag, hoisted by the sepoys, had been given out of Mouiz-Ud-
Deen's house. We killed and took prisoners about five and
thirty sepoys in Mouiz-Ud-Deen's house.[11]

When Marriott was asked whether the feast, which was held in
the palace on the night before the mutiny, was conducted with his
knowledge and consent, he replied affirmatively. The extract of his
reply is this:

> The celebration of the Sultaun Mouiz-Ud-Deen's sister
> marriage, with Syed Nizam-Ud-Deen, had commenced
> some few days before, and it is customary that previous
> to the final ceremonies, dinners would be hosted to their
> respective relations and friends according to the pecuniary
> circumstances of the parties. The four daughters of Tipu
> Sultan, lately married by order of Government, had each of
> them given two dinners and the dinner on the evening of the

---

[11] *Secret Department Sundries*, vol. 2A, 868–75; vol. 2B, 1196–98. Yusuf Khan
(Esoph Cawn) revealed to the commission that Shaik Gansee, havildar of the
Seventh Company and Hussein Ali (Hussain Ally), naik of the First Company,
entered the house of the adjutant, Coombs, at the commencement of the mutiny.
Muthu Samy (Mootoo Sawmy), the naik who commanded the guard at Coombs's
house, did not object to the havildar entering the house but refused to allow
Hussein Ali to enter. Hussein Ali pushed Muthu Samy to one side and entered the
house, but Coombs was not there.

9th July was fixed at the Raymaul [Raj Mahal], by Moiz-Ud-Deen's sister and attended by their relations, living outside of the fort. After the dinner they returned to their houses, the outside of the fort, at eight o'clock the same evening. Ten persons attended on that occasion, as relatives of the family, as ascertained from the register of the gate Harrcarrah. About the time of the marriage, three sets of dancing girls (to the number of 40) were admitted into the palace, in keeping with the custom and they stayed on until after the mutiny.[12]

When asked whether any of the native troops were admitted into the fort to visit the princes on the evening of 9 July, Marriott said no, but added that whenever any of the princes left their houses, a proportion of the guard always accompanied them until they returned to their houses. None of the sepoys or native officers was ever allowed to enter any of the princes' apartments or have any communication with them. On the evening being referred to, a proportion of the guard accompanied as usual whilst Moiz-ud-Din was exercising his horse, and racing with his uncle, Noor Ul Aboor Cawn, within the boundaries of the palace yard, after which they all went to the Raj Mahal for dinner, with the sepoys of the guard remaining, as usual, amongst their attendants outside, until the prince retired to his own house. The *harkaras* were also in attendance along with the sepoys. [13]

Marriott's attention was then drawn to a letter from Gillespie to the governor on 10 July, wherein Gillespie said that Marriott had told him that the princes were innocent. To this, Marriott replied that he did not recollect this. He had met Gillespie in the middle

---

[12] *Secret Department Sundries*, vol. 2A, 863–78.

[13] There was an establishment of *hircarrahs* or *harkaras*, in the rank of peon, at the fort's gates, who took down the names of all persons entering the fort to meet the princes, and stopped all strangers. A similar establishment was attached to each prince's door; no person could enter except the registered servants of the respective princes—the servants of one were not allowed to go to the other's house without permission. They were expected to keep the paymaster informed of every occurrence in both the town and the fort. Of the harkaras, two were shot during the mutiny and one wounded, which would suggest that they were not trusted.

of the parade and accompanied him past the palace gates on their way to the Raj Mahal, which was in the centre of the compound. When they were together, the harkara who had survived reported to Marriott that the four elder princes were safe in their houses, which he then conveyed to Gillespie in English. Almost at the same time, one of the harkaras told him that the flag had been brought from Moiz-ud-Din's house, which, to the best of his recollection, he had mentioned to Gillespie and had begged his permission to place the prince under watch, and this was done before he, Marriott, left the palace. Marriott wanted to place on record that his letter to the governor on 10 July sufficiently showed that he had entertained suspicions against Moiz-ud-Din. He observed that when Gillespie proposed that all twelve sons of Tipu Sultan, five of whom were between nine and eleven years of age, be sent to Madras, he had argued against the measure, since it was improbable that they were all involved. This, he said, was because of his own knowledge of the great hatred and animosity which prevailed amongst the brothers.[14]

Marriott, when asked whether he had any reason to believe that efforts had been made by followers of the palace 'to tamper with the sepoys', he responded saying that he did not know, and had never heard of any such attempts. Some information to that effect was only given to the court of enquiry, of which Forbes was president, he added. Marriott, however, recollected that about a month before the mutiny broke out, the mother of Prince Shakirulah was very earnest in pleading with him not to enforce the order to wear the new turban, 'as they [the sepoys] were our own servants, and to do anything against their prejudices would only make them disaffected, and do no good'. After the arrival of the dragoons on the morning of 10 July, when Marriott went to see if she and her son were safe, the first thing she exclaimed was, 'Marriott Sahib, did not I tell you what would be the consequence of making the sepoys disaffected?'[15]

---

[14] *Secret Department Sundries*, vol. 2A, 863–78.
[15] *Secret Department Sundries*, vol. 2A, 863–78.

When asked whether he had confidential persons employed to bring intelligence of what was happening in the palace, Marriott said he certainly had persons who did give him occasional intelligence of what was going on, amongst their servants, both male and female, besides his own harkara. Asked whether there was any restraint on interaction or communication between the daughters and sons-in-law residing in the pettai, and the royal family at the palace or the fort, he answered that the daughters were allowed, for fixed periods, to come in to see their mothers, and the sons-in-law were occasionally invited to the dinners held on the occasion of their sisters-in-law's weddings, where they might have had personal communications.[16]

Lieutenant Colonel Nathaniel Forbes

Lieutenant Colonel Forbes, at the time of the outbreak of the mutiny, commanded part of a battalion of sepoys, that is, the First Battalion of the First Regiment in the garrison of Vellore, consisting of about 577 rank and file, with ten European officers, besides the native officers. The barracks of the corps were within the fort, but a good many of the sepoys were allowed to stay and sleep in the pettai. This battalion furnished the garrison guards on 9 July; seven privates from the corps were off duty on that night, most of whom, according to Forbes, slept in the pettai.

Forbes highlighted the Mustapha Beg affair before the commission.[17] The sepoy, Mustapha, had visited Forbes's house in the pettai on 17 June 1806 and insisted on seeing him. When Forbes went out to speak with him, he began to say, in an agitated manner, that he had overheard a certain havildar exclaim that he was going to die, and then leave his family to the charge of the man with whom he was conversing in the dark. Being night-time, he could not identify the person, but from this conversation he learnt that they were discoursing on the new turban (which they called a topee), which had just been proposed by the army. Mustapha

---

[16] *Secret Department Sundries*, vol. 2B, 996–97.
[17] *Secret Department Sundries*, vol. 2A, 842–47.

also told Forbes that they were confident that since there were only a few *ferengi*s (foreigners, or specifically, Europeans; whom they called *kafer*s, or turncoats), they could easily defeat them and put them to death. What Forbes understood from what Mustapha told him was that the two men, whose conversation had been overheard, were speaking about the intention to eliminate the 'European officers'. Forbes also noticed Mustapha's agitated mood and the incoherent manner in which he presented himself. He walked with him for some time around his compound, but could not learn anything from him. Mustapha informed him that they had chosen that very night, 17 June, for the execution of their plan, but some apprehension on their part had forced them to defer it. Besides the distracted manner in which Mustapha spoke, Forbes was convinced that what he was saying was unbelievable. Even then, he did not hesitate to urge the naik to find out whether there was any disaffection in the First Battalion.[18]

The naik instantly responded saying that Mustapha Beg was a madman, and that no attention should be paid to what he said, as the battalion was comprised of old soldiers, all well disposed to the government. Many people joined in impressing upon Forbes that Mustapha was mad. When the same question was put to the rest of the guard, they all agreed that the sepoy was deranged. Forbes did not therefore think it necessary to probe further into the matter. He directed his orderly to take Mustapha to the guard to which he had been assigned, with instructions to the jamedar to ascertain from him what he had to say, and to bring him back in the morning, when the guards were relieved. The native adjutant, Jamedar Sheik Ali, waited for Forbes in the morning to make his report. When Forbes asked him if he had heard anything about what the sepoy had been speaking about, the jamedar declared that 'there was not the slightest ground for it, that the Battalions were all perfectly satisfied with the turban, and vying with each other to wear'. He also asserted that the informer, Mustapha, 'was a madman and hence there was no need to pay any attention to him'.[19]

---

[18] *Secret Department Sundries*, vol. 7B, 3687–88.
[19] *Secret Department Sundries*, vol. 7B, 3687–88.

The jamedar brought to the attention of Forbes some previous instances of the Mustapha's 'irregular and extravagant conduct', and had been confined by Forbes himself once during the Muharram fast. The jamedar further stated that he was notorious for running to the commanding officer with flimsy complaints, instead of taking it to his immediate officer, in keeping with the practices of the battalion. Forbes tried, however, to impress upon the jamedar the need for further enquiry into the matter, but the jamedar dissuaded him, insisting that the corps were unfailingly loyal. When dissatisfaction was shown by another battalion to the design of the turban, Forbes informed the native adjutant that if there was really any dissatisfaction in the battalion, it was only fair for them to present it through the regular channels so that the matter would be redressed by a representation on his part to the adjutant-general's office. But the jamedar continued to dismiss his apprehensions, reiterating that there was no objection to the turban. Forbes, as he stated, had no reason at that time to doubt the native adjutant's sincerity.[20]

William Currie

William Currie, assistant surgeon in the Company's service, in his account of the mutiny of the sepoys at Vellore, concluded that the callous attitude of English officials after Mustapha's disclosure, in his opinion, resulted in the gruesome murders of fifteen officers and, killing and wounding of about 200 Europeans. He regretted that the information conveyed by Mustapha to his European officer some days before, about the designs and plans of the mutineers, had been ignored. Instead of arresting and interrogating the native officers accused, they were consulted as confidential advisers. They succeeded in persuading the commanding officer that Mustapha

---

[20] *Secret Department Sundries*, vol. 7B, 3687–88. Rustom Ali, while deposing before the commission, observed that Mohammed Jaffer, formerly an officer in the service of Tipu, and at the time of the Vellore Revolt, a sepoy in the First Battalion, First Regiment, had confided to him that Mustapha Beg was after a promotion and had therefore disclosed this secret to Forbes.

was mentally deranged and so it was ordered he be confined as a lunatic. 'Effecting escape from the guard placed over him, [Mustapha] has since succeeded a munificent reward from Govt. Can you conceive fatality equal to this?', Currie quipped.[21]

Mrs Burke

Mrs Burke, a European woman, claimed to have been a resident of the parachery in the pettai for about two-and-a-half years,[22] and hence could understand Tamil well. She said she had observed meetings and conversations among the natives near her place of dwelling. They were discontented with their subjugation to the Europeans, who they knew were outnumbered and could easily be finished off. When Lieutenant Colonel John Darley's battalion, the Second Battalion, Fourth Regiment, was in Vellore three months earlier, the discontent visibly increased, and meetings (Beach Committees, as they were called) were held frequently from morning till night near her house, and that they used to swear to each other to stay united and fight as one. Mrs Burke considered an old, invalid *tindal* (petty officer) among them, Kaalan (Calah), Parayar by caste, as the principal conspirator. The latter spoke his mind, saying, 'The Europeans had no right to stay in the country; The Europeans are few in number, we shall easily destroy them and then we shall have riches in plenty.'[23] Kaalan, according to Mrs Burke, one day declared before young James Frost, her son, that he was the head of the village and would soon see the day when there would be no Europeans left in the country. The deponent further stated that when she went to Colonel John Fancourt to tell him what she had heard, as well as to apply for prize money for her husband, he dismissed her, calling her a 'bad woman'.[24]

---

[21] William Currie to John Cradock, 17 September 1806, ref. GDI/1153/3(2), National Records of Scotland.

[22] According to Mrs Burke, the inhabitants of the parachery were all Parayars, and these were the people that comprised the Beach Committees.

[23] *Secret Department Sundries*, vol. 2B, 964–66.

[24] *Secret Department Sundries*, vol. 2B, 964–66.

Mrs Potter

The information given by Mrs Potter, wife of David Potter, a merchant in Vellore, under oath, was this: At about a quarter past two, on the morning of 10 July, alarmed by the discharge of muskets at the main guard and at the barracks, Mrs Potter went with her family to the deputy commissary of stores, William Mann, in the commissaries' verandah. At that moment, Mann came downstairs and asked what the matter was. Mrs Potter replied that she did not know. Mann ran upstairs to fetch his sword and came back down, telling them not to be afraid.

He then took them to the conductor of ordnance (a sergeant in charge of manual labourers and military stores). There, a number of sepoys came and called the conductor, by his title, sergeant, saying that Fancourt wanted the keys to the stores to take out ammunition, as the princes were fighting with the sepoys. On seeing Mann, they wanted both him and the sergeant to go along with them to see Fancourt. Thereupon, Mann told them that he would go with them if Fancourt sent another orderly. They then asked Mrs Potter to move away, and shot the conductor. Mrs Potter turned around to make her escape with her children but they were in the way, and she fell over them, as did Mann, while in the act of jumping over them. Mann thus escaped a shot that was aimed at him. The sepoys, incensed that Mann escaped the bullet, took aim at Mrs Potter. She took shelter behind a pillar, but the shot went through her child's knee. They then took shelter in the conductor's house and remained there till dawn, before which time the sepoys fired many shots into the house.

All the European men had left their houses in the wake of the sepoys' uprising, and only the women remained, continued Mrs Potter. The sepoys then went into the houses and plundered them. At dawn, Mrs Potter took her family to the gate, where she saw some sepoys bringing the wounded Lieutenant John Eley from the ramparts. He was making *salams* (gestures) to the sepoys for mercy, at which time a Muslim sepoy struck him, but its impact was taken by the door. Afterwards, he pursued Eley into the guard room and slew him with a long, crooked sword. The sepoys said, 'What can the Europeans do now, they cannot make us wear Topies?'[25]

Mrs Potter also stated that she saw an elderly man, short in stature, and with a large beard, whom she had seen in the fort before. Her guess was that he might have belonged to the palace. She saw him go from the main guard to the ramparts twice, calling out to the sepoys, 'Here are some Europeans; here are some Europeans', at which time Mrs Potter saw a number of Tipu's family members running from the palace towards the Parsee merchant Naoroji's house, crying, 'Dheen, Dheen' (a war cry). She felt scared and hence concealed herself and her family in one of the commanding officers' godowns. Then she heard the announcement of the arrival of the Nineteenth Dragoons. The sepoys ran towards the palace or ran and concealed themselves elsewhere.[26]

Depositions of Indian Soldiers and Officers

After the interrogation of European officials, it was the turn of Indian soldiers and officers. Of them, the testimonies of some key persons are discussed here.

Acting Havildar Major Fakir Mohammed

Acting Havildar Major Mohammed (Fakeer Mahomed) of the Light Infantry, First Battalion, First Regiment, who played an active role in distributing cartridges and guns to the sepoys, disclosed that five days before the mutiny, Subedar Sheik Adam and Subedar Sheik Hussein of the Fifth Company, Second Battalion, Twenty-Third Regiment, and Jamedar Sheik Hussein of the Light Infantry, First Battalion, First Regiment, approached him and insisted that he should take an oath of secrecy. He asked why and refused. They said if he did not, he would be put to death. He took the oath. They then told him that they had been ordered to wear topees, which

---

[25] *Secret Department Sundries*, vol. 2B, 913–16.
[26] *Secret Department Sundries*, vol. 2B, 913–16.

they had decided not to do, and were resolved to revolt. They asked him to be ready to join them on the day of revolt.

At about two o' clock in the early hours of 10 July, while he was sleeping in the barracks, he was awakened, and saw all the sepoys getting ready. Jamedar Sheik Hussein made his troops shoulder their arms and marched them away. Fakir Mohammed said that he remained in the barracks till daylight and afterwards, made his escape.[27]

Muthu Karuppan

Muthu Karuppan (Mootoo Currapah) of the Grenadiers' Second Battalion, Twenty-Third Regiment, told the commission that while he was sleeping in the barracks, at two o' clock in the morning on 10 July, Subedar Sheik Adam, Jamedar Sheik Hussein and Naik Hussein Khan had come to the grenadiers and ordered them to wake up. Several sepoys enquired what business there was for them to get up, as it was not yet four o' clock. The subedar and jamedar replied that the picket in main guard was ready and ordered them to turn out immediately. The subedar, according to Muthu Karuppan, told them that they were being ordered to wear new topees, and that they must all refuse to wear it and must fight and kill all the Europeans that morning.[28]

Sepoy Shiekh Hussein

Shiekh Hussein, sepoy of the Grenadiers' Second Battalion, Twenty-Third Regiment, provided evidence about the events of that morning. According to him, at about quarter past two in the morning, Jamedar Sheikh Hussein went to the sepoys' barracks to wake them up. When he ordered them to fall in line, the sepoys reported it to the subedar of their company, who ordered them to arrest Sheikh Hussein if he came again. Soon, some sepoys of the First Battalion came into their barracks and threatened to shoot if

---

[27] *Secret Department Sundries*, vol. 1B, 308–10.
[28] *Secret Department Sundries*, vol. 1B, 315–20.

they did not join them. When a shot was fired, the panicked sepoys left with them and went to the battalion stores, where Abdul Khadar (Cawdar), lance naik of the First Battalion, First Regiment, handed out ball cartridges. Some of them felt that having 'eaten the company's salt', they should not fight against the Europeans. Abdul Khadar, stating that what was being done was with God's consent, ordered them to join the others at the European barracks, to fire at the Europeans. On hearing this, Shiekh Hussein said, he, along with four or five others, ran away.

Sepoy Murthy

Murthy (Moortee), a sepoy in the Grenadiers' First Battalion, First Regiment, was on duty in the main guard on the night of 9 July. He was posted as a sentry over the arms stores at midnight. A summary of his eyewitness account is this: Jamedar Sheik Kasim volunteered to go on rounds when Subedar Seyed Hussain, who was deputised by the English officer, Captain J. J. Miller, became indisposed. He took an escort, a havildar and two sepoys, with a drummer to carry a lantern, and went around the palace and returned soon. He dispersed his escort and went to sleep. Soon after, Sheik Imam, a havildar, came from the gate to the main guard and met Sepoy Sheik Jaffer, and Lance Naik Mohammed Saib, both of the First Battalion, First Regiment. There, they had a private conversation in low voices and afterwards separated. After the havildar returned to his guard, Sheik Jaffer went and sat down near the *ghurry* (water clock). The other person, Mohammed Saib, ordered those sepoys sleeping outside to go in; some of them declined but he told them that it was an order they must obey, which they did. Thereafter, Mohammed Saib returned to his own bed.

Soon after the clock struck two, when the sentry Murthy was relieved of his duty, he went to bed. He could not sleep as he felt ill at ease. On hearing reports of the firing at the European barracks, as well as the news that Jamedar Sheik Kasim was identifying the Europeans in the main guard and directing his men to shoot them, he asked Kasim, 'What is the meaning of this?' The jamedar replied, 'It is very right, go, take your firelock, join the others.' Murthy did not obey this order; instead, he walked away, which was when he saw Annapah, subedar of the main guard, who came up to him, very frightened; together, they made their way to the coconut garden. Near the magazine, Annapah went into a small hut and Murthy stayed outside. They saw two Europeans run towards the hut, with five or six sepoys pursuing them and firing. Murthy, afraid that they would kill him, pretended to be a supporter. The sepoys asked him what he was doing without his firelock. Murthy responded that his arms were at the main guard and that he was only there to take a break. They then wanted him to take a musket from one of the dead men and follow them.

Murthy followed them to the palace yard where he saw a large crowd of sepoys, most belonging to the Twenty-Third Battalion, and Sheik Adam and Sheik Hussein of the Twenty-Third with Sheik Kasim, jamedar of the First Battalion, First Regiment, and a large party of the princes' followers. Prince Moiz-ud-Din's supporters were giving water to the Muslims and the other princes were giving water to the Hindus, and later, gave them betel nut. The flag was then brought out, by order of Prince Moiz-ud-Din.

Prince Moiz-ud-Din addressed Sheik Adam and told him if they succeeded in this revolt, every sepoy would receive Rs 200 per month, and in case of accidents, their families would be taken care of. The subedar announced this to the crowd. After this, the subedar told the drummers to beat the long roll.[29] The sepoys then assembled and marched off in divisions towards the European barracks, during which time Murthy made his escape.[30]

Sepoy Venkatachalam

Venkatachalam, a sepoy of the First Battalion, First Regiment, Light Company, said that after the firing commenced, he tried making his escape, but Abdul Khadar and Imam Khan stopped him. Abdul Khadar struck him with the butt end of his musket and ordered him to go to the general stores and fetch a barrel of

---

[29] Prolonged beating of drums, which is a signal for troops to fall in line.

[30] *Secret Department Sundries*, 13 July 1806, vol. 1B, 341–46.

ball ammunition. When Venkatachalam refused and ran away, Abdul Khadar immediately took aim with his musket and fired at him, which wounded him in the leg. He fell, and a second shot was directed at his head, which he believed was fired by Imam Khan.[31]

Kasim Ali

Kasim Ali, a native of Tiruchirappalli and formerly a sepoy of the First Battalion, Tenth Native Regiment, who was jobless at the time of mutiny, gave the following information about what he saw: The son of Tipu's confidant Syed Kafur (Syed Geffer), Syed Hussein, along with some sepoys, had wanted to take over one of the hill forts. They had tried to exit through the gate of the main fort, which they found was shut. The sepoys told them not to go through the gate but through the sally port. They went a little way, when some of the sepoys said they had little ammunition left and had to go to the magazine and get some more. When they reached the magazine, they found an old, invalid European gunner, together with an artillery team, bound, and a garrison lascar standing guard over them. The rebel sepoys wanted them to show where the powder and material was stored, which they did. They collected enough and left.

When some of the sepoys cried out that Europeans were coming, they all ran and took shelter in the barracks opposite the Europeans'. They said, 'It is of no use to fire here; let us go out and fire upon the gates at the Barracks and break them down.' They came out and fired four or five shots at the gate, but the Europeans managed to get to the opposite side and ascend the ramparts. When they fired upon the mutineers from the ramparts, the sepoys abandoned their guns and ran away. These sepoys then came around and took control of the north-east bastion. From there, they advanced towards the flagstaff and pulled down the English flag.[32]

---

[31] *Secret Department Sundries*, vol. 7B, 3764–65.
[32] *Secret Department Sundries*, vol. 2A, 903–05.

Hakkim Gulam Mohammed

Hakkim Gulam Mohammed served as the native doctor in different sepoy battalions, and was formerly at the palace during the commands of Lieutenant Colonels Gabriel Doveton and John Darley. He disclosed to Doveton the correspondence that the Mysore princes had with the Marathas, and as a result, incurred the displeasure of the palace. He told the commission of enquiry that he had never heard anything about the intended revolt except for what was said then, that the sepoys were dissatisfied with the new turban and with the order to cut off their whiskers.[33]

Hakkim Gulam Mohammed also testified that on the morning of the mutiny, some people from the palace went to the pettai to call the princes' followers, with their arms, to the fort, and that Sheik Rajah, an attendant of Prince Abdul Khalick, and a cook were employed for this purpose. Some persons then accompanied them into the fort, one of whom was Peer Chan, another attendant of the prince's.[34]

Syed Mahomed

Syed Mahomed, formerly a servant of Abdul Khalick, testified that on the morning of the day of the mutiny, one of the servants of Moiz-ud-Din descended from the ramparts with a rope and, standing by the large banyan tree in the esplanade, announced that the princes had taken the fort, and that all those who wanted to join the armed forces should go in. He then returned with two other men, Peer Chan and Sheik Mohideen, attendants of Khalick.[35]

Mohammed Shroff

According to Mohammed Shroff, a horse-keeper, three bundles of swords had been smuggled into the palace through the princes' stables during the mutiny. However, he feigned ignorance when

---

[33] *Secret Department Sundries*, vol. 2A, 903–05.
[34] *Secret Department Sundries*, vol. 2A, 856–57.
[35] *Secret Department Sundries*, vol. 2A, 857–59.

asked where they had been brought from. Three adherents of Moiz-ud-Din from the palace, Rustom Firoz, Syed Ameer and Munawar Cholak, accompanied by about fifty to hundred soldiers, were sent to bring firearms from the pagoda (a temple which had been converted into a storehouse of arms and ammunition). Just then, European soldiers arrived from the barracks, and started firing. Thereupon, they all ran away.[36]

Sepoy Alagiri

Alagiri, a sepoy in the First Battalion, First Regiment, gave evidence that the son of Syed Jaffar, the commandant, went to the arsenal at the pagoda, opened the doors assisted by some of his people, brought out a gun and went back in to fetch a ball to fit the gun. He brought out grapeshot and a barrel of powder for the gun. He wanted the people around him to each take a shot in hand. Alagiri said one of Syed Jaffar's peons also went in and brought out a bundle of swords, which was sent to the palace. He said, 'If we kill all the Europeans we will beat the great drum over every part of the country.' He also gave orders to a person near him to go to the palace and get the flag and hoist it immediately. Contrary to the claim that the senior-most subedar, Sheik Adam, hoisted the Mysore flag at the request of Moiz-ud-Din, he told the commission that the person who hoisted the flag was the drill havildar of the Twenty-Third, assisted by Humza Beg and Caroder Beg, brothers, and sepoys of the First Battalion, First Regiment.

Alagiri added that he saw a jamedar of the Twenty-Third Regiment with the mat this time, holding a spyglass in his hands and two swords, one of which belonged to a European officer. Alagiri further stated that when he was posted as sentry at the gate of the *zenana* (women's quarters), between the hours of twelve and two on the morning of 10 July, he heard people saying,

> Stand you only firm and staunch we will kill all the Europeans one after the other who are wanting you to wear hats contrary to the Koran; let us assist the cause of the Musselmen until the

---

[36] *Secret Department Sundries*, vol. 2A, 857–59.

sound of the *nakhand* [laughter] shall resound all over the country; you will all be made men of wealth when we get the country into our hands. Only assist us now.[37]

Havildar Yusuf Khan

Havildar Yusuf Khan (Esoph Cawn), of the Second Battalion, Twenty-Third Regiment, deposed to the fact that the subedars were of the view that the 'disaffection of the troops' arose principally because of the intrigues of Tipu's adherents and family. Yusuf Khan informed the commission that the sepoys made no complaints about the regulation on caste marks. They removed their earrings and did not grumble until Tipu's people began to insinuate that the orders were intended 'to make them all of one caste'.[38] He also confessed that Tipu's sons had declared that if the sepoys wore the new turbans, neither them nor their family members would be allowed to be buried in Vellore or in its vicinity when they died. Khan testified that a number of persons, formerly in the service of the sultan and his relatives, were now serving in the Company's native regiments, and that agents and friends of the royal family had been employed all over the country to incite people to revolt. He alleged that Moiz-ud-Din was present at the secret meetings which had preceded the mutiny, and had brought messages from the palace encouraging the mutineers, promising that if the native troops were to defeat the Europeans and hold the fort for eight days, they would be joined by other regiments, and by many of the principal Palayakkarars, with whose support 'the Mohammedan Kingdom of Mysore would be re-established'.[39]

Jamedar Sheik Kasim

Jamedar Sheik Kasim, of the First Battalion, First Regiment, the force behind the mutiny, testified that the secret meetings of the sepoys were well known to every subedar, jamedar and havildar in

[37] *Secret Department Sundries*, vol. 1B, 315–20.
[38] *Secret Department Sundries*, vol. 2B, 1183–89.
[39] *Secret Department Sundries*, vol. 2B, 1173–83.

the corps, 'except those in the margin'.[40] He believed 'that the sepoys throughout the country were all dissatisfied and discontented at the new turband, and that if they seized that opportunity, they might immediately establish the Moghul Government'. This kind of conversation was perpetually heard in the barracks by the non-commissioned sepoys after the introduction of the new turban, observed Sheik Kasim during his deposition. He further added that Sheik Ali, the native adjutant, and Subedar Hussein Khan had made their feelings known to their commanding officer, but the latter suppressed the matter without making a complaint. One day, when the whole grenadier company was feeling very discontented, the subedar wanted to take the 'right men' to complain to Forbes but the jamedar prevented him.[41]

Sheik Kasim said Sheik Nuttar,[42] a sepoy of the Grenadiers' First Regiment, and Imam Khan of the Light Company, had both been very active in contacting pensioners, who were well versed in the management of guns, and the gun lascars, who lived outside the fort, but had promised to come in and assist as soon as they were called upon. A great number of people in the pettai promised they would assist once the date was fixed. According to Sheik Kasim, the day fixed for the insurrection had been changed twice. It was to have taken place before the Second Battalion of the Twenty-Third Regiment was admitted into the plot. It was then put off. It did not take place on the night after they had been acquainted with the idea of revolt either. On the night when Sheik Adam and Sheik Kasim were both on guard duty, it was put off. Eventually, the revolt took place sooner than was finally agreed upon, that is, the succeeding Monday. Jamedar Sheik Hussein of the Twenty-Third, in a drunken state, revealed their plan to revolt, and occasioned its immediate launch on the night of 9 July. At about nine o' clock in the evening, a consultation was held at the barracks and it was resolved that the insurrection would commence at two o' clock in the morning, on Thursday, 10 July. Being a last-minute decision,

---

[40] *Secret Department Sundries*, vol. 2B, 1173–83.

[41] *Secret Department Sundries*, vol. 2A, 700–09.

[42] Sheik Nuttar served as orderly to a European officer, and had offered his services to kill his battalion's commanding officer.

the people in the pettai were not apprised of their intentions and it was too late for them to come in. Sheik Kasim told the commission that it was a sudden decision and that native officers and people in the palace were not aware of it. Otherwise, he thought, the result might have been different.[43]

Sepoy Sheik Nuttar

Sheik Nuttar was found to be active during the mutiny, and was allegedly anxious to shoot Forbes on his arrival at the gates of the fort on the morning of the revolt. So, his evidence to the commission was considered dubious. When interrogated in July, he maintained that the princes played no role in the revolt. With the promise of a pardon, he returned to the commission of enquiry at the fag end of its sitting (7 August 1806) and asserted that the palace had been instrumental in planning the whole affair.

He related the details of the plot, implicating Moiz-ud-Din as a key figure. He identified Jamal-ud-Din, the foster brother of Moiz-ud-Din, as the liaison between the palace and the battalions.

Jamal-ud-Din

Those who planned the plot, according to Jamal-ud-Din, foster brother of Moiz-ud-Din, were of the view that there was a great quantity of money in Vellore, sufficient to pay the troops. One of them said, 'The instant we have gained the fort and murdered all the Europeans we must march to Renepettah [Ranipettai], Arcot, for if we delay and are idle, troops will arrive from Madras but if we are expeditious the cavalry at Arcot will join us and also the cavalry at Canatoor [Kunnathur] will join us.'[44] When asked if any of the troops at Ranipettai had been acquainted with their plan, they replied that on their arrival, as natives, they would certainly join the cause. Imam Khan then said,

---

[43] *Secret Department Sundries*, vol. 2A, 700–09.
[44] *Secret Department Sundries*, vol. 7B, 3717–19.

A short time ago some of the regiments from Kunnathur had come here, amongst whom there was a friend of mine. I acquainted him with our intentions and he promised to assist us; some of the others said we have four companies at Chittoor, and there is also a great quantity of treasure, we had better go there and those companies will join us.[45]

They then wanted Jamal-ud-Din to ask Moiz-ud-Din whether it would be best to remain in Vellore or go to the Ghats. Sheik Kasim then said, 'All these details are known only to eight or nine people,' and cautioned Jamal-ud-Din not to divulge the least part of it.[46]

When interrogated in July, Jamal-ud-Din had feigned ignorance; but on further examination in August, along with Fakir Mohammed, with the promise of a pardon, he also made a disclosure matching the confessions of Sheik Nuttar and of Sheik Kasim.[47]

The following information was derived from their depositions: On 8 and 9 July, Prince Moiz-ud-Din particularly desired that he might be allowed to have the women excluded from his rooms, and that his male servants be allowed to remain with him during the night—an indulgence which was allowed only during Muharram, when they fasted all day, and ate at night. Moiz-ud-Din also sought permission to allow Hyder Hussein Khan, his first cousin, to spend the night with him at his house. Marriott refused both requests, stating that they would set a precedent for the other princes to cite and make similar requests. Another reason for Marriott's suspicion was Moiz-ud-Din's request to buy a horse, which he had refused on account of the heavy debts he had already incurred. Finding that Marriott would not accede to his request, Moiz-ud-Din pleaded with him to be allowed to ride one of the horses that had been brought to the fort, and Marriott swore later in the military court that it was the same horse that was found saddled on the arrival of the dragoons.[48]

---

[45] *Secret Department Sundries*, vol. 7B, 3717–19.
[46] *Secret Department Sundries*, vol. 7B, 3717–19.
[47] Cameron, 'Vellore Mutiny', 96. Also see Bentinck, *Memorial*, 68.
[48] *Secret Department Sundries*, vol. 2A, 829–30.

Havildar Kasi Singh

Kasi Singh, havildar of the Second Battalion, Twenty-Third Regiment, in his statement, recalled what he saw: The sepoys had dropped into the fort from the pettai by means of ropes. Singh had gone to Fancourt's stables and when he came out, he saw Fancourt lying wounded on the ground and the flag of Tipu hoisted. He saw prince Mohi-ud-Din, Sheik Adam, Jamedar Mohammed Kasim, and a number of sepoys of the two battalions nearby. He saw a sepoy come out of the palace with a dagger in hand. The sepoy attempted to kill the harkara, whereupon a number of sepoys and people from the palace stopped him.

Kasi Singh saw the subedar, the jamedar and sepoys, about twelve in number, speaking to Prince Mohi-ud-Din. The prince said to them, 'Don't be afraid of any children; kill the remaining Europeans that are alive.' Mohi-ud-Din then asked if Marriott was dead or alive. A sepoy standing near Jamedar Mohammed Kasim bluffed that Marriott and his brother had shot themselves. The prince gave betel to Mohammed Kasim and to the commandant in celebration, who received it with a salam (a gesture of respect). So, it seemed, Marriott was also on their hit list. Kasi Singh also told the commission that he saw a horse saddled at Moiz-ud-Din's door at the ready. He recalled that the other princes' doors remained shut, but those of Mohi-ud-Din and Moiz-ud-Din had been opened.[49]

Sepoy Ramany Sawany

Ramany Sawany, a sepoy, testified that he heard Moiz-ud-Din and Mohi-ud-Din call the jamedar of the First Battalion and the jamedar of the Second Battalion of the Twenty-Third Regiment and give orders to provide a band of sepoys to accompany Syed Kafur's son to take possession of the hill fort. Prior to that, he heard the two princes making offers to the jamedars and sepoys, saying, 'If you succeed in securing the country, you shall possess wealth and be men of great consequence, have elephants and horses and

---

[49] *Secret Department Sundries*, vol. 7B, 3717–19.

everything you wish and each sepoy shall have 25 rupees per mensem as pay and as long as your families exist, they shall be provided for.'[50] The deponent later stated that there were orders issued to kill Marriott once they had taken possession of the hill fort, and to take his body to Mohi-ud-Din, who would then mount his horse and parade himself through the city. However, Neil B. Edmonstone, secretary to the government, remarked, 'All that is ascribed to the two princes has with some variations been ascribed by other evidences exclusively to Moiz-Ud-Deen ... Great doubt therefore exists whether the evidence is applied to Mohi-Ud-Deen as well ... No attempt appears to have been made to unravel this confusion.'[51]

Probe into the Acquisition of Tipu's Flag

Moiz-ud-Din admitted to Marriott that the flag had come from his house, but maintained that the sepoys had plundered it, along with many other things. Marriott enquired how he came to possess it, to which Moiz-ud-Din replied that he had bought it from the Parsee merchant, Naoroji, during Doveton's command. The flag was produced before the special commission of enquiry too, and it appeared to be an old one, bearing the late sultan's insignia—a sun in the centre, with green tiger stripes on a red field. On enquiring, the Parsee merchant denied that he had ever sold such a flag to the princes. When questioned further, he admitted that he did sell some cloth of the same sort, but without the image of the sun on the flag. Asked where he obtained it, he said he had purchased a box of cloths at the public sales, after the capture of Srirangapatnam, in which the piece of cloth was found. When Moiz-ud-Din's servants purchased it, they told him it was intended as cloth for an elephant, which they planned to buy from Skardon, the paymaster of Vellore. Upon further interrogation, the merchant said that the flag was not made from the cloth he had sold to the princes. On that cloth,

---

[50] *Secret Department Sundries*, vol. 4A, 1934–35.
[51] *Secret Department Sundries*, vol. 4A, 1934–35.

the tiger stripes had been sewn on with a needle, whereas on the flag, the stripes had been woven in. And the witness, to elucidate, produced another piece of cloth woven in the same fashion.[52]

Military Court of Enquiry

There was also a military court of enquiry with Lieutenant Colonel Ross Lang presiding and George Read and W. S. Wright as members. The military court, which functioned as a court martial, after recording the depositions of all those who had been detained in Vellore and Madras, summed up its findings thus:

> It is unnecessary to go through the painful recital of the atrocious Revolt and Massacre on the 10th of July at Vellore; the fatal occurrences are within universal information. They comprehend every case of disloyalty, treachery, and horror. The whole was planned with unequalled secrecy and concealment. The object was to destroy every European, and place a son of Tippoo at the head of a Moorish Government. With this view letters were ready, or even were dispatched to the Mahrattas and to disaffected Chieftains at Cuddapah [Kadapa], in the ceded districts, and Vencatigherry [Venkatagiri], in the Carnatic, to excite a general hostility. Indiscriminate fury and slaughter raged for many hours and wretches were seen tottering from the Hospital to partake in the bloody scene; whilst the British soldiers were dragged from the same asylum and devoted to a deliberate death. Fatal instruction extended so far that the sepoy boys armed themselves with their carbines of exercise, and lent their aid to the general destruction.[53]

Many officials, realising that the safety of the Empire depended on the connection between the native army and their British officers, pressed for admonition and not for 'barbarous punishment'. They used means fair and foul to extract confessional statements from the sepoys, so as to fix and punish the ringleaders. A. Campbell,

---

[52] *Secret Department Sundries*, vol. 2A, 882–84.
[53] Bentinck, *Memorial*, 79.

commanding officer of the southern division of the army at Tiruchirappalli, was the first to take such a tactical line. He offered to give fifty pagodas to every sepoy who turned approver.[54] The special commission recommended, and the government instantly approved, the idea of granting immunity to those who were prepared to help in discovering the cause of the mutiny. It was notified that persons providing information about the mutiny on 10 July would not suffer 'any pains or penalties for any acts which they themselves may have done, nor be deprived of any pension or allowances which they now enjoy.'[55]

As a preliminary to the trials, the commander-in-chief, at the instance of the governor, had earlier directed Forbes and Coombs to investigate and classify the prisoners at Vellore under the following heads: 'innocent', 'most guilty', 'less guilty' and 'in arms' on 10 July, but with no specific charges of guilt (see Appendices 4–10). The report prepared by the officers was presented to the council on 9 November 1806.[56] An important conclusion of the report was that the revolt had been caused by 'a conspiracy so formidable and daring in its nature, aiming at no less an object than subverting the British authority.'[57] Thomas Oakes, a member of the governor's council, and Forbes, were of the view that it was not possible to procure enough evidence to individually convict these 600 men before a court martial.[58]

II

Experienced civilians like William Petrie, the second member of the council at Fort St George, believed that the loyalty of the Indian sepoys was a crucial component of British power. As he observed, 'With Indian on our side, we may set our European foes at defiance,

---

[54] *Military Department Consultation*, vol. 354, 5094–95.
[55] *Secret Department Sundries*, vol. 2A, 67–173.
[56] Bentinck, *Memorial*, 32.
[57] Quoted in Cameron, 'Vellore Mutiny', 100–01.
[58] *Secret Department Sundries*, vol. 3B, 1565–66; vol. 3A, 1442–45.

but if we lose the affection of our native subject, our sovereignty in the East will vanish like a dream.'[59]

Petrie expressed hope that the native troops 'will soon return to the habits of subordination and obedience and therefore I do not think their removal from service is either expedient or necessary'. He, however, was of the view that the native officers of the First Battalion of the First Regiment of Native Infantry should be discharged from the Coast Army.[60] Governor William Bentinck, who was stubborn before the outbreak of the mutiny that the new regulations and dress code should be enforced without yielding to pressure from the Indian soldiers, was all for clemency. But the commander-in-chief pushed for stringent punishment for those who were proved guilty.

So, the disposal of the prisoners remained undecided until the arrival of Lord Minto, the governor general of British India, in Madras, on his way to Bengal. It was then resolved that 'a final investigation should take place, and, with the exception of those against whom proof of plunder and murder could be adduced, and who were to be punished accordingly, the whole should be gradually enlarged, being dismissed from the service and declared incapable of being again enlisted'.[61]

A general pardon was granted to 516 mutineers, who were allowed to continue in service without any restraints after the revolt on 10 July. The officers and men who were absent at the time of the mutiny, or who had shown proof of their fidelity on the day of the mutiny, remained in armed service, while 'the rest were discharged forever from the service, with the grant to the officers of small pensions for their support, and the numbers of the regiments were erased from the army list'. However, based on depositions before the court of enquiry, the court martial awarded death sentences and banishment to select individuals, which were carried out by the commanding officer of Vellore on 23 September

[59] Hoover, *Men Without Hats*, 180.
[60] *Secret Department Sundries*, vol. 3B, 1723–27. The Madras Army was called Coast Army by the British.
[61] Mill and Wilson, *History of British India*, vol. 7, 87–88.

1806. The following is the text of the letter sent to the adjutant-general by the fort commandant:

Sir,

I request you will be pleased to communicate to His Excellency the Commander-in-Chief, that I have this morning carried into execution the approved sentences of the Native General Court Martial; six of the convicted mutineers were blown away from guns, five were shot with musketry (by a detachment of the 1st of the 1st, and 2nd, 23rd) and eight were hung. The two men that were acquitted are released, and those sentenced to be discharged the service and to be transported, remain in confinement awaiting His Excellency's further orders.

The execution took place on the western glacis of the fort, and the painful duty was performed without a single failure or accident.

(Signed)
Geo. Harcourt
Colonel[62]

Table 3.1 gives the details, rank-wise, of mutineers whose sentences were carried out in Vellore, as notified by Colonel George Harcourt.

TABLE 3.1: Mutineers' sentences carried out at Vellore

First Battalion, First Regiment	
Blown from a gun	1 havildar, 1 naik
Shot	1 naik, 4 sepoys
Hanged	1 jamedar, 4 sepoys
Transported	3 havildars, 2 naiks, 1 sepoy
Second Battalion, Twenty-Third Regiment	
Blown from a gun	2 subedars, 2 lascars
Hanged	2 havildars, 1 naik

Source: Wilson, History of the Madras Army, vol. 3, 188.

---

[62] Colonel Harcourt to the Adjutant-General, Vellore, 23 September 1806, in Wilson, History of the Madras Army, vol. 3, 188–89.

The following is an eyewitness description of the scene of the execution:

> The names and crimes of the convicts with the sentences of the General Court Martial and warrant for the execution were then read in presence of the troops and interpreted loudly in Moors to all the Sepoys ... The sentence appeared to make a great impression on the sepoys in general, but the prisoners were hardened and apparently reconciled to their approaching fate. A gallows was erected on the side of the square which was open to the country, where six field pieces were also drawn out and loaded on the spot and a small space was left, in the centre for a detachment of musquetry. The firing party consisted entirely of Sepoys selected from the two corps which had mutinied. The criminals were then marched out to their respective stations to meet the different deaths which they had been condemned to suffer. Upon a given signal, the general execution took place ... Almost all the inhabitants of the pettah were out upon the occasion, and made a violent cry and noise when the explosion took place— but they retired very peaceably after the business was over.[63]

Another spectator described how a number of kites accompanied the party to the place where prisoners were being blown from a gun,

> flapping their wings and screeching as if in anticipation of the bloody feast, till the fatal flash scattered the fragments of bodies in the air, when, pouncing on their prey, they caught in their talons many pieces of quivering flesh before they could reach the ground. At sight of this, native troops employed on this duty, together with the crowd assembled to witness the execution, set up a yell of horror.[64]

The officers and men engaged in the suppression of the mutiny were thanked for their services. One month's pay was presented to each of the non-commissioned officers and privates of the Nineteenth Dragoons who were involved in the operation. To all the native commissioned officers of the cavalry, a gold medal was

---

[63] Quoted in Cameron, 'Vellore Mutiny', 191–92.
[64] Quoted in Cox, *Manual of North Arcot District*, 86–87.

presented, and a silver to each of the non-commissioned officers and privates who accompanied the troops to Vellore on 10 July.[65] The native cavalry detachment, that consisted of 107 men of the Seventh Regiment, under Doveton, and 305 men drawn from all ranks of the other seven regiments, under Mason, of the Fifth Regiment, was rewarded with a special pay, in addition to the salary they were drawing, for their loyalty to the British cause. Accordingly, subedars, jamedars, havildars and naiks or privates were to get Rs 21, 14, 7 and 3.5, respectively. This special pay was to continue till they were discharged or pensioned off. It was also resolved at the time that medals, with a suitable inscription, should be presented to the detachment—gold for the native officers, and silver for the other ranks—but this resolution was not implemented.[66]

Sir John Cradock believed that Gillespie's prompt and decisive actions helped to destroy the dangerous confederacy that was shaping up against the Company government. On this, the commander-in-chief remarked in his dispatch that 'Colonel Gillespie's party was enabled to perform a deed that demands the gratitude of India'.[67] Cradock appreciated the immense value of the service rendered by Gillespie, calling it 'a military wonder'.[68] Quoting military historian, Sir John Fortescue's assessment of Gillespie that, 'I still think him the bravest man who ever wore the King's uniform,' Ferdinand Mount describes Gillespie as follows:

> [Gillespie] was the most impetuous, umbrageous, impatient, ruthless and unstoppable soldier there ever was. He was the epitome of Wellington's dictum that what a great commander in battle must have above everything else was *dash*. Gillespie's tiny frame pulsed with a ferocity that welled up in a nanosecond at the faintest provoking. His red hair crackled with energy. He was in your face before you were out of your chair. His life was not so much a military career as a series of uncontrolled explosions. [emphasis as in original][69]

[65] Vibart, *Madras Engineers and Pioneers*, vol. 1, 408.
[66] Wilson, *History of the Madras Army*, vol. 3, 188.
[67] Quoted in Vibart, *Madras Engineers and Pioneers*, vol. 1, 408.
[68] Quoted in Vibart, *Madras Engineers and Pioneers*, vol. 1, 104.
[69] Mount, *Tears of the Rajas*, 50.

William Thorn, the author of Gillespie's memoir, however, felt that the Company government did not appreciate Gillespie's service adequately. He wrote:

> Such was the unexpected result of his heroic zeal, at the moment, when, it may be said, that on his single determination hung the fate of our eastern possessions, and the existence not of a single fortress or an army, but of an extensive empire, consisting of millions of inhabitants of various denominations, countries and pursuits. This is not the exaggerated language of oriental declamation and hyperbolical panegyric, but the serious expression of truth and feeling, occasioned by a sense of what this valuable man did for British India, and regret that his services should have passed in a manner unrequited.[70]

In appreciation of Gillespie's gallant conduct, he was appointed by the government to the control of the whole cavalry, and 200 pagodas a month was fixed for this appointment.[71] Gillespie was also rewarded 'with a vote of thanks very handsomely expressed', accompanied by a monetary gift of 7,000 pagodas (Rs 24,500).[72]

Sergeant Brady of the Sixty-Ninth Regiment was recommended for a commission, which he exchanged for an appointment as conductor of ordnance. He was also presented with 800 pagodas (Rs 2,800) in acknowledgment of his service. Mrs Fancourt was granted an annuity of 100 pounds so long as she remained a widow, and each of her two children was given an allowance of 25 pounds per annum, to be continued until the age of sixteen in the case of the boy, and twenty-one in the case of the girl.[73]

Mustapha Beg, one of those involved in the early planning of the uprising, who escaped during the revolt, returned to the fort a few days later, and was rewarded with 2,000 pagodas and a subedar's pension for playing the role of a betrayer. The dubious character of Mustapha stood exposed when the adjutant-general,

---

[70] Thorn, *Memoir of Major-General Gillespie*, 106, 240. A monument was erected in his memory at Meerut by the officers who served under his command.

[71] Vibart, *Madras Engineers and Pioneers*, vol. 1, 408.

[72] Vibart, *Madras Engineers and Pioneers*, vol. 1, 105

[73] Wilson, *History of the Madras Army*, vol. 3, 187, 200.

Lieutenant Colonel Patrick A. Agnew, received an anonymous letter from the Hyderabad Subsidiary Force, in which the authors wrote,

> In the affair of Vellore, when the mutiny first commenced it was on account of Mustafa Beg; and the gentlemen of the Company's Government have bestowed upon him a reward of two thousand pagodas from the public treasury, with the rank of Subahdar. The same Mustafa Beg, Sepoy, was the man who gave the signal for revolt to the people at Vellore, and this is the man whom the Company have distinguished by their favour.[74]

Later, after the enquiries conducted by the military court and the special commission appointed by the Madras Government concluded, Harcourt recommended to Lieutenant Colonel Reynell, on 3 December 1806, to grant 'either preferment or pecuniary reward' for the loyalty demonstrated by some of the men of the First Battalion, First Regiment of the Native Infantry during the Vellore Revolt. In the list furnished, there were Hindu as well as Muslim men. It was recommended that Naiks Subbarayan, Perumalu and Arunchalam, and Lance Naik Samy be made havildars, and Sepoys Muthu, Venkatachalam and Ramaru, and Lance Naiks Mohammed and Syed Ahmed be promoted to naik. Harcourt recommended monetary rewards for Sepoys Muniappan and Muthukrishnan, for the loyalty demonstrated during the revolt. Sepoys Thonda Murty and Ramaswamy were acquitted of the charges and ordered to be released. The reason that promotions or pecuniary rewards were recommended for select sepoys and officers was because they assisted European officers and their family members during the revolt and obeyed the orders of English officers fighting against the mutineers.[75]

A collision of opinions took place with regard to the abolition of regiments that indulged in the revolt. Commander-in-chief

---

[74] Quoted in Kaye, *Sepoy Army in India*, vol. 2, 227.

[75] *Military Department Consultation*, 1806, vol. 360, 8853–56. One cannot miss the discrimination shown by the English colonel in extending promotion or monetary reward, suggested for Hindus, to the Muslims.

Cradock was of the strong view that regiments which were implicated in the revolt should be expunged from the army list. On this question, the members in the governor's council disagreed with Bentinck and concurred with the commander-in-chief. Bentinck set aside the decision of the council, and determined that the regiments in which the revolt had occurred should remain on the list. His act of setting aside the opinion of his council was annulled by the Supreme Government in Calcutta. The governor general then directed that the names of the implicated regiments be struck off. The conduct of the governor in indiscreetly exercising the extraordinary powers vested in him was reprimanded in England. The higher tribunals of the British government held the chief authorities of Madras, namely the governor, the commander-in-chief, and the adjutant-general, responsible for the bungling and ordered their recall. The adjutant-general was subsequently restored. The deputy adjutant-general was probably made a scapegoat and ordered to return to England.[76]

The obnoxious regulations to which the soldiers objected were withdrawn and repealed on 24 September 1806. A government order issued on 17 July, and reissued on 24 September, prohibited all unauthorised alterations in dress, or interference with the native soldiery in regard to their national observances. It was further directed that the turban previously sanctioned by the government on 15 March 1797 should continue to be the pattern for the army. The order read as follows:

> The order of Government under date the 15th March 1797 fixing a pattern Turband shall continue to be in force— leather cockades and plumes shall not be worn. Stocks of every description shall be abolished ... The Jacket shall be worn as received from the contractor, without any additional ornament of distinction, and the half-mounting shall in no particular way differ from the patterns lodged in the office of the Military Board and already in use ... The fullest permission shall be given to the native troops to wear their marks of caste at all times and in any manner they shall be granted with respect to the hair on the upper lip and wearing

---

[76] Furnell, *Mutiny of Vellore*, 25–28.

of toys and ornaments peculiar to different families and castes. The imposition of any restraint, either by order or by request, on the inclination of the sepoys in these particulars is positively forbidden. The Governor-in-Council also requires that every practicable indulgence shall be shown to the sepoy in the observance of his domestic custom.[77]

Bentinck and his colleagues in the council agreed upon a proclamation and issued it on 3 December. This they sent, after translating the contents into Hindustani, Tamil and Telugu, to every native battalion in the army, with orders to commanding officers to circulate and make its contents known to every native officer and sepoy under their command. After referring to the unrest that had prevailed in the Madras Army, and the news spread for malicious purposes that it was the intention of the British government to convert the troops forcibly to Christianity, the proclamation proceeded to declare that

> the constant kindness and liberality at all times shown to the sepoy should convince him of the happiness of his situation, "greater than what the troops of any other part of the world enjoy," and induce him to return to the good conduct for which he had been distinguished in the days of Lawrence and Coote, and "other renowned heroes." If they would not, they would learn that the British Government "is not less prepared to punish the guilty than to protect and distinguish those who are deserving of its favour."[78]

III

The Court of Directors reviewed the varied views expressed on the mutiny and conveyed their concluding remarks in a lengthy dispatch sent on 29 May 1807:

> The immediate cause of the discontent among the sepoys was the introduction of certain innovations in their dress, which were offensive, and, as they held, degrading to them; and that

---

[77] *Secret Department Sundries*, vol. 2A, 850–51.
[78] Quoted in Kaye, *Sepoy Army in India*, vol. 2, 244.

the captive sons of the late Tippoo Sultan, with their adherents and abettors, took occasion, from the dissatisfaction of the sepoys, to instigate them to insurrection and revolt with the view to effecting their own liberation and the restoration of the Mahomedan power.[79]

They focused their attention on the danger of interfering with the sepoys 'in any manner which, however erroneously, they might consider as affecting their castes'. They also questioned the course of action taken by the governor and the commander-in-chief.

> When it was found that the sepoys discovered great reluctance to the adoption of these novelties, the important question to be solved was, not whether the use of the turband was indeed inconsistent with the purity of caste, or whether the prohibition of marks and whiskers was sanctioned by any former practice; neither was it enough that the Mahomedan priest and Hindoo brahmin, who were consulted, both admitted that there was in the turband, or in those other articles, nothing contrary to their castes; but the matter of enquiry should have been whether the sepoys, ignorant and bigoted as they might be, were really persuaded that the usages imposed upon them did trench upon their castes, because, if they were, no compliance was to be expected from them, whatever might be the sacrifice.[80]

The Court of Directors lamented that when the commander-in-chief reported on 29 June 'an almost universal objection' to the new turban, Bentinck failed to make a thorough enquiry before permitting the change to be carried out. As to the commander-in-chief, they observed that it was impossible to exonerate him from responsibility on the plea that he had acted under the advice of his staff.[81]

The special commission, presided by Pater, that commenced its enquiry on 21 July, submitted its findings to the government

---

[79] Quoted in Wilson, *History of the Madras Army*, vol. 3, 198.

[80] Quoted in Wilson, *History of the Madras Army*, vol. 3, 198–99.

[81] Wilson, *History of the Madras Army*, vol. 3, 199.

on 9 August,[82] together with the depositions recorded during the enquiry. The commission in the first instance, observed that, 'the turban was highly offensive to the prejudices of the sepoys'.[83] The commission added that both Hindus and Muslims adhered stubbornly to their customs and it was no wonder that they felt the new military dress code violated the doctrines of their religion. Thus, 'the dissatisfaction arose out of a religious prejudice and was therefore converted to a common cause'.[84]

On the residence of the family of Hyder and Tipu at Vellore, which was identified as another cause, the commission said:

> Their [the princes'] followers had emigrated in great numbers to Vellore ... These persons naturally brought along with them their former attachments and prejudices ... Speaking the same language, and following the same religion, connections were easily formed, and amongst men who were not much occupied with engagements of trade or business, schemes of power and ambition would naturally occur to those who had been born to enjoy them ... When we look back to some former insurrections amongst the troops ... the civility with which the men distinguished their officers, and the point of honour which they seemed to feel in doing so, we cannot but think that the outrages on the late occasion are of foreign growth and could only have been inspired by a barbarous enemy.[85]

The commission summarised the report in a single sentence: 'The late innovations as to the dress and appearance of the sepoys was the leading cause of the mutiny, and the other was the residence of the family of the late Tippoo Sultan at Vellore.'[86] The government of Madras, and the governor general concurred with the commission's conclusion. Cradock, however, expressed dissent. In his report to the Court of Directors on 21 September

---

[82] Not 4 August, as stated in Gupta, 'Vellore Mutiny, July 1806', 26. See *Secret Department Sundries*, vol. 2A, 821.

[83] *Secret Department Sundries*, vol. 2A, 821–22.

[84] *Secret Department Sundries*, vol. 2A, 821–40.

[85] *Secret Department Sundries*, vol. 2A, 839–40.

[86] *Secret Department Sundries*, vol. 2A, 840.

1806, he argued that the 'alterations in dress had been nothing more than a pretext; the real object having been the restoration of the Mahomedan power'.[87]

In contrast, Bentinck felt that the cause of the mutiny was the new army regulations, and therefore supported Marriott who had reached the same conclusion. Marriott, in a letter to his wife on 20 August, while travelling to Bengal with the ten oldest sons of Tipu, his brother and two nephews, disclosed that he was upset about the decision of the government to transfer the male members of Tipu's family to Bengal even before the commission of enquiry presented its findings. Characterising the move as political, Marriott summed up his view in his letter thus:

> You will easily believe how actively Govt. must have been alarmed, at so general a disaffectation of the native troops. The corps in Fort St. George went so far as to stick their turband on their bayonets while sentries on the ramparts wear the rear to the front, with the violent symptoms of mutiny—I must not forget to say that the order for the removal of princes to Bengal was passed before the Commissioners had made this report to Govt, so that the resolution was not passed upon the strength of the princes being implicated in having exited the mutiny, but only to prevent the possibility if any future inconveniences by having them so near Mysore.[88]

It was thus ordered that the Mysore princes be sent to Calcutta, as their complicity could not be established 'to such a degree as to warrant more extreme measures'. They were removed from Vellore on 20 August 1806, amidst 'an immense concourse of spectators, who manifested no sympathy in their fate' (see Appendix 11 for details).[89] They arrived in Calcutta on 12 September. The second son of Tipu, Abdul Khalick, died on arrival. The rest were placed 'in suitable residences near Calcutta, under official surveillance, but no personal restraint'. They lived and left their legacies in Calcutta. Moiz-ud-Din, against whom there was still suspicion,

---

[87] Wilson, *History of the Madras Army*, vol. 3, 192–193.
[88] Thomas Marriott to his wife, 20 August 1806, *Madras Political Proceedings*, British Library, London.
[89] *Secret Department Sundries*, vol. 6A, 2984–86.

was kept for some time in confinement, but was eventually freed. The women of Moiz-ud-Din's family were not removed to Bengal. Eight of the retainers of the Mysore princes were tried before a special commission at Chittoor in April 1807, and the proceedings were confirmed by the government in May. One was sentenced to death, two to transportation for life, one to imprisonment for life, one to imprisonment for ten years, and three were acquitted.[90]

The monthly allowance paid to Tipu's family was drastically cut down. Fateh Hyder, who had a large family, was permitted Rs 1,500 per month, while Abdul Khalick, Mohi-ud-Din, Moiz-ud-Din and Shakirulah were sanctioned Rs 1,000 each. Subhan Saib and Siraj-ud-Din were allowed Rs 800 and Rs 400, respectively. Yassim Saib, Munir-ud-Din and Jamal-ud-Din, brothers by the same mother, received a total sum of Rs 660 per month. The caretaker, Marriott, suggested that the princes, in order to reduce their expenses, sell their horses and elephants, which they had to comply with before leaving for Bengal.[91]

Bentinck defended his decision to send the princes to Calcutta, citing the intelligence he got from the commander-in-chief, based on the voluntary disclosure of 'a Subedar of distinguished character and services'. This, he said, was consistent with the confession of 'a principal conspirator', who had asserted that the native cavalry,

> of whom as yet no suspicion had been entertained, were no less infected with a spirit of disloyalty than the infantry. On the receipt of these depositions ... it was determined to send the sons of Tippoo Sultan instantly to Bengal and to submit to the Supreme Government a proposal for the augmentation of the European force on the coast by a supply from that Presidency ... The escort of the Princes was, as usual, composed of a mixed force of European and Native troops.[92]

When the news of the Vellore Uprising reached England and the ensuing debate became intense, the Court of Directors

---

[90] *Secret Department Sundries*, vol. 6A, 2984–86.
[91] *Secret Department Sundries*, vol. 4A, 1794–95.
[92] Bentinck, *Memorial*, 30–32.

appointed one of its members, George Holford, a loyal servant of the Company for many years, to probe into the causes of mutiny. While conducting the investigation, Holford relied mostly on the accounts contained in the official papers dispatched by the Madras government. These papers, routed through the Supreme Government, also carried the opinions of the acting governor general, Sir George Barlow. Barlow had earlier rejected the view that revolt in Vellore was the handiwork of the Mysore princes and strongly held that the mutiny erupted solely because of the new military regulations. Influenced by Barlow's thinking, Holford, in his report, rebuffed the gullibility of the governor and commander-in-chief in believing that there were objections to the new turban, and thereby failing to probe the matter further. He placed the blame on several individuals wielding power at Fort St George for the tragic event. The Court of Directors accepted the verdict of Holford's report and decided to dismiss Bentinck, Cradock and a few others.[93]

The government, both in India and in England, held Bentinck and Cradock responsible for the Vellore Uprising and firmly resolved to recall both. The following reasons were given for this recall of the governor and the commander-in-chief:

> It seems to us that the Government, considered generally, did not exercise the discernment and vigilance which all the circumstances of the time required. Besides the application of this observation to Sir J. F. Cradock in particular, the injudicious regulations enforced under his authority, the remarkable degree in which he was unacquainted with the state of his own army just at the eve of an insurrection, when he thought all was calm; and the unpopularity which, it is too justly to be apprehended, the fatal issue of the whole would entail upon him, rendered it, in our opinion, impossible, whatever regret we felt on the occasion, to continue him in the command of the army.[94]

---

[93] Cameron, 'Vellore Mutiny', 233–35.
[94] Quoted in Wilson, *History of the Madras Army*, vol. 3, 199.

In the case of Cradock, the Company conveyed its anger by refusing to even pay for his passage home. Deprived of his position, he was without income, and had to wait till the arrival of the next convoy. It cost him a sum of 3,500 pounds for his family and servants.[95] Bentinck was also sent home in this fashion, which he mentioned in his memorial presented to the Court of Directors: 'It was ordered that I should immediately cease to be Governor; no measures were taken for my return home; and had it not been for the voluntary kindness of Sir Edward Pellow,[96] I should have been obliged to remain in India, stripped of all authority, till the departure of the homeward bound Fleet had afforded me a passage.'[97]

With regard to Bentinck, the statement issued by the Court of Directors ran as follows:

> Of the uprightness of his intentions, and his regard for our service, we have no doubt; and we have had pleasure in expressing our satisfaction with different measures of his government; but others which we felt ourselves obliged, in the course of the last year, to disapprove, impaired our confidence in him; and after weighing all the considerations connected with the business of Vellore, we felt ourselves unable any longer to continue that confidence to him which it is so necessary for a person holding his situation to possess.[98]

Apart from Bentinck and Cradock, 'Lieutenant Colonel Agnew, and Major Pierce were considered to have shown so little acquaintance with the disposition and prejudices of the native troops that they were removed from their respective appointments, and ordered to return to England.'[99]

The government dissolved the First and Twenty-Third Regiments on 31 December 1806, and in their places, stationed two regiments of two battalions each, numbered the Twenty-Fourth and the Twenty-Fifth Regiments, respectively. Petrie, senior

---

[95] Mount, *Tears of the Rajas*, 68.
[96] Bentinck, *Memorial*, 32. Pellow was a ship owner, who offered his own ship for the conveyance of the Mysore princes to Bengal.
[97] Bentinck, *Memorial*, v–vi.
[98] Quoted in Wilson, *History of the Madras Army*, vol. 3, 199–200.
[99] Wilson, *History of the Madras Army*, vol. 3, 199–200.

member of the governor's council in Madras and provisional governor, assumed office as governor on 11 September 1807, and Lieutenant-General Hay MacDowall took command of the army on 17 September 1806.[100]

Bentinck presented a memorial to the Court of Directors, as vindication of his actions, in which he wrote,

> I have been removed from my situation, and condemned as an accomplice in measures with which I had no further concern than to obviate their evil consequences. My dismissal was effected in a manner harsh and mortifying; and the forms which custom has prescribed to soften the severity of misfortune at all events sufficiently severe, were, on this single instance been violated as if for the express purpose of deepening my disgrace ... I have been severely injured in my character and my feelings: for these injuries I ask reparation; if, indeed, any reparation can atone for feelings so deeply aggrieved, and a character so unjustly compromised in the eyes of the world.[101]

Notwithstanding this appeal, the Court of Directors did not withdraw their censure or offer him the reparations he claimed. Their reply stated,

> While again expressing their sense of his lordship's uprightness and zeal, and disclaiming any intention of personal disrespect, they still adhered to their original view, and regretted that greater care and caution had not been exercised in examining the real sentiments and disposition of the sepoys before measures of severity were adopted to enforce the order respecting the use of the new turban.[102]

Evidently, there had been a strained relationship between Bentinck and the Court of Directors even before the Vellore Mutiny. At the beginning of his career as governor, Bentinck dismissed the collector of South Arcot, George Garrow, without consulting the Board of Revenue. Oakes was then appointed to the governor-in-council

---

[100] Wilson, *History of the Madras Army*, vol. 3, 199–200.
[101] Bentinck, *Memorial*, 49
[102] Quoted in Boulger, 'Lord William Bentinck', 38–39.

by the Court of Directors, much against the decision of Bentinck. Bentinck later supported Thomas Munro in his policy against the Palayakkarars of Andhra, whereas the order of the Court of Directors was to restore the Palayakkarars dispossessed by Munro. Therefore, when news of the Vellore Revolt first reached London, the Court of Directors desired that the confusion in Madras be set at naught by a change of authority, by appointing a person having the confidence of the British government.[103]

Ironically, the directors of the East India Company, who had rejected Bentinck's appeal in 1809, after eighteen years, entrusted to him the charge of not a single presidency, but the whole of India. Curiously, when Bentinck later opted to relinquish the post of governor general on health grounds, the directors, in contrast to the 'uncharitable words' conveyed when he was to demit his governorship, passed the following resolution, carried by a majority of fifteen to two:

> That this court deeply lament that the state of Lord William Bentinck's health should be such as to deprive the company of his most valuable services; and this court deem it proper to record, on the occasion of his Lordship's resignation of the office of Governor General, their high sense of the distinguished ability, energy, zeal and integrity with which his Lordship has discharged the arduous duties of his exalted station.[104]

IV

Seemingly, the storm had passed. But the fear that the 'disaffection of the native army' would always pose an internal threat to the British caused anxiety and worry for a long time to come. A military official who took part in the recapture of the fortress gave vent to this feeling when he wrote, 'No one knew how deeply rooted or

---

[103] Sipra Mukherjee, *Indian Administration of Lord William Bentinck* (Calcutta: K. P. Bagchi, 1994), 9–10.
[104] Quoted in John William Kaye, *Lives of Indian Officers*, vol. 1 (London: A. Strahan, 1867), 428.

extensive might have been the plot. The English seemed to stand as it were on a volcano, one eruption of which had been experienced, and which might be succeeded by others they knew not how soon. Indeed, it was a considerable time before this feeling subsided.'[105]

After withdrawing the controversial military regulations and the new dress code, the government earnestly believed that there no longer existed 'the slightest danger of a repetition of this dreadful tragedy'. But it was not to be. As the year 1807 dawned, there was fresh commotion, as Marudhu Pandian's testament, calling for unity across castes and religions to resist British rule before being hanged by the British in 1801, was found on the walls of the nawab's palace in Tiruchirappalli and Srirangam temple. Later it was claimed that it was found pasted on the doors of houses, and walls of streets and bazaars in Triplicane, Madras (see Appendix 15).

There are two anonymous documents, dated 26 February 1807 and 4 March 1807, cited by Alan D. Cameron in his unpublished PhD thesis, that are relevant. He laid his hands on them while looking through the records of the Secret Department Series of the Madras Government. Extracts of the two documents are given here, to understand the panic that prevailed in the Madras Presidency in the aftermath of the Vellore Revolt:

> After the affair at Vellore, suspicion and alarm spread through every garrison. Rumours propagated by Mussulman or French interests that the extirpation of the English was at hand. Emissaries in the disguise of Fakirs daily apprehended, exciting disaffection among the troops. A French flag was hoisted at Seringapatam ... Placards posted full of threats against the English. *Choultries* [resting places for travellers] scribbled with mutinous expressions. Christmas Day and New Year's Day were said to be appointed for a general massacre ... Rajah of Calastry [Kalahasti] and other Polygars have taken a threatening attitude. Reported that 400 of our sepoys intended to join them, after having cut off their officers. If the French on hearing of the Vellore business send out their emissaries and spies, the country must be lost to

---

[105] Quoted in Cox, *Manual of North Arcot District*, 86–87.

England, unless she sends out a man of uncommon capacity to accomplish the task successfully.[106]

The proclamation of Marudhu Pandian and the developments highlighted in the aforesaid documents testify to the panic in this situation. In this panic, Barlow, the acting governor general of India, considered it necessary, for the security of the Company's interests in Bengal, to put a stop to the activities of Serampore's missionaries, lest the natives regard them as an interference with their religion.[107] Minto, who succeeded Barlow as governor general, imposed a ban on the publications and preachings of the Serampore missionaries for 'imprudently attacking the Hindu religion'. When Minto asked for guidance from the home government as to his future policy in this matter, a draft was ably and tactfully prepared by Henry Dundas, president of the Board of Control, for the governor general's reference. It read as follows:

We are very far from being averse to the introduction of Christianity into India … but nothing could be more unwise than any imprudent or injudicious attempt to induce it by means which should irritate and alarm their religious prejudices … When we sanctioned the dispatch of missionaries of India it was far from being in our contemplation to add the influence of our authority to any attempts they might make … It is desirable that the knowledge of Christianity should be imparted to the natives, but the means to be used for that end shall be only such as shall be free from any political danger or alarm … Our paramount power imposes upon us the necessity to protect the native inhabitants in the free and undisturbed possession of their religious opinions.[108]

In a letter to Robert Dundas, the chief baron of the exchequer of Scotland, Sir John Anstruther, a privy counsellor, asserted that the

---

[106] Quoted in Cameron, 'Vellore Mutiny', 299–300. My attempt to locate these documents did not fructify.

[107] Marshman, *History of India*, vol. 2, 214.

[108] C. H. Philips, *East India Company, 1784–1834* (Manchester: Manchester University Press, 1940), 158–60.

government had lost confidence in the native army and suggested the elimination of the ranks of native officers. He observed,

> There is no doubt that the confidence of the Government in the native army is nearly lost. They have felt their own strength. They know also that we suspect and fear them— some officers have added to this by absurd conduct. Colonel Campbell of the 74th disarmed all the native Battalions at Trichinopoly; others have followed the example and these men are once again with Arms in the hands.[109]

Dundas followed up the instruction with further elaboration on the subject of the Company's policy towards religion in British India, in August 1808. He advised Minto to continue the government's policy of 'recognising the religion of the country by collecting taxes from "the pilgrims thronging the great festivals of Juggernaut" and by supervising the management of the temple'. Charles Grant and Edward Parry, chairman and deputy chairman, respectively, of the East India Company, shocked by this attitude, retorted to Dundas, 'Let me beg you will not yourself sign nor require us to sign to the principle that a Christian government may appoint the priests and direct the worship of a heathen temple.' To this, Dundas replied,

> On a principle of religion we are not at liberty under any circumstances ... to meddle in the idolatrous ceremonies of the Hindus. I think that there can be no doubt that it is extremely unwise to interfere in any degree beyond what the public welfare and safety absolutely require ... Political sovereignty gives the Company the obligation to preserve the public institutions.[110]

Based on the above discourse, the advice doled out by the Court of Directors was to base the religious policy of the Company government on political expediency rather than on Biblical principles.[111]

---

[109] John Anstruther to Robert Dundas, 20 October 1806, ref. GD51/3/434/1–2, National Records of Scotland.
[110] Anstruther to Dundas, National Records of Scotland.
[111] Anstruther to Dundas, National Records of Scotland.

The Madras government, taking into consideration the explosive situation prevailing in the presidency, exercised utmost caution while releasing the prisoners, which commenced in October 1807. With a view to avoiding the risk of prisoners 'forming a kind of renegade force' against the Company, they were released in several batches, with an interval of a few days between each batch. They were sent back to their native villages with police escorts. The collectors of all districts were alerted to the arrival of these men, so that their movements could be kept under surveillance. Before being released, the age, caste, colour and place of origin of each man was recorded so that it would be possible for the military administration to identify them if they subsequently made any effort to re-enlist in the Company's service. They also declared that the penalty for any such attempt would be banishment for life.[112]

Summary

Immediately after suppressing the outbreak at Vellore, Colonel Gillespie ordered an enquiry into the circumstances that led to it. However, the Madras government—the governor-in-council—preferred a special commission of its own to investigate. There was also a military court of enquiry set up in Vellore, with Lieutenant Colonels Forbes and Coombs assisting with their input. It is likely that many of the depositions were either tutored or done at the instance of English officers under an offer of pardon or monetary reward. The deponents were also keen to wriggle out of the impending punishment. Yet the findings of all these enquiry committees are helpful, to know the role of every person implicated in the revolt.

The Second Battalion of the Twenty-Third Regiment was recruited from Sankaran Kovil in Tirunelveli district, and the sepoys, erstwhile soldiers of the Palayakkarar chiefs of south

---

[112] Cameron, 'Vellore Mutiny', 252.

Tamil Nadu, were mostly drawn from the lower castes, namely Parayars, Pallars and Arunthathiers.

The caretaker of Tipu's family in Vellore Fort, Marriott argued that the only grievance he had heard from sepoys in the garrison was about the new turban. Marriott, Lieutenants Coombs and Gunning, the adjutant of the Twenty-third Regiment and acting adjutant of the European regiment (the Sixty-Ninth), and Marriott's brother, Captain Charles Marriott, escaped by hiding themselves in rooms. Around ten o' clock, when a regiment of cavalry from Arcot arrived on the parade ground, all the surviving Englishmen rallied behind Gillespie. Lieutenant Colonel Marriott informed the commission that thereafter, they killed and took 530 sepoys as prisoners in Moiz-ud-Din's palace.

Marriott affirmed that none of the sepoys or native officers was allowed to have any contact with the princes, but admitted that the wedding ceremony of one of Tipu's daughters was held with his knowledge. Though Marriott later wrote to his wife that he believed the princes were innocent, he told the commission that he had conveyed his suspicions against Moiz-ud-Din to Gillespie.

Forbes highlighted the Mustapha Beg affair before the commission. Though the incoherent manner in which Mustapha spoke to Forbes indicated his madness, he had asked the naik and Jamedar Sheik Ali to check whether there was any genuine grievance over the new turban. All of them affirmed that the battalions were happy with the new turban.

Mrs Burke spoke about the attitude of people in her neighbourhood, when she was living in the parachery. Her well-meaning effort, she testified, to apprise Colonel Fancourt of conversations she had overheard was uncharitably spurned by him. She recalled how, under the leadership of a Parayar leader named Kaalan, a few notables in the village would meet and discuss the evils of foreign rule in their 'Beach Committees'. Kaalan, she said, was the principal conspirator.

Mrs Potter related the harrowing experiences she had when she went to Mr Mann's residence with her children to seek protection. The sepoys came rushing in, saying that they were sent by Fancourt to get the keys to the gunpowder storeroom. As the conductor was not willing to oblige, the sepoys shot at him. Mann, fearing a threat to his life, jumped over Mrs Potter's children and escaped. Angered by his escape, the sepoys then targeted Mrs Potter. Fortunately for Mrs Potter, there was a pillar to hide behind. She spent the entire night hiding herself and her children in the conductor's house.

After completing the enquiry with the English officers and some of the deceased officers' wives, the commission started interrogating Indian soldiers and officers. Havildar Fakir Mohammed revealed the key role played by Subedars Sheik Adam and Sheik Hussein of the Fifth Company of the Second Battalion, Twenty-Third Regiment, and Jamedar Sheik Hussein of the Light Infantry. Fakir Mohammed was witness to Sheik Hussein arming the troops and marching them away. According to Muthu Karuppan, Sheik Adam had asked the sepoys not to wear the new turban, and to fight and kill all Europeans. His deposition also helped to add Naik Hussein Khan to the list of active insurgents, in addition to the previous three. The instigation of sepoys to rebel was done by Syed Jaffar, as testified by Alagiri.

Sepoy Hussein testified that Lance Naik Abdul Khadar had distributed ball cartridges taken from the battalion stores and urged everybody to fire at the European regiment. Venkatachalam related how he was wounded by gunshots from Abdul Khadar and Imam Khan while trying to escape from the scene of the mutiny. Murthy, who was on sentry duty, stated that Captain J. J. Miller, who was to go on rounds, did not go. Instead, Jamedar Sheik Hussein was the one who did the rounds. Murthy was the one who testified that the Mysore flag was brought from the house of Moiz-ud-Din. The senior-most subedar, Sheik Adam, hoisted the flag at his request. Later, Kasi Singh disclosed the princes' promise to hike their salary to Rs 25 and to take care of their families.

Kasim Ali, in his deposition, testified to Syed Kafur's (Tipu's confidant) son, Syed Hussein's role in leading the battalions to the east bastion of the fort. He pulled down the English flag from a flagpole nearby. Dr Hakkim Gulam Mohammed brought to the notice of the commission that some of the palace servants visited the pettai to call the supporters of the princes, with their arms, into the fort. Syed Mahomed, a former servant of Prince Abdul

Khalick, also confirmed the visit of one of Moiz-ud-Din's servants to the pettai. Mohammed Shroff made known the smuggling of three bundles of swords into the palace before the mutiny.

Yusuf Khan and Sheik Kasim did not mince words. The former claimed that the intrigues of Tipu's followers and family led to the Vellore uprising. Their alleged object was to re-establish the Mysore Sultanate. Sheik Kasim, who is considered the originator of the mutiny, told the commission that the mutiny was planned even before the arrival of the Second Battalion, Twenty-Third Regiment to the fort, but it was deferred twice. The third time, the plan was to raise the standard of revolt the following week. Because of the blabbering of Jamedar Sheik Hussein in his state of drunkenness on the night of 9 July, the mutiny commenced in the early hours of 10 July. Had it gone as planned, he said, the outcome would have been different, as people from pettai as well as the Palayakkarars from the north Arcot region were desirous of joining the Vellore insurgents.

Sheik Nuttar and Jamal-ud-Din, on the promise of pardons, turned approvers. Moiz-ud-Din's involvement in the conspiracy was disclosed by Sheik Nuttar. He also helped the commission identify Jamal-ud-Din, a foster brother of Moiz-ud-Din, as the mediator between the palace and the battalions. Nuttar brought to the notice of the commission Marriott's refusal to buy Moiz-ud-Din a horse, and to permit his first cousin, Hyder Hussein Khan, to stay overnight with him in the palace. According to Nuttar, the horse that Moiz-ud-Din rode with Marriott's consent was found saddled in front of his house when the dragoons from Arcot arrived at the fort. Jamal-ud-Din pointed out why Vellore was chosen for the revolt, and the plan to follow up the victory with assistance from cavalry stationed in Arcot and Kunnathur, thereby precluding the possibility of European forces being sent from Madras to crush the rebellion. This indicates the pre-planned attempt to extend the revolt.

Kasi Singh spoke about Mohi-ud-Din's anxiety over the fate of Marriott and his brother. This concern was to make sure that his enemies were totally wiped out and there was no one to carry on the fight from the English side. Ramany Sawany testified that

Moiz-ud-Din and Mohi-ud-Din called the jamedars of both regiments and asked them to send Syed Kafur's son along with a band of sepoys to take possession of the hill fort. But this order could not be carried out. If it had been, the course of events might have been different.

Lieutenant Colonel Ross Lang, with George Read and W. S. Wright as members, constituted the court martial that concluded that the mutiny occurred because of a plot to place a son of Tipu at the head of a Muslim government. They had, with this end in mind, sent communication to chieftains of Kadapa and Venkatagiri to embark on a general revolt.

The confessional statements extorted from the sepoys were mostly on the promise of a pardon or enticement. As a result, many of them turned approvers. The English realised that without the native army, Company rule could not be sustained. Oakes, a member of the governor's council, and Forbes also argued that proving the guilt of 400 prisoners before the court martial would be a difficult task.

William Petrie, senior member of the governor-in-council, pleaded for a general pardon for the 516 accused, who continued in service without any restraint from 10 July. However, he wanted all Indian officers of the First Battalion, First Regiment to be discharged from the Madras Army. Governor Bentinck was also for mercy. Only the commander-in-chief, Cradock, persisted in his stand to award stringent punishment for those found guilty.

Twenty-five subedars, jamedars, havildars, naiks, lascars and sepoys, belonging to the native infantry in Vellore garrison, convicted by the court martial, were executed. We know the number of people and their designations, but not the names of those sentenced to death and banishment.

The princes, excepting Moiz-ud-Din, were shifted to Calcutta on 20 August 1806. Later Moiz-ud-Din was exonerated and also removed to Bengal along with his family. Eight of the princes' retainers were tried by a special court at Chittoor in April 1807. One was sentenced to death, two transported for life, one to imprisonment for life and one for ten years. Three were acquitted.

The officers, sepoys and privates who helped to quell the rebellion were presented with gold and silver medals, according to their status and the role they played. The native cavalry detachment, comprising 117 men under Lieutenant Colonel Doveton, and 305 men belonging to all ranks of the other seven regiments, under Captain Mason, were rewarded with additional pay. Gillespie, apart from receiving a promotion and an increase in salary, was presented with a monetary gift of Rs 25,000. Mrs Fancourt was granted 100 pounds per annum, while her two children were given an allowance of 25 pounds per annum.

Mustapha Beg was rewarded with 2,000 pagodas and a subedar's pension for playing the role of an informer. The natives who demonstrated loyalty were given promotions. In the list of such persons, there are two Muslims and nine Hindus.

The special commission, presided over by J. Pater, which commenced its enquiry on 21 July, presented its findings to the government on 9 August. The primary cause of the mutiny, according to the special commission, was the forced change of dress and appearance of the sepoys. The other factor was the residence of Tipu's family at Vellore, a view endorsed by the governor general and the government of Madras. The dissenting voice was the commander-in-chief's.

The Court of Directors, of their own volition, conducted an investigation through one of their trustworthy servants, Holford, who held Bentinck and Cradock responsible for their negligence, leading to the revolt. So, the Court of Directors, based on Holford's report, decided to dispense with their services, along with the adjutant-general, Lieutenant Colonel Agnew, and deputy adjutant-general, Major Pierce. Bentinck appealed against the decision of the Court of Directors, but to no avail.

The government also dissolved the First and the Twenty-Third Regiments on 31 December 1806, and in their places, stationed the Twenty-Fourth and Twenty-Fifth Regiments in Vellore.

The odious military regulations objected to by the native soldiers were withdrawn. Thereafter, the government believed that there was no longer any threat to their rule. But the new year greeted the government with new alarms. The late Marudhu Pandian's testament calling upon natives to revolt against the ferengis was found written on walls in Tiruchirappalli and Triplicane. In Srirangapatnam, the French flag was hoisted. There were desperate attempts to seek the intervention of the French. The situation of panic that prevailed in the Madras Presidency prompted the acting governor general, Barlow, to put a stop to the activities of Serampore's missionaries. Lord Minto, later as governor general, imposed a ban on their publications.

The rewards to those who played a crucial role in quelling the revolt, and death sentences to the ringleaders and front-liners, were carried out after receiving the findings of the two enquiry commissions. The enquiries, it seems, were not fairly conducted, as most of the deponents identified Muslim officers and sepoys as the villains, either under the threat of reprimand or lured by financial incentive. The government manipulated the list of persons who swore to overthrow Company rule, originally obtained from a sepoy, by adding more Muslim names to the list, as evidenced from Appendices 2 and 3.

The disagreement between the governor and the commander-in-chief over the cause of the revolt led to the recall of both by the Company administration in England. Based on their dispute—the commander-in-chief insisting that the revolt was due to innovations in the military dress code, and the governor attributing the crisis to a conspiracy by Tipu's sons—public opinion in England also got polarised. Those who subscribed to the viewpoint of the commander-in-chief focused on the activities of the Christian missionaries that caused apprehension among the native Hindus.

However, there can be no monocausal explanation for the standard of revolt the native troops raised in Vellore. We explore the multiple causes of the revolt as we move to Chapter 4.

4

Causes and Consequences

I n the early narrative accounts of the mutiny by Company officials and military personnel, only the recapture of the fort was highlighted. Historians also articulated these viewpoints, echoing the deeply divided opinions of civil and military authorities. The new turban was seen as the cause of the mutiny. But the causes of this event in 1806 are evidently complex and manifold. Though the insurgency was confined to military cantonments, it is simplistic to attribute it to grievances relating to military affairs.

The soldiers in the Madras Army were drawn from the peasant community and were in touch with their native villages, and were kept informed of developments of every kind, positive and negative. When they returned after vacations from their home towns, they would share their concerns and worries with fellow soldiers. In this way, they were very much part of a society that was going through a phase of violent change in all spheres of life in the context of British rule. The provocation in the cantonment, therefore, could have been only a trigger. There were other underlying factors that stirred the Indian soldiers to revolt. Hindu and Muslim soldiers buried their religious differences and turned against their common adversary, the British. This chapter attempts a detailed analysis of the causative factors that led to the tumult, not only in Vellore Fort but in almost all British cantonments of southern India at that time.

I

On the eve of the Vellore Revolt, the service conditions of Indian sepoys in the Madras Army were abominable. The pay of the sepoy was Rs 7 a month, less than half of what a European private received, and less than what Tipu Sultan had paid.[1] Things had come to such a pass that if one were to spend one's whole life in the Company's service, despite an immaculate record of experience, one could barely rise to the rank of subedar. In an army of nearly 150,000 natives, the highest pay a subedar could receive was 20 pagodas (less than Rs 100) a month. No consideration was given to the subedar who had served for up to forty years, to save him from the harshness of a young European officer who would have just joined the corps.[2]

The prestige of Indian officers (sardars) had declined towards the close of the eighteenth century. Their status diminished as more and more British soldiers arrived in India. The position of officer was becoming increasingly the preserve of Europeans. The military reforms of 1796 accelerated this trend. The rank of killadar, fort commandant, to which Indian army officers could formerly aspire, was abolished. 'From having previously occupied positions of considerable power and influence in the army, and being treated accordingly by the British, the sardars found themselves relegated to a situation where their rank tended to count for little,' remarked historian Raymond Callahan.[3]

A letter from members of the Subsidiary Force at Hyderabad, received by Lieutenant Colonel Patrick A. Agnew, to which a reference was made in Chapter 3, contained thirty-two paragraphs enumerating sepoys' grievances and complaints.[4] It particularly focused on the ill-treatment suffered by Indian officers, while dilating on the causes of the outbreak.

> When in consequence of the new turbans a certain event
> occurred at Vellore, it is reported that some Gentlemen

---

[1] Mount, *Tears of the Rajas*, 70.

[2] Malcolm, *Political History of British India*, 501–02.

[3] Quoted in Cameron, 'Vellore Mutiny', 138.

[4] Hoover, *Men Without Hats*, 27. Having perused the Wellington Papers at Southampton University Library, Hoover found that the anonymous authors of the petition were eleven native commissioned officers of the Subsidiary Force at Hyderabad, and that the letter, originally written in Urdu, was translated into English by J. Munro, Persian interpreter to the adjutant-general.

declared that it was occasioned by the sons of Tippoo
Sultan. This declaration is false. If at that conjunction all
the Subidars, Jemidars, Havildars, Naiques, Sepoys had been
united, Vellore would not have been retaken. The cause of
the mutiny, proceeded from the folly of a few persons, and
from the European officers having ill-treated the Subidars
and Jemidars on every occasion.[5]

Focusing on the specific grievances of Indian soldiers, the
petitioners pointed out that they could attain the rank of subedar
only after spending their whole life in the Company's service. After
attaining that rank, there was no scope for further advancement.
According to the Company's service rules, one was expected to
pass through the ranks of sepoy, naik, havildar and jamedar, and
on attaining the position of subedar, at the end of eighteen years,
they would receive a pay of 20 pagodas.[6]

The racial prejudice entertained by the English seems to
have hurt Indian officers and soldiers beyond repair. On this, the
anonymous authors of the petition had the following to say:

Almighty God has created all mankind whether white
or black men; the same desire that are possessed by white
men, whether to eat, to drink, or to enjoy the pleasures of
life, equally prevail in the hearts of black men; and if the
European Gentlemen shall consume three parts of the
Company's revenues it is well, let them assign a fourth part
at least.[7]

The petitioners asserted that the sepoys of the nizam and the
Marathas were better off than the subedars and jamedars of
the Company army. They ate and drank with their families and led
comfortable and happy lives. They said that the truth or falsehood
of their account could be ascertained by getting a report from any
English officer who had marched through the nizam's or Marathas'
country. A comparison of the scales of pay for European officers

---

[5] Minto Papers, file no. 93–112, MS 11322, National Library of Scotland, in
Cameron, 'Vellore Mutiny', 139–56.
[6] See endnote 41 in Hoover, *Men Without Hats*, 45–46.
[7] Quoted in Hoover, *Men Without Hats*, 45–46.

with those of their Indian counterparts was also attempted in the anonymous letter. The Company was accused of fixing the rates of European officers' pay at some 100, 200, 300, 400, 500, 600 and 1,000 pagodas, while jamedars and subedars, according to their regulations, were granted a pay of 7 and 12 pagodas, respectively.[8]

Relations between European and native officers had been estranged by the former's contemptuous apathy for the feelings and opinions of the latter, and by their lack of acquaintance with the native languages. The petitioners pointed out how European officers had earlier considered subedars and jamedars as their equals, and had treated them with kindness and respect. In contrast, every new European officer who had arrived from Europe in the previous ten years, they alleged, showed no consideration or regard towards the subedars and jamedars, and treated them worse than their cooks.[9]

The Court of Directors made a pointed reference to this view in one of their letters while giving their remarks on the Vellore mutiny: 'We have too much reason to apprehend, that, to the neglect and disrespect manifested to the native officers by the European officers, the disposition to foment and conceal the disaffection of the men is principally to be attributed.' They also observed, 'It has been represented to us that the deficiency in the knowledge of the languages of the country prevalent amongst the officers of the army may have operated as another cause of the absence of confidence between the European officers and the native troops.'[10]

Military historian, John William Kaye, provided an exhaustive account of the grievances of Indian officers and soldiers. He noted that a sepoy on duty always carried arms to the English officers, but an English soldier never cared to salute his Indian officer when he crossed him. Senior Indian officers who had served for several years were publicly insulted by young European officers. English sergeants, equivalent to only havildar in rank, commanded Indian officers of the highest rank in a parade, and during military

---

[8] Hoover, *Men Without Hats*, 31.
[9] Hoover, *Men Without Hats*, 34.
[10] Court of Directors to Fort St George, 29 May 1807, quoted in Mill and Wilson, *History of British India*, vol. 7, 125.

marches, Indian officers had to stay with the sepoys, sharing the same tents. In the armies of Indian rulers, elephants or palanquins were provided to Indian officers for their transportation, but in the Company's army, whatever be the distance they had to travel, they were denied this privilege. If a sepoy were to die while on duty in faraway places, his wife and children were left in the lurch. The Indian rulers had also dispensed land grants to soldiers who had distinguished themselves in war, but the Company government gave them only 'sweet words'. Kaye concluded that

> the concubines of the English gentlemen were better paid than the native officers, and their grooms and grass-cutters better than the native soldiers; that the English officers could import into their Zenanas the most beautiful women in the country, whilst the natives hardly dared look at the slave-girls; and, to crown all, it was declared that General Arthur Wellesley had ordered his wounded sepoys to be mercilessly shot to death.[11]

S. S. Furnell highlighted this grave aspect in his brilliant analysis:

> Between an army composed of Hindoos and Mahomedans and the Europeans who command them, there can be but little community of feelings. Differing, as they do, in country, in religious belief, in habits of life, in form and complexion, they have not even the bond of a common tongue; the European officers generally possessing but a slender knowledge of a language of the men under their command, and the men no knowledge at all of the language of their officers. The elements of discontent are, therefore, sufficiently powerful, while the means of allaying it are small.[12]

The imperious attitude of the European officers only added insult to injury. A widely condemned incident reported to Lord Cornwallis in 1792 helps illustrate the situation. An English officer owed money to a native and when he was asked for it, he paid the debt not in money, but in blows. The matter did not end there. By order of the commanding officer, accompanied by the adjutant of

---

[11] Kaye, *Sepoy Army in India*, vol. 2, 221–22.
[12] Furnell, *Mutiny of Vellore*, 2.

the regiment, the man was sent back to the debtor who 'received him "with the money that was due to him and the stick that was prepared to beat him lying on the same table," and administered a second correction to him, which "divided his ear.'" But the sympathy of the court martial was with the white man, who was 'acquitted as though this "new way to pay old debts" were quite in consonance with the acknowledged usages of officers and gentlemen'.[13]

Major Joseph Haslewood, of the Second Battalion of the First Regiment, served for seven years in the battalion that revolted in Vellore and was personally acquainted with all the ringleaders. He was in Wallajahbad at the time of outbreak of the revolt at Vellore. In a letter to his friend Hall Plumer,[14] Haslewood related how the sepoys were no longer treated with respect, which, according to him, started from the time of General John Braithwaite, the commander-in-chief in 1800, who, without understanding the language and temperament of Indians, took decisions based on the opinions of others. Many officers opposed changes made to the military regulations. But given the power that the adjutant-general wielded over the commanding officers and the commander-in-chief, any attempt to apprise them of the serious implications of the new regulations was viewed contemptuously, and those who attempted to do so came to be dubbed as the 'weak and bigoted disciples of ridiculous prejudices of antiquated doctrines'. Haslewood wrote,

> The Sepoy was now taught that his officer was not the important man he had hitherto considered him; that it was derogatory to them to do any menial office for him or to run after his horse or Palanquin, as his forefathers had always taken pride in doing; that if the officer ordered, the sepoy had no right to obey, unless what the officer ordered was proper.[15]

---

[13] Kaye, *Lives of Indian Officers*, 88–90.
[14] Hall Plumer was his influential friend, and brother of the famous British judge, Thomas Plumer, who later became the first vice-chancellor of England.
[15] Major J. Haslewood to Hall Plumer, as to Origin and Causes of the Mutiny of the Madras Sepoys at Vellore, Madras, 13 October 1806, ref. GD51/3/432, National Records of Scotland, 385.

In 1802, Haslewood wrote a letter to the confidential adviser of Lieutenant Colonel Charles Stuart, to convince the general that the 'novelties introduced at that time had ... checked all ardour and [were] changing entirely the disposition of the sepoys'. In this letter, he noted that although 'promotion was quicker; pay considerably greater in all ranks', and territories extended, it remained difficult to recruit; desertions too had 'alarmingly multiplied'. He also expressed his conviction that '[his] battalion would willingly give back all the advantages lately conferred by quicker promotion and greater pay, to get back the former habits, manners, customs of the service'.[16]

Haslewood asserted that despite the advantages of the new systems of discipline, the Indian soldiers were vexed, as they knew very well that there would be no advantage whatsoever, from the military point of view, for them, by acquiescing to the 'revolting innovations'. Haslewood further wrote,

> They therefore considered them as wanton insult on their feelings, and as the warning of premeditated intention to degrade all casts to the level of a Pariah. Whilst the Pariah thought the time arrived for him to be degraded with the rest, to the despised rank of Christian; and their disaffection to the service and Europeans in general became so evident that the most blind might observe it, and most ignorant avail themselves of it, provided their proposal was hostile to us and our service.[17]

II

Though the Palayakkarars had been crushed by the close of the eighteenth century, they were not reconciled to their vanquished state. The *zamindars* (tax farmers for the state) of Venkatagiri and Kalahasti were still collecting arms and ammunitions, and

---

[16] Haslewood to Plumer, 13 October 1806, ref. GD51/3/432, National Records of Scotland.

[17] Haslewood to Plumer, 13 October 1806, ref. GD51/3/432, National Records of Scotland, 183.

recruiting retainers. Gurram Gondah, which was under the hereditary killadars since Mughal rule, had established contact with Hyder Ali, and great reliance was placed upon these Palayakkarars by the mutineers.[18] Besides, a large number Tipu Sultan's disbanded troops were in Gurram Gondah. So the involvement of the family of the hereditary killadar of Gurram Gondah was suspected. But Thomas Munro did not think that 'it has sufficient weight to be at all dangerous'. Munro, who was in the Ceded Districts—Kadapa, Karnool and Bellary—in a letter addressed to Governor William Bentinck, stated,

> On the first alarm of the conspiracy at Vellore, I dispatched orders to watch the proceedings of the principal people of Gurrum Condah, for I immediately suspected that the sons of Tippoo Sultan were concerned, and I concluded that if they had extended their intrigues beyond Vellore, the most likely places for them to begin with were Chitteldroog, Nundidroog, Gurrum Condah and Seringapatam … The poligars, I am convinced, never will run any risk for the sake of Tippoo's family. Some of them would be well pleased to join in disturbances of any kind, not with the view of supporting a new government, but of rendering themselves more independent. The most restless among them, the Ghuttim-man, is fortunately in confinement; and I imagine that the others have had little or no correspondence with the princes. Had it been carried to any length, I should most likely have heard of it from some of the poligars themselves.[19]

But contemporary records and recent studies tell us how the Palayakkarars were always looking for an opportunity to free themselves from servitude to the Company government and assert their independence. Historian Kate Brittlebank has shown that the taking of Srirangapatnam by itself did not eventuate in British control of the Mysore territory. Rebellions broke out in various

---

[18] Gleig, *Life of Thomas Munro*, vol. 1, 361–63.

[19] Thomas Munro to William Bentinck, 11 August 1806, quoted in Gleig, *Life of Thomas Munro*, vol. 1, 363–64.

parts of Mysore, which had to be subdued before the British could establish their supremacy over the newly conquered territory.[20]

The Palayakkarars of Chittoor had been refractory and turbulent until 1805. Not only did they not pay the tribute, they also refused to acknowledge the authority of the British. They also wielded influence over the Palayakkarars of the Ceded Districts. The detachment sent to force the Palayakkarars of Chittoor into submission was opposed by open rebellion, and though they were finally brought to heel, it caused 'continued anxiety to the Company administration'.[21]

Major Haslewood's letter to Hall Plumer revealed the entire plan of the rebel army: The battalions at Hyderabad were to depose the nizam, who was friendly with the Europeans. Letters had been written to different Palayakkarars and rajas, as well as to the Marathas, inviting them to join in a general attack on the English. Every European was to be killed or reduced to the status of a mercenary in the native armies. These conversations were held by the sepoys even when on guard. Evidence of this was presented to the committee of which Haslewood was a member. Even the Christian sepoys were involved in the conspiracy against the English having been promised that their condition would be bettered under the new dispensation. The English were accused of treating all Christian converts with greater contempt than all other castes, not allowing them to rise above the rank of a sepoy.[22]

H. H. Dodwell considered French intrigue to be one of the contributory factors for the lingering hopes of the Palayakkarars. Though French rule had ended in India after the Treaty of Amiens in 1802, that permitted them to retain only Pondicherry, the French were very active in conspiring against the English. Louis Binot, the chief of staff to Charles Decaen, the newly appointed captain-general of French India, had established relations with the rajas

---

[20] Quoted in Janaki Nair, 'Tipu Sultan, History Painting and the Battle for "Perspective"', *Studies in History* 22, no. 1 (February 2006): 97–143.

[21] W. K. Firminger, ed., *Affairs of the East India Company*, vol. 1 (1812; repr., Delhi: Neeraj Publishing House, 1985).

[22] Haslewood to Plumer, 13 October 1806, ref. GD51/3/432, National Records of Scotland.

of Thanjavur and Travancore, and had kept one of his officers in contact with the Marathas. Binot had agents at Tranquebar in the south and Serampore in the north, when these two places passed into the hands of the English from the Danes. These French agents, with their spies active throughout the country, deemed India ripe for rebellion against the English. In a communiqué addressed to rebellious chiefs of the palayams in southern India, Decaen urged them to attack the Company with their collective force if they wanted to save themselves from the fate that had befallen Oudh, Arcot and Mysore.[23]

The Treaty of Amiens in 1802 gave the French access once more to south India by re-establishing their sphere of interest in Pondicherry. Major Haslewood, of the Second Battalion, First Regiment, the one that had demonstrated unrest at Wallajahbad, volunteered to provide evidence before the enquiry commission, and in his deposition stated,

> I have lately met Mr Salter, who was recently a prisoner in Isle of France and is at present at Madras, who mentioned that it was the common report in the Island and generally believed that a number of young men were training upon the Island for the express purpose of qualifying them to proceed to India by way of Tranqubar for the purpose of sowing the seeds of sedition and revolution among the minds of the natives of the Peninsular India.[24]

Fateh Ali, Tipu's nephew, himself reportedly claimed that he had established friendship with an influential Frenchman.[25]

For the commander-in-chief, Sir John Cradock, the mutiny was a part of a conspiracy by the descendants of Tipu. The author of Colonel Robert Gillespie's memoir, William Thorn, also held a similar view. The splendour that the Company government provided to the sons of Tipu and the liberty they enjoyed in interacting with 'a continual influx of strangers, contributed to

---

[23] H. H. Dodwell, ed., *The Cambridge History of India*, vol. 5 (1929; Indian repr., New Delhi: S. Chand, 1963), 329–30.

[24] *Secret Department Sundries*, vol. 9, 955.

[25] Unknown author to Major Haslewood, Minto Papers, in Cameron, 'Vellore Mutiny', 301.

strengthen the activities of the conspirators'. According to Thorn, the unsuspecting nature of English officers and the mildness of the government encouraged the insurgents to carry out their wicked designs on the very day that Gillespie was to have dined with his friend, Colonel John Fancourt, at Vellore Fort. In his view, it turned out to be 'a fatal supineness' for many valuable men, who were 'neither apprehensive of evil designs in others, nor meditating oppression themselves'.[26]

As we have seen, some historians pointed an accusing finger at the extravagant lifestyle provided to the relatives of Tipu in the *mahal*s (palaces) of the fort (see Figures 4.1 to 4.4). No officer except Lieutenant Colonel Thomas Marriott was allowed to enter the palace without the permission of the princes, and no European sentinel did duty within its precincts.[27]

The army officers' perspectives are in agreement with this viewpoint. They were of the view that if Tipu's family

> had not been left to disport themselves at will in Vellore—
> if they had not been gorged with money, and attended by
> countless Musulman followers eager to recover the posts
> and the privileges which they had lost, there would have
> been no massacre and no mutiny, and not even a murmur
> of discontent.[28]

The funds set aside after the takeover of Mysore by the British in 1799 for the maintenance of the families and descendants of Hyder Ali and Tipu Sultan amounted to 200,000 star pagodas per annum. The break-up for each prince, as furnished by Marriott, is as follows: The four eldest princes, namely, Fateh Hyder, Abdul Khalick, Mohi-ud-Din and Moiz-ud-Din, were to receive Rs 50,000 each per annum in monthly payments. The next three in age, namely, Muhammad Yassin, Muhammad Subhaun and Shakirulah, were to receive Rs 25,000 each per annum. The five minor princes were to receive Rs 25,000 each on attaining the age of fifteen, and until that time, two of them, Sirur-ud-Din and

---

[26] Thorn, *Memoir of Major-General Gillespie*, 99–100.

[27] Mill and Wilson, *History of British India*, vol. 7, 83.

[28] Kaye, *Sepoy Army in India*, vol. 2, 247.

Jamal-ud-Din, would receive Rs 700 each month and the others, namely, Munir-ud-Din, Gulam Muhammad and Gulam Ahmed, were to receive Rs 500 each per month.[29]

The enquiry commission, appointed by the government, received no evidence to suggest that the communications sent to the 'conspirators' in the princes' names had emanated from them. There was little evidence to establish that prior to the mutiny, they had personal interaction with any of the insurgents. It appeared from the depositions of some sepoys that during the insurrection, some of the rebels had refreshments at the houses of the princes, Mohi-ud-Din and Moiz-ud-Din, and that the Mysore flag was brought from the residence of the latter. But then there are facts which inveigh against such conclusions. Tipu's sons had refrained from accepting the tempting invitation by the crowd to assume the leadership of the insurgents and had cautiously avoided making utterances which could implicate them in the mutiny.

Military leaders, in order to wriggle out of the situation in which they were caught napping, insisted that the whole episode was a political movement. They said that three representative men—a Hindu (Havildar Major Karuppan), a Muslim (Subedar Sheik Imam) and a Rajput (Chaing Singh)—belonging to the Madras Army, had approved the new cap, and one or two regiments had been paraded in it without complaint.[30] They alleged that the mutiny had been engineered by the deposed family of Tipu Sultan with the object of restoring, in the first instance, Muslim rule in southern India, and eventually, to recover the imperial throne for the Mughals. Kaye, after examining these two divergent points of view, concluded, 'But for the intrigues of Tipu's family there would have been no outbreak at that time, and but for the new military regulations they might have intrigued in vain.'[31]

Believing that the revolt was the outcome of a larger conspiracy by the descendants of dethroned chieftains and petty rulers, in connivance with Tipu's family interned in Vellore, S. S. Furnell

---

[29] *Secret Department Sundries*, vol. 2A, 961–63.
[30] Documents Connected with the Case of Colonel P. A. Agnew, 1808, British Library, London.
[31] Kaye, *Sepoy Army in India*, vol. 2, 225–27.

wrote, 'Vellore was, at that time, the seat of deep and dark intrigues, directed to the destruction of the British Government, and the elevation of a Mahomedan sovereignty upon its ruins.' Furnell explained the sequence of events thus: The fortress of Vellore, the residence of Tipu's sons, and the whole neighbourhood, was inhabited by the relatives and friends of the deposed family. The Muslim rulers had declined and the number of those whose fortunes depended on them declined with it. Many of these persons entered the British army. Thus, the ranks in the Company army came to be dominated by a body of persons whose interests were aligned against the British. The result was that in the fort and garrison of Vellore, their numerical strength became greater than that of the Company government that held them in captivity.[32]

Historians James Mill and H. H. Wilson exonerated Tipu's sons by arguing that the younger sons of Tipu were at too tender an age to get involved in such a sordid project, and the elder sons were at loggerheads, to the extent that Moiz-ud-Din had attempted to poison Fateh Hyder, the eldest of his brothers. They concluded that the sons of Tipu were not personally the originators or instigators of the mutiny.[33]

Mill and Wilson, while agreeing on the proposition that Muslims were dissatisfied with the change of rulers, doubted the probability that the discontent of the Hindus in the army led to intrigues in favour of a Muslim power. Rejecting the 'conspiracy theory' that the mutiny was attributable to the presence of the descendants of Tipu and their retainers in the fort, they wrote, 'A conspiracy of the Mohammedan princes was a mere shadow, created by an alarmist imagination, or by a wish to shift the responsibility from the real cause, the military orders, to one wholly visionary.' In support of their contention, they pointed to the decision of Colonel Thomas G. Montresor, commander of the Subsidiary Force at Hyderabad, who withdrew the orders of the commander-in-chief to adopt the objectionable military regulations and dress code. For him and

---

[32] Furnell, *Mutiny of Vellore*, 16–20.
[33] Mill and Wilson, *History of British India*, vol. 7, 98–104.

the resident, Thomas Sydenham, the unrest was caused by the interference of the government in matters of religion and faith.[34]

It is a great error to suppose that the people of India are so sensitive upon the subject of their religion, either Hindu or Mohammedan, as to suffer no approach of controversy, or to encounter adverse opinions with no other arguments than insurrection and murder … It was not conversion which the troops dreaded, it was compulsion; it was not the reasoning or the persuasion of the missionary which they feared, but the arbitrary interposition of authority. They believed, of course erroneously, that the Government was about to compel them to become Christians, and they resisted compulsory conversion by violence and bloodshed.[35]

But there is no denying the fact that Muslim sepoys in several cantonments saw in the descendants of Tipu a legitimate authority to overthrow the illegitimate Company rulers. In Vellore, the presence of Tipu's sons provided a rallying point for the aggrieved and the disaffected. There was no restriction on the native soldiery meeting and deliberating with the occupants of the palace in Vellore Fort. So the latter went about jeering at the sepoys and telling them that they would soon be made Christians. Here is Kaye's passionate portrayal of the scene:

The different parts of their uniform were curiously examined, amidst shrugs and other expressive gestures, and significant "Wah-wahs!" and vague hints that everything about them in some way portended Christianity. They looked at the sepoy's stock, and said, "What is this? It is leather! Well!" Then they would look at his belt, and tell him that it made a cross on his breast, and at the little implements of his calling, the turn screw and worm, suspended from it, and say that they also were designed to fix the Christian's cross upon his person. But it was the round hat that most of all was the object of the taunts and warnings of the people from the Palace. "It only needed this," they said, "to make you altogether a Faringhi. Take care, or we shall soon all be made Christians—Bazaar-people,

---

[34] Mill and Wilson, *History of British India*, vol. 7, 135–37.
[35] Mill and Wilson, *History of British India*, vol. 7, 140–41.

Ryots, everyone will be compelled to wear the hat; and then the whole country will be ruined."[36]

III

Munro, in a letter addressed to Bentinck, debunked the theory that the restoration of the sultan was the only motive for such a conspiracy. He refused to believe that it was 'a Mohammedan plot, involving adherents and members of Tipu family',[37] for such an event could hardly have been desirable to any of the Hindus who formed the bulk of the native troops. Munro's argument was that despite the Company's native troops not being paid for ten to twelve months during Hyder Ali's invasions of the Carnatic, and being exposed to privations of every kind, they still remained loyal. Though many who had gone over to Hyder's side were raised to distinguished positions, they were not tempted by offers of reward. At no point did they show any signs of discontent. Munro was firmly of the view that the orders on military regulations paved the way for the revolt by spreading discontent amongst the soldiers. Though the object of regulations was not to attack the religious customs of the natives, Munro observed, 'The prohibition of the marks of castes was well calculated to enable artful leaders to inflame the minds of the ignorant, for there is nothing so absurd but that they will believe when made a question of religion.'[38]

On the regulation that ordered that every soldier be cleanly shaved on the chin, Munro made the following humourous remarks:

> A stranger who reads the Madras regulation would naturally suppose that the sepoys' beards descend to their girdles, and that they are bearded like the pard; but this is so far from being the case, that they are now, and have been, as long as I

---

[36] Kaye, *Sepoy Army in India*, vol. 2, 225–26.
[37] Munro to Bentinck, 11 August 1806, quoted in Gleig, *Life of Thomas Munro*, vol. 1, 363–38.
[38] Munro to Bentinck, 11 August 1806, quoted in Gleig, *Life of Thomas Munro*, vol. 1, 364.

can remember, as smooth on the chin as Europeans, making a due allowance for the difference of the razors employed on the two subjects. And as to the hair upon the upper lip, its form is so much like that which sometimes appears upon the upper lip of our own dragoons and grenadiers, that none but the critical eye of a shaver could distinguish the difference. Had the grand projected shaving-match terminated without accident, it might have amused the spectators like a pantomime upon a large stage; but when it is considered how many brave men lost their lives by it, one cannot help feeling for the national character.[39]

Munro asserted that the general opinion of the native intelligentsia in southern India at the time was that the regulations were intended to convert the sepoys to Christianity. He wrote, 'The rapid progress of the conspiracy is not to be wondered at, for the circulation of the General Orders prepared the way, by spreading discontent; and the rest was easily done by the means of the tappal, and of sending confidential emissaries on leave of absence.'[40]

The sepoy, 'forbidden to wear the distinguishing marks of Caste on his forehead, stripped of his earrings … and ordered to shave himself according to a regulation cut, was put into a stiff round hat, like a Pariah drummer's, with a flat top, a leather cockade, and a standing feather'. It was distinctly different from the turban they had previously. It was now a cap, a *topee*. A *topee-wallah*, or hat-wearer, was, in local parlance, a synonym for a ferengi, or Christian.[41] As Kaye wrote, the Muslim soldier 'had no distinguishing marks of caste to be rubbed off on parade … but he venerated his beard and his earrings'. The hat issue fuelled the feeling and made him fear that some planned assault on caste and religion was on the cards. The soldiers and officers, apprehending assault on their customs, turned to religious teachers and warrior-saints for advice. The prejudice against lower castes was also

---

[39] Munro to his Father, Anantpoor, 4 September 1806, quoted in Gleig, *Life of Thomas Munro*, vol. 1, 367–68.
[40] Munro to Bentinck, 11 August 1806, quoted in Gleig, *Life of Thomas Munro*, vol. 1, 364.
[41] Kaye, *Sepoy Army in India*, vol. 2, 218.

evident among the native sepoys. To confound the matter, the new hat was discovered to be an abomination in terms of material too. 'It was made in part of leather prepared from the skin of the unclean hog, or of the sacred cow, and was, therefore, an offence and a desecration alike to Muhammadan and Hindu.' The talk of the sepoys was, 'We shall next be compelled to eat and drink with the outcaste and infidel English, to give them our daughters in marriage, to become one people, and follow one faith.'[42] As Kaye observed, 'Moved by the sense of a common danger, and roused by a common hope, [Hindus and Muslims] forgot their differences and combined against a common foe.'[43]

Dilating upon the outbreak of rebellion, Kaye remarked that the mutiny broke out in the spring of 1806 because, relieved of exercises in the cold, parades, field days, and inspections, the soldiers had more leisure time at their disposal to reflect on the wrongs done to them. The Europeans were also haunted by the impending heat and rain, a factor that emboldened the Indian soldiers and officers to share their grievances with each other and plan to mutiny. Elaborating on this, Kaye wrote,

> In April and May the English officer sees little of his men; his visits to the Lines are few; few are his appearance on parade. He is languid and prostrate. The morning and evening ride are as much as his energies can compass. The sepoy then, disencumbered of dress and dismissed from drill, can afford to snatch some hours from sleep to listen to any strange stories told by wandering mendicants, with the odour of sanctified filth about them, and to discuss the most incredible fables with all the gravity of settled belief. There is always more or less of this vain talk. It amuses the sepoy, and for a while excites him with a visionary prospect of higher rank and better pay, under some new dispensation.[44]

---

[42] *Proceedings of the Court of Inquiry*, in *Home Miscellaneous Series*, vol. 507, 92, 220.

[43] Kaye, *Sepoy Army in India*, vol. 2, 218–19.

[44] Kaye, *Sepoy Army in India*, vol. 2, 219–20.

Captain Homes, in a memorandum to the Court of Directors, argued,

> The causes of the mutiny are to be found unquestionably in the local ignorance and the martinetism [severe punishment policy] of the Commander-in-Chief and his advisers ... By altering the shape of the turban and causing it to approach the form of Drummer's cap / a Christian's cap, he [the commander-in-chief] disgusted the whole body of sepoys. By directing the whiskers of the sepoys to be reduced in size and trimmed to uniformity ... and by ordering the Hindoos to obliterate the marks of their casts invariably worn on their foreheads, he made mutiny and murder their duty. Thus disposed, the slightest degree of excitement from the sons of Tippoo precipitated an explosion which cost the lives of seventeen valuable officers and near hundred soldiers.[45]

However, Major General Campbell, in a letter dated 13 September 1806, observed, 'Since the General Orders issued about eight years ago, the Marks of Caste have been generally discontinued throughout the Army; and I am confidently assured that many instances of Native Officers of their own accord chastising Sepoys for appearing in the Ranks so distinguished.'[46]

For Furnell, the change of turban, the ostensible cause of rebellion, was only a trifling affair and not the trigger for the revolt. He opined that the opposition against the new turban was certainly far from universal. In many instances, there was much enthusiasm shown in adopting it, and after the mutiny, some corps even requested permission to wear it as testimony to their unshaken loyalty. Had no political causes intervened, the changes might have been effected as quietly as others, he observed. Therefore, the military regulations to which the revolt was attributed was not the decisive cause.[47]

Furnell mentions the role of travelling fakirs in exciting alarm and animosity. To quote his words, 'Fanatical mendicants

---

[45] Captain Homes to the Court of Directors, Memorial, ref. GD51/3/429, National Records of Scotland.
[46] Bentinck, *Memorial*, 79.
[47] Furnell, *Mutiny of Vellore*, 16–17.

prowled about, scattering the seeds of sedition and revolt, and astrology was called in to predict the downfall of the Europeans and the ascendancy of the Mussulman power.'[48] These Muslim holy men prophesied an imminent end to British rule, as the French and the supporters of Tipu Sultan were coming together to drive the 'infidel' English out of the country. The prophecies they pronounced, the puppet shows they performed and the ballads they sang conveyed the impending disaster awaiting the British. To quote Kaye, 'Strange writings were dropped by unseen hands, and strange placards posted on the walls. At all the large military stations in the Carnatic and in the Deccan, there was an uneasy feeling as of something coming.'[49]

As Cradock stated in his deposition,

> Fakirs with their puppet shows exhibit military conflicts, which end with the flight of the English. Songs resound with the praises of our enemies and reports are industriously spread to rouse the native troops and inferior classes of inhabitants into action. The government is charged with mediating dishonour and even destruction to their pagodas and mosques. The very salt we manufacture is said to be mixed with the blood of cows or swine, as applied to vitiate the Hindus and the Musalmans.[50]

Charles Kirby, the author of *The Adventures of an Arcot Rupee*, described how this group of fakirs emerged after the fall of Mysore. According to him, many who were deprived of their livelihood, or in a bid to run away from exploitative creditors, took to the 'profession of Faqeers'. In a state of destitution and want, they were constantly looking for opportunities for disturbances, 'to thrive and prosper'.[51]

The activities of the fakirs were considerable in Vellore. On the eve of the mutiny in July, Rustom Ali, a fakir from Kadapa, had forecasted the impending murder of Europeans in the streets. 'One sepoy has joined with many ... yet in seven days, all the kafirs will

---

[48] Furnell, *Mutiny of Vellore*, 20–21.
[49] Kaye, *Sepoy Army in India*, vol. 2, 217–56.
[50] *Secret Department Sundries*, vol. 4B, 339–43.
[51] Kirby, *Adventures of an Arcot Rupee*, vol. 2, 173–74.

be killed ... Rivers of blood will flow; heaps of dead will be carried away ... [A Muslim] flag will be hoisted.'[52] On 18 November 1806, in Palayamkottai, there was one fakir from Vellore who allegedly had a meeting in the street at night, in which a resolve to kill the European officers within ten days was made.

The district collectors and magistrates had been issued notices about what was considered the 'fakir menace'. Bentinck noted this in a minute:

> From the extreme activity which had been practiced by religious mendicants and other secret emissaries in all parts of the peninsula in exciting a spirit of discontent among the native troops, we had deemed it proper to counteract such machinations as far as may be practicable by orders which have been issued to the Magistrates and other local authorities.[53]

Reporting that he had unravelled a plot by a group of seven fakirs, Campbell named some of them. Under directions from the head fakir based in Lalgudi in Tiruchirappalli, Nur Ali and Moideen Shah operated from Thanjavur and Sankaran Kovil, respectively. The magistrate of Chittoor suggested, and the Company government implemented, the grant of a generous reward for the spies employed to inform on the activities of the fakirs.[54] In Tiruchirappalli, during Ramzan celebrations, the British officers noticed a large presence of fakirs, but they cautioned against any precipitate steps.

> We entirely agree in opinion as to the hazard incurred of estranging the fidelity of the Native Troops by the extraordinary number of Fakeers and Mendicants assembled at the moment at Trichinopoly; at the same time we feel the delicacy of risking at the height of the Festival an interference which might be construed by the industrious malevolence of the disaffected into a determined violation of their customs and religions.[55]

---

[52] Hoover, *Men Without Hats*, 101–102.
[53] *Secret Department Sundries*, vol. 6, 3071–72.
[54] *Secret Department Sundries*, vol. 5, 2572.
[55] *Secret Department Sundries*, vol. 6, 2894.

The administrative officers, headed by Mark Wilks, a historian of southern India, then representing the British in Mysore, poured scorn on the views of the military officers and said, as described by Kaye, that

> [t]he things which they spoke of as so portentous were in reality only phenomena of every-day appearance, familiar to men acquainted with the feelings and habits of the people. He [Wilks] derided all that had been said about seditious conversations in the Bazaars and the Lines, the wild prophecies and the mysterious hints of wandering Fakirs, and the suggestive devices of the puppet-shows. There was nothing in all this, he contended, of an exceptional character, to be regarded as the harbingers of mutiny and massacre. And his arguments culminated in the chuckling assertion that the military authorities had discovered a cabalistic document of a most treasonable character, which appeared to their excited imaginations to be a plan for partitioning the territory to be wrested from the English, but which, in reality, was nothing more portentous than the scribblement of the Dervesh Bazi, or "royal game of goose".[56]

IV

Some military officials attributed the mutiny to the supposed activity of Christian missionaries and of certain 'missionary chaplains'. Sepoys were led to believe that attempts were on to convert them forcibly to Christianity. With a view to adding strength to this belief, rumours were circulated for the consumption of the general public that the Company was selling salt sprinkled with the blood of hogs and cows, with the sole intention of polluting Muslims and Hindus. As a result, some stopped using salt altogether, and others purchased it at high prices and kept it in store sufficiently, along with other the articles of necessity to pre-empt any of the above-stated acts.[57]

---

[56] Kaye, *Sepoy Army in India*, vol. 2, 246–47.
[57] Kaye, *Sepoy Army in India*, vol. 2, 248–49.

Another rumour described the actions of the collector of Triconamalai in Ceylon, who was building a church in his district, adjacent to a Hindu temple. Rumours soon spread that the collector had forbidden all from entering the temple to worship the deity, and people protested. The collector, however, asserted that there was nothing unusual in what he was doing, as the government had ordered that similar such churches should be built in every town.[58]

Even more interesting was a story floating around in Hyderabad, referenced in Chapter 2. A temple oracle had allegedly prophesied that there was treasure at the bottom of a well in the European barracks, and that it could only be located if a certain number of human heads were offered to the tutelary deity of the place. The rumour suggested that the British were planning to massacre all Indians, except those who fixed the sign of the cross (the symbol of Christian faith) on the doors of their houses.[59]

Cradock flatly denied that the cause of the mutiny in Vellore could be traced to an interference with the religious observances of the soldiers. He pointed out:

> From the total absence of religious establishments in the interior of the country, from the habits of life prevalent among military men, it is a melancholy truth that so unfrequent are the religious observances of officers doing duty with battalions that the sepoys have not, until very lately, discovered the nature of the religion professed by the English.[60]

Echoing Cradock, John Clark Marshman, nineteenth century historian of British India, in his analysis of the Company's policy towards Indian religious traditions and customs, scouted the view that missionaries played a role in creating an atmosphere of hostility and mistrust amongst Hindus. He believed that of all the presidencies, Madras had been the most obliging in patronising the religions of the country. Forgetting the duty due to their own creed, the Madras functionaries had been in the habit of firing

[58] Kaye, *Sepoy Army in India*, vol. 2, 248–49.
[59] Furnell, *Mutiny of Vellore*, 20–21.
[60] *Secret Department Sundries*, vol. 6, 3071–72.

royal salutes on festive occasions in temples, of pressuring their own Christian servants to make offerings at different shrines in the name of the Company, and of employing the police to enable poor peasants to drag the cars of idols. At the same time, he argued that the cause of Christianity was utterly neglected, so as to lead the natives to believe that their European conquerors had no religion. But all these did not deter the government from the suspicion of a design to destroy the religion of the people, and to force a foreign faith upon them.[61] Marshman dealt with the subject extensively.

> The previous conquerors, the Hindu, the Buddhist, and the Muslim, identified their religion with their policy. They supported it with their full political and military power and persecuted those who professed a different faith. In contrast the English were the first conquerors who did not interfere with the creed of their subjects ... The East India Company, from the apprehension that an opposite course might evoke stiff opposition to their rule from the natives, adhered to the principle of religious tolerance. It was on this score the Court of Directors set their faces sternly against all missionary efforts.[62]

'To an European, the very imputation of an intention on the part of the Government to interfere with the religion of the people of India, excluding all considerations of the means by which it was supported, can appear only ridiculous,' commented Furnell. In his critique, he asserted that no government had ever exercised such perfect toleration towards religions differing from those of the rulers, as that of the British in India. He wrote,

> Indulgence has been pushed even to excess—the most horrible atrocities were long allowed to be perpetrated with impunity, from a fear of giving offence to the votaries of the gloomy creed in which they originated. Impartial observers have sometimes complained of the indifference of the ruling powers to the cause of Christianity; but never has there been

---

[61] Marshman, *History of India*, vol. 2, 212–14.
[62] Marshman, *History of India*, vol. 2, 212–14.

a shadow of reason for ascribing to them an indiscreet zeal to accelerate its progress.[63]

The Company's policy in the eighteenth century was against interference in the religious and social customs of Indians. But, as the century closed, numerous fanatical religious groups in England, such as the Wesleyan Methodists, the Baptists and the Calvinists, had begun to press for 'universal dissemination of Christianity in India'. William Wilberforce, Charles Grant, Henry Thornton and Edward Parry, the frontline activists of the Clapham Sect, an evangelical group, took the lead in this direction.[64]

Grant, the chairman of the East India Company, wrote in 1792 that the social and moral conditions among the Indians were barbarous, that Hinduism was inherently ignorant and that it was only English education that would 'open to the people a knowledge of Christianity'. Grant and his associates, therefore, worked to influence policy, establish Christian missions, and send a number of evangelical clergymen to India, prominent amongst them being Reverend Dr Claudius Buchanan and Henry Martin. About twenty missionaries came to India between 1793 and 1813.[65] The soldiers in India had heard, and talked, about their recent arrival from England.

Buchanan dashed off a letter to the government of Bengal refuting the view held in certain circles that the Vellore Mutiny was the outcome of the activities of Christian missionaries.

> I travelled for two months immediately afterwards in the province adjacent with the sanction of the Government, and I heard the evidence of Christians, Mohammedans, and Hindus, on the subject. That the insurrection at Vellore had no connexion with the Christian religion, directly or indirectly, immediately or remotely, is truth which is capable of demonstration.[66]

---

[63] Furnell, *Mutiny of Vellore*, 20–21.
[64] Cited in Philips, *East India Company*, 158–60.
[65] Philips, *East India Company*, 158–59.
[66] Claudius Buchanan to the Governor General, 7 November 1807, quoted in Mill and Wilson, *History of British India*, vol. 7, 92–94.

But this was the very same Buchanan who, as a part of his lobbying efforts, was against the 'indifference of the Hindus to any form of Christian teaching'. He urged in a pamphlet, 'A wise policy seems to demand that we should use every means of coercing this contemptuous spirit of our native subjects.' This became controversial and a subject of acrimonious debate amongst the Board of Directors.[67] If England itself received this information, at a time when communication from India took three months to arrive, at home, such provocative utterances patently reached the natives and stirred them into action fearing the loss of their religion.

The most influential historians of nineteenth-century British India, Wilson and Kaye, held contrasting views on the role of religion. Wilson placed the responsibility for the revolt on the interference in the sepoys' religions, stating, 'The essential and mainspring of the mutiny was religious principle.' He believed 'that the mutiny of Vellore was of a purely political character and arose out of a conspiracy to replace a Mohammedan dynasty on the throne of Mysore—an opinion that was strenuously advocated by those who wished to shut their eyes against the evidence of its religious connexion—was wholly incapable of demonstration.'[68]

Kaye on the other hand, was of the considered opinion that 'an insane hope engendered in the breasts of the princes of the house of Tipu—a hope of recovering their lost dominion in Mysore—was the origin of the movement'.[69] Here, it must be noted that Kaye was an evangelical, and keen that the blame for the mutiny not be laid at the door of the missionaries. In his book *Christianity in India* (1859), Kaye wrote,

> I believe that I should best convey my opinion of the connection of the Vellore massacre with the subject of this work by taking no further note of it. But although it was in no degree the result of Christianity in India, it was the cause of many grievous charges against Christianity in India.[70]

---

[67] Philips, *East India Company*, 160–61.
[68] Quoted in Cameron, 'Vellore Mutiny', 323–24.
[69] Quoted in Cameron, 'Vellore Mutiny', 323–24.
[70] Quoted in Cameron, 'Vellore Mutiny', 323–24.

The debate on the causes of the mutiny at Vellore divided opinions into two camps:

> One, which included Bentinck and other officers, held that imposing British norms of dress had outraged the soldiers' profound commitment to their communities' customs; the other, largely expressed by officials in London, was that a group affiliated with a religion they deemed inherently hostile had been the unprovoked aggressor, even an invader ... and that a group affiliated with a religion they deemed inherently submissive had been entirely innocent.[71]

The debate, while pitting officials in India against those in Britain, eventually contributed to a polarisation of British discourse on proselytisation in India.

Lieutenant Colonel Alexander Dow, who served the East India Company until he died in 1779, argued against missionary work in India on the basis that Hinduism guaranteed civil order under the pressures of colonialism.

> The Hindoo religion, in other respects, inspires the purest morals. Productive, from its principles, of the greatest degree of subordination to authority, it prepares mankind for the government of foreign lords. It supplies, by its well-followed precepts, the place of penal laws; and it renders crime almost unknown in the land. The peaceable sentiments which it breathes, will check the more warlike doctrines promulgated by the Coran. The prudent successors of Timur saw that the Hindoo religion was favourable to their power; and they sheathed the sword, which the other princes of the Mohammedan persuasion employed in establishing their own faith, in all their conquests.[72]

Thus, the Hindu soldiers were represented as naturally loyal and subservient, and so the outrage was foreign-grown and inspired by

---

[71] Julia M. Wright, *Ireland, India and Nationalism in Nineteenth-Century Literature* (Cambridge: Cambridge University Press, 2007), 87.

[72] *An Account of the Origin, Progress and Consequences of the Late Discontents of the Army of the Madras Establishment* (London: T. Cadell & W. Davies, 1810), 84. Also see Alexander Dow, *The History of Hindostan*, vol. 1 (1772; repr., London: J. Walker, 1812), 146.

a 'barbarous enemy'. The barbarous enemies deemed responsible for inciting rebellion among the troops at Vellore were the sons of Tipu.[73] The enquiry commission concurred with Dow's assumption that the Hindus were capable of 'the greatest degree of subordination', while Muslims were 'warlike'. Vellore was thus represented as a Muslim insurgency instead of an attempt to regain their traditional power in the region. This conspiracy theory was adopted notwithstanding Bentinck's view that the cause of mutiny at Vellore was 'a lack of regard for the religious feelings of the sepoys in some instituted regulations'.[74] However, it was recorded in the minutes of a meeting of the Court of Directors in 1809 that 'the impressions universally entertained, both in India and Europe, at the breaking out of the Vellore Mutiny, was that it was occasioned by the wanton or needless violations of the religious usages of the Natives'.[75]

V

Grant and Parry, chairman and deputy chairman, respectively, of the East India Company, in a bid to distract the attention of those who were protesting against missionary activity in India, conceded that the 'positive causes' of the mutiny were the changes in the dress of the sepoys and the intrigues of the Muslim adherents of Tipu Sultan's family. But, in their opinion, there were equally important predisposing causes. The Company's government in India, they said, had become (except in religious matters) apathetic, as more men came from England to occupy leading positions in the Company's service. The governor general had become absolute and unsympathetic to the freedom of opinion. New men and European ideas of policy had been too rapidly introduced into India. At the same time, policy measures to further the British

---

[73] Wilson, *History of the Madras Army*, vol. 3, 192.
[74] Wilson, *History of the Madras Army*, vol. 3, 86.
[75] Bentinck, *Memorial*, 53.

interests in different parts of India had gradually dispensed with natives in higher posts.[76]

Here, insinuation is made against Cornwallis, whose responsibility has been overlooked even by Indian scholars who studied the Vellore Mutiny. 'Full of the aristocratical ideas of modern Europe, the aristocratical person [Cornwallis] now at the head, avowed his intention of establishing an aristocratic [government] upon the European model.' Such are the illuminating words of Mill on Cornwallis.[77]

Cornwallis introduced a law in 1791 which excluded Indians from the higher posts of government. By doing so, he set the pattern for racial estrangement. His policy of Permanent Settlement, under which the decennial leases of *zamindari*s (estates of zamindars) were made permanent, was a disaster in the Madras Presidency. Bentinck, who advocated the system of *ryotwari* settlements,[78] said, 'It was apparent to me, that the creation of zemindar, where no zemindaries before existed was neither calculated to improve the condition of the lower orders of the people, nor politically wise, with reference to the future security of this government.'[79] The judicial reforms of Cornwallis, apart from causing friction amongst civil and military officials, estranged the local notables, especially the village headmen, who had to travel frequently from their villages to the district headquarters, at their own cost, on summons from the magistrate to give evidence.[80] Every district was divided into police circles or *thana*s, each of which was about 20 square miles, and was under a *daroga*, an Indian police officer. The police organisation was by no means efficient, and 'the daroga

---

[76] Cameron, 'The Vellore Mutiny', 162.

[77] Quoted in Kaye, *Lives of Indian Officers*, vol. 1, 88–90.

[78] The system under which land tax began to be collected directly from cultivators, eliminating all middlemen. It was first introduced by Thomas Munro in the Ceded Districts, and later in the entire presidency (1822) after he became governor.

[79] Firminger, *Affairs of the East India Company*, vol. 3, 454.

[80] For a detailed account, see A. Sarada Raju, *Economic Conditions in the Madras Presidency, 1800–1850* (Madras: University of Madras, 1941).

... enjoyed almost unlimited power of extortion, and became the scourge of the country.[81]

There is no denying the opinion of the British bureaucracy, expressed in survey documents of that time, that the nawab as well as Tipu levied oppressive taxes on the peasantry and subjected people of all classes to greater exaction under their regimes.[82] Yet, the fact of the matter was that the levy collected during their time was irregular and evasion was rather widespread. Munro, with respect to Salem district, stated, 'A long series of oppressive governments, and particularly under Tippu, had reduced the country, when delivered over to the Company, to such a state that a rich farmer was nowhere to be found; not one among them perhaps was worth 100 pagodas (Rs 350), exclusive of his farming stock.'[83]

Haripado Chaudhuri, in his article, 'The Vellore Mutiny: A Reappraisal', pointed out how the failure of British revenue policies to win the confidence of the peasants brought about a deep disenchantment with Company rule and contributed to the outbreak of 1806.[84] His view finds endorsement in the anonymous document found by Cameron in the records of the Secret Department. The author of the document made the following remarks:

> The present revenue system is not satisfactory to the people. The husbandman is exposed to greater vexations than he was before its introduction. The local attachment which formed so striking a feature in the native character, and which it is our policy to encourage, has been destroyed by it. Many of the ryots flock to the large towns for subsistence and discontent is prevalent amongst the whole.[85]

---

[81] Quoted in R. Sathianathaier, *A Political and Cultural History of India*, vol. 3 (Madras: S. Viswanathan, 1972), 252.

[82] Raghavaiyengar, *Memorandum on the Madras Presidency*, 301.

[83] Raju, *Economic Conditions in the Madras Presidency*, 49, 259.

[84] Haripado Chaudhuri, 'The Vellore Mutiny: A Reappraisal', *Modern Review* 98 (August 1955): 125–28.

[85] Cameron, 'The Vellore Mutiny', 303.

Thomas Munro described to his father how the revenue administration functioned in south India. He wrote:

We see every day collectors, who always lived above their salary, amassing great fortunes in a very few years ... The numerous band of revenue servants require no encouragement to exercise the trade which they have always followed; but they now act without restraint, and are joined by the head farmers, in stripping the unfortunate husbandmen of the great part of the produce of their labours. This is the system under the Nabobs, under Tipoo, under the Company, and, I believe, under every government in India.[86]

Devadas Moodley, in a study, attempted to trace the economic origins of the revolt. He drew attention to the drought and consequent crop failures in 1805 and 1806, which caused enormous distress in the South Arcot, North Arcot and Nellore districts. The prices of food grains at the time, the highest in North Arcot, would have impinged on Indian soldiers and their families. But Moodley, instead of highlighting incidents of distress at the grassroot level, jumped to the conclusion that 'the self-destructive eagerness of the sepoys to disperse in the search for plunder during the mutiny, explains the economic distress the warrior class came to experience at that time.'[87] K. Rajayyan also suggested that the Madras Army's revolt was attributable to the agrarian crisis of that time, though he does not elaborate on it.[88] The fact that the land-owning Vellalar and Naidu communities too had to take up arduous military assignments for their survival substantiates the viewpoint of Moodley (see Appendices 12 and 13).

As land tax was considered the mainstay of government finance, the British, through the Board of Revenue, attempted several experiments in land revenue administration to exact as much as possible from landholders. Permanent Settlement for

---

[86] Munro to his Father, 31 January 1795, quoted in Gleig, *Life of Thomas Munro*, vol. 1, 155–56.

[87] Devadas Moodley, 'Vellore 1806: The Meanings of Mutiny' (seminar, Ohio University); also see his chapter in Hathaway, ed., *Rebellion, Repression, Reinvention*.

[88] Rajayyan, *South Indian Rebellion*, 286.

land revenues was enforced in the presidency in 1802 and under this system, the districts of Chengalpattu, Salem and Dindigul were parcelled into a number of *mittas* (a farm of several villages) and sold to the highest bidders. In these newly created mittas and in the traditional palayams-turned-zamindaries, 'the only limit to the exaction to which the ryots were subjected was their ability to pay'. In Salem, the *mittadars* (person who possesses a mitta) had a trying time because of the distress caused by the combination of Permanent Settlement and monsoon failures. A reduction of 15 or 20 per cent on the permanent rent would have saved many an estate from defaulting in Salem. But the government's refusal to give even that small amount of remission inevitably led to the failure of estates and their eventual confiscation. The peasants, under the new dispensation, did not want to take land on lease and hence had to move out of the villages. When the mittas were sold, they fetched only 19 per cent land revenue in the annual *jamabandhi* (settlement of the assessed revenue amount).[89]

The status of cultivating peasants also declined as a result of Permanent Settlement, since the system turned peasant-proprietors into tenants. The accounts of Francis Buchanan, who passed through Coimbatore in 1800, and Abbe Dubois, who lived in the presidency from 1792 to 1823, portray the abominable living conditions of peasants on account of oppressive land tenure.[90] To add death to debility, 1806 was a famine year. In severity and duration, the famine of 1805–07 was unprecedented. The impact of distress was felt in North and South Arcot, Madurai, Dindigul, Chengalpattu, Thanjavur and Tiruchirappalli. As for the extent of mortality, though no district-wise figures are available, in Madras alone, more than 17,000 people perished, not to mention the loss of cattle, whose numbers far exceeded the human toll.[91] Thus, the discontent among the peasantry was widespread.

---

[89] Firminger, *Affairs of the East India Company*, vol. 3, 495, 581.
[90] Raju, *Economic Conditions in the Madras Presidency*, 121.
[91] Raju, *Economic Conditions in the Madras Presidency*, 284.

The state of the Madras economy during 1806–07 was highlighted in the anonymous document found in the *Secret Department Sundries*:

> Whole coast threatened with the horrors of famine … Failure of the public revenue from a failure of crops … When the rains failed it was known there would be a famine. Advertisement for encouraging the importation of rice delayed too long and produced a scarcity at Madras, and some stores were broken open and plundered. Sepoys continue to guard the bazaars. After the advertisement grain came from Bengal in abundance but it is still dear. Nevertheless great distress is apprehended.[92]

In North Arcot, the collector, David Cockburn, extended the ryotwari land revenue system enforced in Salem and forcibly collected land revenue, notwithstanding the bad monsoons and crop failures from 1803–05. This caused peasant protests in Denkanikottai and Rayakottai in North Arcot district (now Vellore district). About thirty peasants who went to Madras to present a petition to the Board of Revenue refused to return to their native villages, despite the collector's arrest orders. In Rayakottai, about 900 landholders, including *mirasidars* (landholders through inheritance), demonstrated against the land revenue policy of the Company government. Of them, as a government report notes, nearly 150 were 'carrying matchlocks, pikes and swords'. A military contingent consisting of eighty sepoys, accompanied by several commissioned and non-commissioned officers brought from Sankagiridurg, was no match for them. Therefore, additional forces had to be drawn from Vellore and Erode to suppress the movement.[93]

Cradock spoke the truth when he wrote,

> The general belief is that the condition of the people is not so happy, as it was, that their own arrangements, their own

---

[92] Quoted in Cameron, 'Vellore Mutiny', 301.

[93] D. Subramanyam Reddy, 'The Ryotwari Land Revenue Settlements and Peasant Resistance in the "Northern Division of Arcot" of the Madras Presidency during Early British Rule', *Social Scientist* 16, no. 6/7 (June–July 1988): 39–40.

institution pleased them better than our regulations. It is reasoned, with apparent force, that slaves as they are, to their own customs and habits, in every trifle of their lives, the introduction of all our systems (which it is in vain to make them comprehend) alarms, and annoys them, and they view them only as preparatory to greater innovations, which may extend to every circumstance that surrounds them. It is said, while the treasures of the state are expended on judicial establishments throughout countries without distinction, where even military force, at times, is unable to preserve subjection, it would be better to enquire into the state of the inhabitants and regulate the means of subsistence, so that the numerous dependants on former power and ancient establishment, the crowds of moormen in the different provinces ... may not remain in distress and continue to excite discontent.[94]

Summary

This chapter covered the views of prominent historians, opinions conveyed in anonymous letters from the Hyderabad Subsidiary Force, and the standpoints of the Court of Directors, company officials, the commander-in-chief and the governor-in-council in Madras, as to the causes and consequences of the Vellore Mutiny.

The abominable service conditions and lack of avenues for promotion for native soldiers and officers were pointed out as important causes for the revolt by the Subsidiary Force at Hyderabad. The Court of Directors attributed the trouble to the estranged relationship between the European and native officers, caused by the racial arrogance of the former and their lack of acquaintance with native languages. This view was endorsed by the military historian Kaye, and elaborated on by Furnell. Rigorous military discipline and the changing dispositions of the Madras sepoys caused the mutiny, according to Major Haslewood of the Second Battalion of the First Regiment at Wallajahbad.

---

[94] John Cradock to the Chief Secretary, 21 September 1806, *Secret Department Sundries*, vol. 4B, 2095.

The historian Dodwell considered the refusal of the erstwhile Palayakkarars and rajas to reconcile to Company rule, the incitement and interference by the French, and the contact between Fateh Ali, Tipu's nephew, and the Marathas and the French in Pondicherry to be contributory factors. The commander-in-chief, Sir Cradock, ascribed the outbreak of mutiny to the conspiracy by the descendants of Tipu. Thorn, the biographer of Colonel Gillespie, also expressed the same view.

Historians Mill and Wilson ruled out this possibility, as they doubted the probability of discontent among the Hindu section of the army that would have led to their collaboration with the Muslim soldiery to establish a Muslim power. According to them, the interference of the government in matters of religion was disastrous. Munro was of the firm view that the general orders on military regulations paved the way for the revolt. Some of the East India Company's officials held the commander-in-chief responsible for the innovations in dress and turban, and the eventual revolt.

The role of fakirs in inciting the people and the army against the government was emphasised by Furnell. Some military officials attributed the mutiny to the activity of Christian missionaries. Marshman, supported by Furnell, Wilson and Kaye, refuted this contention. This debate led to the division of opinion-makers into two camps. The enquiry commission acquitted the Hindus saying that they were meek and submissive and hence manageable, while alleging that the Muslims were belligerent and intractable.

Governor Bentinck's view was that English officials were apathetic towards the religious sentiments of the sepoys while formulating institutional regulations. The chairman and deputy chairman of the East India Company subscribed to the view that the causes of the mutiny were the changes in the dress code of sepoys and the conspiracy by the Muslim followers of Tipu Sultan's family.

The perspective of Moodley was that successive droughts in the Madras Presidency, aggravated by the revenue policy of the Company government, affected the land-owning communities, which sent a large number of soldiers to the Madras Army. The outcome of the soldiers' general discontent was their disgust with

Company rule, and revolts in Vellore and other cantonments in south India.

The crucial aspect emerging from our analysis is the effect of foreign domination in south Tamil Nadu, that resulted in new judicial processes, oppressive land revenue policies and evangelising activities. All these stirred up anti-imperial feelings among the well-informed Indian soldiery. We take up these issues, as well as the multiple other causes that led to the upheaval in 1806, in Chapter 5.

5

CONCLUSION

British officials and historians, who wrote histories on the Vellore Mutiny from a colonial perspective, attributed it to a conspiracy by the Mysore princes, to the introduction of changes in military regulations that supposedly violated the religious sentiments of both Hindus and Muslims, and to the change in attitude of the younger generation of English officers, whose inept handling led to the outburst in 1806.

William Bentinck, as governor at Fort St George at the time of the revolt, attributed the mutiny to the intrigues of Tipu's sons. The chief conspirators, according to him, were Fateh Hyder and Moiz-ud-Din. Contrary to Bentinck's view, Thomas Munro, principal collector of the Ceded Districts at the time, asserted that the mutiny was not political. He believed that 'the proportionate cause was religious disquietude, induced by certain vexatious military regulations'.[1]

From the beginning, the commander-in-chief, Sir John Cradock, was apprehensive about the negative reactions of the Indian officers and soldiers to the new military regulations and changes to the turban. However, under pressure from the adjutant-general, Lieutenant Colonel Patrick A. Agnew, he had no other option but to enforce them. When the matter snowballed, he took it up with the government. Bentinck considered both Agnew and his deputy, Major Frederick Pierce, to be men of ability and

---

[1] G. D. Oswell, *Sketches of Rulers of India: The Company's Governors*, vol. 2 (Oxford: Clarendon Press, 1908), 96.

experience, and so naturally looked to them for advice. Both insisted on remaining unyielding.[2]

When the special commission concluded that the military regulations were the reason for the mutiny, Cradock was against holding the army responsible, and so he kept up the pressure for further investigations by articulating his views on the matter at every given opportunity. At one meeting of the governor-in-council, he stated that he had received intelligence from prisoners in various quarters and on examination, was convinced that one could draw much stronger conclusions than those arrived at by the commission. He also argued that this information should be placed in the public domain so that the government would become aware of the exact state of affairs. He was emphatic that the sepoys' disaffection had its foundation in the manoeuvring of the princes and their adherents. In his view, the discontent, to a very serious extent, arose when unfounded fears were instilled in the innocuous minds of the sepoys.[3]

Historians James Mill and H. H. Wilson were critical of the Company's failure to conduct a proper investigation into the rejection of the new turban by the soldiers in May 1806. They thought that had this grievance been fully examined at the time, it 'would in all likelihood have prevented the mutiny of July'.[4] Governor General George Barlow also held this view. Military historian, John William Kaye, asserted that the mutiny of 1806 was 'no mere military revolt'. Though he attributed it to multiple causes, he laid great emphasis on the role of Tipu's descendants. But his charges that 'the inmates of the Palace were fraternising with the Sipahis [mutineers]', that '[f]rom the apartments of the Princes went forth food to the insurgents', that 'the third son of Tipu [Moiz-ud-Din] personally encouraged the leaders of the revolt', and that 'from his apartments [came] the tiger-striped standard of Maisur, which amidst cries of "Din! Din!" was hoisted',

---

[2] Letter by unknown author, 20 October 1806, enclosed in Anstruther to Dundas, April 1807, ref. GD51/3/434/1–2, National Records of Scotland.

[3] Quoted in Cameron, 'Vellore Mutiny', 182.

[4] Cameron, 'Vellore Mutiny', 104.

were, however, deemed untenable by the special commission of enquiry.[5]

The chairman and deputy chairman of the East India Company, Charles Grant and Edward Parry, respectively, held the disdainful attitude of the new generation of English officers responsible for the turmoil. They pointed out that these new officers, who had occupied key positions in the government and the army, were drawn from the English elite, and had no knowledge of India, and no concern for its people or tolerance for their beliefs.[6]

John Malcolm, who was the first to incorporate the event into history books, agreed with the views expressed by the top brass of the East India Company. Justifying the grievances of Indian sepoys, Malcolm, a Scotsman, concurred that the young officers drafted from England had exacerbated the situation with their imperious attitude. Admitting that this new generation of officers 'practised a severity and harshness altogether unsuited to the character of the men under their command', he said, 'Qualities such as knowledge of the languages and customs of the men under their command, a kindness of manner, and solicitude for their comfort, and a frequent and intimate intercourse with the native Officers, appeared to be in a great degree forgotten, or neglected.'[7]

John Clark Marshman reiterated the findings of the special commission set up by the Madras government. Though convinced of the designs of the Mysore princes and their adherents, Marshman did not fail to focus on the religious dimension of the issue. He thought that the introduction of new regulations and European headgear, which was seen as the 'precursor of an attempt' to force Christianity on native soldiers, provided 'the mine for … Tipu's family to torch'.[8] The activities of missionaries, according to him, thus created fear in the absence of any proselytising efforts from Muslims. Historian R. E. Frykenberg highlighted the proselyting activities of Christian missionaries at Palayamkottai, in

---

[5] Kaye, *Sepoy Army in India*, 250.
[6] *Military Department Despatches from England*, 1806, Tamil Nadu Archives. Volume and page number not available.
[7] Malcolm, *Political History of British India*, 502.
[8] Marshman, *History of India*, vol. 2, 212–14.

Tirunelveli, from where many of the battalions stationed in Vellore Fort, notably the Second Battalion of the Twenty-Third Regiment, were drawn. Palayamkottai, a cantonment town, witnessed large-scale conversions, particularly amongst Nadars. Between 2 April 1802 and 24 January 1803, forty-six baptismal services were held and 5,629 persons were baptised.[9] As the result of an attack by the Hindus on Christian converts, the latter had to move out of their homes and settle in a village raised exclusively for Christians. In 1805, the Society for the Promotion of Christian Knowledge succeeded in getting orders from the Court of Directors to ensure that converts were not persecuted.[10] Thus, for the soldiers recruited from Tirunelveli, the threat of conversion must have seemed real.

At the time, there existed an organised movement of fakirs in south India. Abdulla Khan, who served Tipu as *ashoph* (lord lieutenant), was the prime mover of this movement under whose aegis emissaries were sent to different regions in the guise of fakirs. These fakirs inspired and incited those in the native infantry to take collective action against the British to restore the dethroned regional potentates to their seats of power. Notable among them were the fakirs Alam Ali Sha and Nur Khalil Shah, who succeeded in winning over the subedar and two prominent sepoys of the Second Battalion of the Seventh Regiment at Bellary. Fakirs like Rustom Ali travelled as puppeteers, as a part of this conspiracy to overthrow the British.[11]

All British historians stressed the role of rumours spread by fakirs in exciting the minds of native military men. What Tapti Roy says in the context of the year 1857 is worth quoting here: 'Rumours precede or follow the actual outbreak of rebellion; they do not cause it … Rumours reinforce popular fears.' As in the case of the rebellion in 1857, 'such rumours-turned-beliefs acted as

---

[9] Stephen Neill, *A History of Christianity in India, 1707–1858* (1985; repr., Cambridge: Cambridge University Press, 2002), 201.

[10] Penelope Carson, *The East India Company and Religion, 1698–1858* (Woodbridge: The Boydell Press, 2012), 64–66.

[11] See P. Chinnayan, *The Vellore Mutiny* (Madras, 1982).

forces of mobilisation and as transmission and rebellion against authority in 1806.[12]

The policy of territorial conquest pursued vigorously by the Company and the consequential dethronement of Indian potentates caused resentment amongst erstwhile rulers. Marudhu Pandian's glowing testament calling for unity across castes and religions to fight a last-ditch battle against the British, released before he was hanged by the British in 1801, and found in the centre of Madras shortly after the uprising in Vellore Fort, was supportive of this view.

II

Devadas Moodley, perusing the diaries and accounts of contemporary British officials, to which he had direct access in London, belittles the significance of the mutiny by concurring with the opinion of Lieutenant John Blakiston, the engineer who blew up gates to clear the way for Colonel Robert Gillespie's operation in Vellore Fort. Blakiston reminisced in his memoir that the 'sepoys were actually duped into the uprising'. Forgetting for a moment that the confessional statements of the accused were but desperate attempts to save their skin, Moodley concludes,

> The overwhelming evidence of the men (and their behaviour would endorse this) indicates that they were either led into the mutiny as hapless tools of their native officers or were uninvolved and that they fled as soon as the cavalry arrived from Arcot ... Sepoys interrogated after the event all claimed—indeed repetitiously so—to have fled on the approach of the cavalry and its indiscriminate killing. There is very little evidence of sustained resistance.[13]

Moodley's assumption, probably based on Blakiston's prejudiced version, is problematic. In a letter addressed to the

---

[12] Tapti Roy, *The Politics of a Popular Uprising: Bundelkhand in 1857* (Delhi: Oxford University Press, 1994), 231–33.

[13] Moodley, 'Vellore 1806: The Meanings of Mutiny', 9.

commander-in-chief, Gillespie himself states that on reaching the inner gate, while in the process of breaking the lock, he lost several men because of the continuous firing of musketry, and hence decided to await the arrival of the guns of the Nineteenth Light Dragoons in order to blow the gate open. Then, about the operation, he writes, 'At this moment the enemy kept up an incessant fire and I have to regret the loss of many of the 69th.'[14] That a pitched gun battle between the mutineers and the forces of Gillespie had taken place is, therefore, more than evident. This apart, most of the depositions were tutored and obtained under the promise of a pardon. The Company government was keen on getting statements implicating the Mysore princes.

In fact, Gillespie's forces were brutal and indiscriminate, while the mutineers were discriminating and compassionate in dealing with the enemies. Sergeant Solomon Frost was killed in the mutiny (see Figure 5.1), but his son James Frost was not. While deposing before the commission, James recalled how a solider allowed him to escape saying, 'I suffer you to escape because you are country born, were you a European I would stab you at this moment.'[15] Significantly, European women and children were spared. At the intervention of palace servants, presumably under orders from the Mysore princes, Frost's Indian wife and Sergeant James Watters's European wife, Charlotte, were protected by the sepoys of the native infantry.

In directing their anger towards white men, the Indian soldiers were almost always governed by feelings of revenge for an individual officer's acts of high-handedness in the pre-mutiny period.[16] Significantly, though the princes would have liked Lieutenant Colonel Thomas Marriott to be killed, the Indian soldiers chose to overlook his presence inside the fort. The officers who were let off by the mutineers could, therefore, congregate in the ramparts quickly and consolidate their position.[17] Those who were outside the fort

---

[14] Colonel Gillespie to Sir Cradock, *Secret Consultations*, vol. 19, 830–38.
[15] *Secret Department Sundries*, vol. 2A, 895–97.
[16] Moodley, 'Vellore 1806: The Meanings of Mutiny', 10–11.
[17] See Blakiston, *Twelve Years' Military Adventure*, vol. 1, 288–89. Blakiston observed in his memoir, 'It is surprising that the mutineers did not, at this time,

saw to it that no soldier attempted to escape through the sally port. In contrast, having exhausted all the ammunition at their disposal, the rebel soldiers could hardly cope with the demonic contingent that had arrived from Arcot. Gillespie, formerly a soldier in the Revolutionary and Napoleonic Wars, had gained notoriety for his brutality and, as Moodley pointed out, had 'all the makings of a psychopath', and the Nineteenth Light Dragoons had, for its part, earned a reputation for being the 'terrors of the East'.[18]

Gillespie and the dragoons threw to the wind all civilised conventions of warfare. After the suppression of the revolt, Gillespie unilaterally declared the appointment of a court of enquiry, which was subsequently superseded by a duly authorised commission constituted by the government. He behaved in such a high-handed fashion that, as discussed in Chapter 2, Marriott had to be firm in restraining him and his troops from putting Tipu's family and retainers to the sword. Paradoxically, the Seventh Regiment cavalry, which consisted mostly of Muslims, threw its full weight behind Gillespie.

No mercy was shown to soldiers found inside the fort premises and Gillespie's summary justice was even appalling to some of the British officials present on the scene. About 100 sepoys who had sought asylum in the palace were dragged out, lined up against the wall and blasted with canister shots[19] until everyone fell dead.[20] Moodley cites a letter from Marriott's wounded younger brother Charles, a captain, which indicated that Indian soldiers were hunted down until the morning of 12 July:

> The Europeans have been hunting for any of the mutineers who may have hid themselves these past two days, and every son of a bitch that has been found they either pistol'd or bayoneted ... Near seven hundred have been killed inside and outside and the work of death has only stopped this

make some serious attempts to force the gate. Had they done so the surviving Europeans must have fallen an easy prey.'
[18] Moodley, 'Vellore 1806: The Meanings of Mutiny', 10–11.
[19] A tin container filled with musket balls, used before the invention of shrapnel.
[20] Cox, *Manual of North Arcot District*, 85–86.

morning. I never in my life experienced such horrid, horrid sentiments and scenes.[21]

William F. Butler, a nineteenth century military officer who later served as commander-in-chief in South Africa, relishing the indiscriminate violence that Gillespie indulged in, provided details of the Vellore 'massacre' in his book, *A Narrative of Historical Events Connected with the Sixty-Ninth Regiment*:

> Between the great pagoda and the eastern rampart there was situated a large oblong court ... Into this court, the mutineers, to the number of three hundred, were now placed; they filled almost the entire space between the walls ... The order given to the dismounted troops, who stood round these guns, was one apparently easy of fulfilment; it was to fire until the living crowd became a heap of dead; but it is said that half-an-hour afterward there were arms moving and a few bodies writhing amidst the confused shapeless mass of black corpses which lay four and five deep upon the flagged floor of the blood-saturated fives' court.[22]

The exact number of soldiers killed is deliberately not enumerated in the official records. In the same way, the number of men awarded capital punishment, blown to pieces and hanged is given, but not their names. Gillespie reported that the casualties following the suppression of the mutiny included fourteen European officers, nine Indian officers and 168 European soldiers. According to his estimate, seventy-eight Europeans were seriously injured, clearly indicating that there was stiff resistance by rebel forces. Blakiston, who was an eyewitness to Gillespie's outrage in the fort, wrote, 'Upwards of 800 bodies were carried out of the fort, besides those who were killed after they escaped through the sally port.'[23]

---

[21] Quoted in Moodley, 'Vellore 1806: The Meanings of Mutiny', 13–14.

[22] W. F. Butler, *A Narrative of the Historical Events Connected with the Sixty-Ninth Regiment* (London: W. Mitchell, 1870), 44–45. Fives is a ball game played by two or four players in a court enclosed on three or four sides. In England, this game was played by boys in public schools.

[23] Blakiston, *Twelve Years' Military Adventure*, vol. 1, 298. Also see Vibart, *Madras Engineers and Pioneers*, vol. 1, 409.

III

The special commission formulated certain principles by which the guilty could be punished. The principles determined were as follows: native officers who were involved in the mutiny, native soldiers who were on the main guard on the night of the event, and others held guilty of committing atrocities were to be punished in such a manner as the Board of Control thought prudent. In the event that the Board decided to make a distinction in the punishment of the classes, native officers were to be banished, and the more atrocious offenders were to be subjected to some other form of punishment within the limits of the presidency. As for the remainder of the prisoners in confinement, the opinion of the Board was that they should be released on the clear understanding that they would never be re-admitted into the Company's service.[24]

In keeping with these principles, the commission suggested that Subedar Syed Hussain, who had feigned illness and permitted Jamedar Sheik Kasim to go on rounds on the night of 9 July, Subedar Annapah, who had been on duty on the main guard but was found inside the palace during the revolt, and Jamedar Ramasamy, who was on duty at the outer gate but was seen inside the fort, be dismissed from service. Jamedars Ramsingh and Rangappa, and Havildars Gopalu and Appa Rao were also dismissed from service 'for involvement in the whole conspiracy, betraying the trust enjoined on them'.[25]

Some of the officers who abstained from duty during the time of the uprising were also ordered to be dismissed from service. But taking into consideration their long period of service, they were granted a small amount as pension. Subedars Ismail Khan, Sheik Madar and Tirumalai Naickan, and Jamedars Ramasamy, Venkatiah and Gulam Singh were also listed in this category.[26] Of them, Rangappa, Gopalu and Appa Rao had taken an oath

---

[24] Special Commission Report, *Secret Department Sundries*, vol. 2A, 821–40.

[25] *Secret Department Sundries*, vol. 3B, 1663–73; vol. 11, 1592–1605.

[26] Special Commission Report, *Secret Department Sundries*, vol. 2A, 821–40. There were also a few other names identified during interrogation. See, for instance, Appendix 4.

along with other Muslim gentlemen to rebel.[27] There was also a long list of sepoys who indulged in plundering and looting.[28] The commission expressed the view that 'their crime has been already sufficiently punished; and their confinement should cease with the release of the other prisoners.'[29]

Lieutenant Colonel Ross Lang, George Read and W. S. Wright formed the military court of enquiry in Vellore. They painstakingly collected data and classified the mutineers based on the nature of their involvement in the revolt. In these lists, they presented the number for each category to the government (see Appendices 4–10.)

According to their classification, those who actively took part in the revolt numbered fifty (22 Muslims, 27 Hindus, 1 Christian). Twenty-one men (7 Muslims, 14 Hindus) entered the fort from outside and actively took part in the revolt. On duty and off duty soldiers who deserted and absconded numbered 157 (55 Muslims, 101 Hindus, 1 Christian). A group of 123 persons (35 Muslims, 88 Hindus) proved their innocence and hence were released.

The court martial, based on the verdict of the military court of enquiry, executed nineteen 'mutineers'. Of them, only four names have been identified. Subedar Sheik Adam, who was considered the unquestioned leader amongst Indian soldiers and officers, was blown from a gun. Jamedar Sheik Kasim, who was ordered to be dismissed from service by the special commission, was fixed as a chief conspirator by the military court. He was hanged to death, and his body exhibited in chains thereafter for public view. Sheik Meeran, a naik of the First Battalion, First Regiment, was shot by musketry, and Abdul Khadar, a lance naik of the Second Battalion, Twenty-Third Regiment, accused of supplying ball cartridges,

---

[27] *Secret Department Sundries*, vol. 3B, 1668–71.

[28] The looters identified by the special commission were: Havildars Gopalu and Appa Rao; and Sepoys Sheik Chan, Ismail, Rama Ramasamy, Pichamuthu, Perumalu, Subramani, Venkatraman, Rangappa, Sheik Moideen, Nalla Thampi, Sidhu Ali, Kulandaivelan, Lingappan, Moideen Khan, Venkatram, Alagu, Sheik Kussain, Andi, Balu, Sudalai Muthu and Anthony. See Appendices 5–10 to identify these persons with their rank and background.

[29] *Secret Department Sundries*, vol. 3B, 1663–73.

was 'hung by the neck until dead'.[30] The names of the other fifteen rebels executed along with them are not mentioned in any of the records examined during the research for this book.

The names of prisoners awaiting trial at Madras, those domiciled in Madras, and their personal details, are listed separately (see Appendices 12–13). These details, prepared by R. Barclay, town major at Fort St George, were sent to the governor-in-council on 9 November 1807. In two separate lists, the governor was provided with 207 names (49 Muslims, 158 Hindus). These lists contained information about the caste to which each individual belonged and their native place. The caste-wise representation in the Vellore Mutiny of 10 July 1806 is provided in Appendices 12–13 to drive home the point that it was a united fight of militia men, cutting across caste, religion and region. The land-owning communities, the Tirunelveli Pillais and Balija Naidus, formed a large part of the prisoners, twenty-eight and thirty-eight, respectively; this is reflective of the acute agrarian distress in the region that forced them to opt for a military career. The Parayars, twenty-seven in number, outnumbered their oppressors, the Vanniars, from which there were two prisoners, together with seventeen Pallars, constituted the largest contingent of participants in the revolt. There was also a significant presence of the Mukulathor people (16 in total; 9 Agamudayars and 7 Maravars). The Chettiyars, Kuravars, Edayars, Marathas, Asaaris (goldsmiths), Mutharayars and Telugu Jangams each had one member on the list.[31]

In the two lists of the prisoners, the native Christians were all persons belonging to the Parayar caste. In government prison records, the names of the prisoner, his father and paternal grandfather were given. Invariably, the names of the fathers of the Parayar Christians involved in the revolt bear their Christian names. As pointed out previously, European officers did not treat Christian converts with respect. At the same time, the Parayars who did not take to Christianity, detested the white people probably because of the increasing incidence of conversions in

---

[30] Quoted in Cameron, 'Vellore Mutiny', 191.
[31] *Secret Department Sundries*, vol. 11, 1628–1705; vol. 10B, 1448–52.

their community. This debunks the view of certain scholars that the mutiny failed because the lower castes did not support it. This is probably based on the assumption that a similar outcome to that of the battle of Bhima-Koregaon in Maratha country, in which the Mahars were involved, would have prevailed here too. In that battle, fought on 1 January 1818, the Mahars, having joined the British army, helped to trounce Peshwa forces.

In the Telugu and Tamil regions, individual caste identities were less important than collective ones, like *Valangai–Idangai*.[32] As Susan Bayly rightly pointed out, individual identities came to be articulated only after the left–right distinction disappeared in the middle of the nineteenth century.[33] Unlike in the Peshwa army, where lower caste groups like the Mahars were denied a place, in Tamil Nadu, the early regional rulers who resisted Company rule, whether it was Puli Thevan or Kattabomman, had a separate army division of Pallars. There was no exclusion of the 'untouchable' castes from military service in pre-British Tamil Nadu.

Studies undertaken in south Tamil Nadu in the eighteenth and nineteenth centuries indicated that caste organisation was weak because of the powerful presence of the Nattars (the ruling class in Tamil Nadu) as headmen of villages. Nattar authority was based not on caste structures but on their control over local territories. Thus, territory was a marker of social identity rather than caste in the social system of south India.[34]

In a letter addressed to the directors of East India Company, Agnew wrote of the bonhomie that prevailed amongst various grades of militia men drawn from different caste groups. Caste

---

[32] *Valangai* (right hand) and *idangai* (left hand) are terms appearing in Tamil inscriptions from the eleventh century and in British records from the eighteenth century. They denote two opposing and conflicting social groups. Right-hand groups comprised castes engaged in agriculture, while trading and artisan groups formed the left-hand group.

[33] Susan Bayly, *Caste, Society, and Politics in India from the Eighteenth Century to the Modern Age* (Cambridge: Cambridge University Press, 2001), 145–87.

[34] Nicholas B. Dirks, *Castes of Mind: Colonialism and the Making of Modern India* (Delhi: Permanent Black, 2002), 78, 116–17.

and religious sentiments were certainly played upon, but they only helped to stir the soldiers into revolt.

The special commission had received a list of twenty-three persons who swore to resist the new hat. The Madras government, however, notified more names, thirty-eight in total, all Muslims, and declared them the principal conspirators. But Sheik Kasim in his deposition mentioned that 300 men of the First Battalion, First Regiment had taken this oath of loyalty, and every native officer in the Twenty-Third Regiment, with the exception of Subedar Syed Mali, who was killed, and Subedar Ramalinga Naik, who was on command, was involved in the conspiracy. The names of these officers are Subedars Sheik Adam, Sheik Hamid, Noor Mohammed, Sheik Imam, Sheik Ahmed; Jamedars Sheik Kasim and Sheik Hussein; and Havildar Fakir Mohammed.[35] We have to presume that those who were at the forefront of the revolt, twenty-one in number according to the government, were executed. In all probability, these officers were among those executed in the fort.

IV

The Vellore Revolt, from the point of view of historian K. Rajayyan, who worked on eighteenth century colonial south India, was an offshoot of the Palayakkarars' rebellion of 1801. For Rajayyan, the rebellion in Vellore was the culmination of revolutionary activities sustained by men who were discharged from the troops of native rulers and chieftains. They had formed a network and were in touch with the aggrieved erstwhile rulers and chieftains, with the aim to overthrow the rule of the Company. In the words of Rajayyan, the patriots involved in the south Indian rebellion made a valiant but final endeavour when they recouped their eclipsed energies in the organisation of the revolt in 1806. They also managed to infiltrate the native infantry of the British to a great extent.[36]

---

[35] *Secret Department Sundries*, vol. 3B, 1663–73.

[36] Rajayyan, *South Indian Rebellion*, 286.

The adjutant-general of the army, Agnew, considered Mohammed Jaffer, formerly an officer in the service of Tipu, and a sepoy in the First Battalion, First Regiment, at the time of the revolt, as the principal agent who acted as liaison between the Mysore princes at Vellore Fort and the descendants of the dethroned chieftains in the south.[37] Agnew had been in command of the forces in Tirunelveli and had led the assault on Veerapandya Kattabomman's Panchalamkurichy in 1799, and had headed the European forces that quelled the rebellion of the Marudhu brothers of Sivagangai in 1801. So, he rightly suspected the role of the supporters of the deceased Marudhu brothers in the conspiracy, as the entire contingent of the Second Battalion, Twenty-Third Regiment had been recruited in south Tamil Nadu. William Thorn, the author of *A Memoir of Major-General Sir R. R. Gillespie*, remarked,

> The confederates intended that all those who were brought to join in the insurrection should act upon a preconcerted plan, which had been digested and privately circulated by some of the Marawa chiefs: and in connexion with them were some Frenchmen disguised as Fakeers, who went about the country inveighing everywhere against the English as robbers and tyrants.[38]

Moiz-ud-Din and Abdul Khalick were the two sons of Tipu held hostage by the English for two years according to the Treaty of Srirangapatnam, signed in 1792. Moiz-ud-Din was five years old then. In 1806, he was nineteen. The robust Moiz-ud-Din must not have forgotten the humiliation he suffered at the hands of the British. Abdul Khalick, who was eight years old in 1792, was twenty-two years old at the time of the revolt. He must have maintained poor health, because after the revolt, when his family and their attendants were transported to Calcutta, he died on arrival. As we have seen, his servants were actively involved in the mutiny. It seems Mohi-ud-Din, another son of Tipu, was equally

---

[37] P. A. Agnew, *Letter to the Honourable Court of Directors of the East India Company*, 1808, ref. W 2430(b), India Office Library, 12.
[38] Thorn, *Memoir of Major-General Gillespie*, 99.

involved in urging the native army battalions to raise the standard of revolt. Thus, both Moiz-ud-Din and Mohi-ud-Din must have looked for an opportunity to avenge the humiliation meted out to their family. But neither did they take the initiative, nor did they openly labour to organise resistance.

In fact, the sepoys' intention to revolt was conveyed to Moiz-ud-Din by Jamal-ud-Din, his foster brother, as revealed by Sheik Nuttar. After the Second Battalion of the Fourth Regiment was sent out of Vellore, he began to follow the developments in the fort. The vanquished regional forces elsewhere were awaiting an opportune moment to restore their rule. The French were ready to support the displaced chieftains, to regain their 'little kingdoms'. Maravar chiefs were in touch with them and were negotiating with them on behalf of Sultan Fateh Ali (Tipu's nephew). So the caste-breaking military regulations were only the proverbial straw that broke the camel's back. The grievances of the army's personnel came in handy for them. Ramu, a sepoy, drew the attention of the court of enquiry to the utterances of emotion-charged Mohammed Jaffer during the uprising: 'They will all think we are fighting for the turband. No.' Pointing to the Mysore flag that was flying, Jaffer thundered, 'It is for that we are fighting.'[39] The discontent, as seen in Chapter 2, was widespread, and none of the regional forces were reconciled to the conditions to which they had been reduced by the British.

A careful analysis of the figures, provided in the appendices, nails the lie that it was a 'mutiny of Mohammedans'.[40] The Second Battalion of the Fourth Regiment, which was the first to be dissolved, was composed of high-caste Hindus and Muslims.

That the Muslim soldiery took the initiative is evident from the names of those who were at the forefront of the revolt. Mohammed Jaffer, for instance, was formerly a jamedar in the service of Tipu, and at the time of rebellion, was a sepoy in the First Battalion of the First Regiment. Jaffer Beg, who had served Tipu Sultan as his bodyguard, was Mohammed Jaffer's associate,

---

[39] *Home Miscellaneous Series*, vol. 50B, file 4253, India Office Library, London.
[40] Military Officials' Petition to William Bentinck, *Home Miscellaneous Series*, vol. 507, India Office Library, London.

and two sepoys, Imam Khan and Syed Moideen of the First Battalion, First Regiment, were constantly in their company. Secret parleys were held at the residence of Sheik Adam, of the Second Battalion, Twenty-third Regiment. Syed Hussein, who was accused of acting under the orders of Moiz-ud-Din, was the one who woke up the sepoys at 2 a.m. on 10 July. Grenadier Mohammad Ali killed Major Charles Armstrong, Havildar Yusuf Khan killed Lieutenant Colonel James McKerras, Havildar Abdul Qadir killed Lieutenants Popham and O'Reilly, Subedar Ismail Khan indiscreetly killed European officers, Syed Hamid killed the European sentry in Colonel John Fancourt's house, Lance Naik Bawah Sahib set fire to the European quarters, and Grenadier Sheik Nuttar urged the sepoys at the gate to shoot Lieutenant Colonel Nathaniel Forbes.

The records relating to prisoners kept in Vellore and Fort St George suggest that the Muslims in two battalions, the First Battalion, First Regiment and the Second Battalion, Twenty-Third Regiment, put together, formed barely 40 per cent. Hindus constituted 60 per cent.[41] Venkatachalam, a sepoy of the First Battalion, First Regiment, admitted that he himself had killed four Europeans.[42] Similarly, the military court recorded that Balu, of the Eighth Company of the First Battalion, First Regiment, and Muthusamy, havildar of the Fifth Company, Second Battalion, Twenty-third Regiment, had killed a European soldier and a 'Sergeant's woman', respectively. Another Muthusamy of the Fifth Company, First Battalion, First Regiment, was found distributing ball cartridges, while Muthaian, sepoy, Light Company, was found loading a musket. Muthuveeran, sepoy, Eighth Company of the First Battalion, First Regiment, was accused of pointing out to the mutineers the hideouts of the Europeans in the fort, which resulted in huge loss of life to the European force.[43]

Thus, the Vellore Uprising was a united revolt of Indian soldiers against a common adversary, the British. Bentinck, after being stripped of his office as governor, wrote in a memorial presented

---

[41] *Secret Department Sundries*, vol. 11, 1628–1705; vol. 10B, 1448–52.
[42] *Secret Department Sundries*, vol. 10B, 1458–1552.
[43] *Secret Department Sundries*, vol. 10B, 1458–1552.

to the Court of Directors, 'In several of the disturbances that took place, the Hindoos were equally implicated with the Mussulmen. At Sankerydroog [Sankagiridurg] the principal was said to be a Hindu; and the Minister Purneah gave it as opinion that the Hindoos were more alarmed and dissatisfied than the Mussulmen.'[44] But for the imperial government, it was a question of survival. So, they opted for political measures. In Blakiston's words, 'It appeared to throw the odium of the conspiracy upon them, instead of permitting it to rest on the native army, whose loyalty and attachment it would not have been prudent to question.'[45]

The Company government first attempted to treat the Vellore episode as an isolated disturbance. But when it became evidently known, after the public execution of those who masterminded the revolt,[46] that the discontent had not receded but was spreading and that the cause was more political than military in nature, every effort was made to reconcile with the native infantry.

It has been argued by many a scholar that the uprising was not one of organised resistance and hence it floundered. But one has to remember that 'the natives had their own ways of secret counsel and distant confidential communication which entirely escaped the vigilance of the British authorities, when there were no railways, no telegraphs, no newspapers as the organ of public opinion.'[47] In the arrangements made for the Vellore Uprising,

> there was a manifestation of the capacity to devise and the means to execute, however imperfectly, very extensive schemes of combination. Partly through the action of hired emissaries, who, more readily to elude suspicion, assumed the varied guise of wandering devotees; and partly by clandestine correspondence conveyed through special

---

[44] Bentinck, *Memorial*, 45.

[45] Blakiston, *Twelve Years' Military Adventure*, 311–12.

[46] Minto Papers, MS 11322, National Library of Scotland. The petitioners of the Hyderabad Subsidiary Force had warned that 'if another insurrection should occur in the army, all the men will be united in the sentiment and action, in consequence of Colonel Gillespie's undistinguishing vengeance'. It was to that extent that the bloody episode affected the south Indian soldiery.

[47] Letters of Indophilus to the Editor of the Newspaper, *Bengal Hurkara*, *Mutiny of Vellore: Its Parallelisms and its Lessons*, 1857, India Office Library, London.

messengers, an insurrectionary spirit, under the pretext of violent interference with their religion, was simultaneously fomented at far distant and widely scattered stations— Palamcottah [Palayamkottai] and Bangalore, Nandydroog [Nandydurg] and Bellary, Wallajahbad and Hyderabad.[48]

Sheik Adam and Sheik Kasim planned and executed the insurrection ably. But for the bungling of Sheik Hussein, whose drunken behaviour betrayed their plan to revolt before the set date, the outcome might have been different. But ifs and buts have no value in history.

The soldiers did not act on impulse and emotion. They hated the new imperial policy and confidently planned to overthrow British rule. In this, they went by the saying of the English poet, Arthur Hugh Clough, 'It is better to have fought and lost, than never to have fought at all.' The groundswell of discontent among the people was considered essentially patriotic. The soldiers epitomised this in their revolt. The remarks of Mountstuart Elphinstone, made with reference to regions annexed from the Peshwas and incorporated into Bombay Presidency, are relevant to Madras also:

> The whole of the soldiery and all connected with them— all who lived entirely by service, all who joined service and cultivation, all who had a brother in employment, who is now thrown back on the family, and all who had horses and were otherwise maintained by the existence of an army—detest us and our regular battalions and are joined by their neighbours from sympathy and national feeling.[49]

In sum, the near extinction of regional and sub-regional rulers and chieftains resulting in the loss of power, status and wealth to those who served them in the army and bureaucracy, the oppressive land revenue policies of the Company government leading to the impoverishment of peasants, and increasing instances of the

---

[48] Letters of Indophilus to the Editor of the Newspaper, *Bengal Hurkara*, 1857, India Office Library.

[49] Quoted in L. S. S. O'Malley, ed., *Modern India and the West: A Study of the Interaction of their Civilisation* (1941; repr., London: Oxford University Press, 1968), 55–56.

evangelical activities of European missionaries, which caused fears of forced conversions to Christianity, all created a highly charged situation in south India. For the descendants of the dethroned rulers and chieftains who had been plotting to advance their cause, and maintaining correspondence with adversaries of the English, like the French and the Marathas, the new military code proved to be the powder keg.

Realising that the outbreak was political in nature, the government in Madras and the Supreme Government in Calcutta, notwithstanding the findings and recommendations of the special commission and military court of enquiry, decided to conciliate with the 'rebels', as it was impossible for them to raise the required number of troops from England. This was because of the unwillingness of the English to face the climate in India. From the viewpoint of the Company too, it was considered expensive. So, as we have seen, 500-odd prisoners were released and permitted to rejoin duty.

The proceedings of the special commission in Vellore were not conducted fairly. Lured by offers of financial reward or pardon by English officials, the deponents turned quislings and parroted what Forbes and Coombs had tutored them to say. Sheik Nuttar and Sheik Kasim, who initially refused to appear before the special commission, under the threat of reprimand, made what they called confessional statements. But the nefarious Company government reneged on its word and awarded death sentences to both. The imperial government singled out Muslim officers and soldiers for punishment, with death or dismissal. The fact that Major James Welsh was admonished by the court martial, despite his anti-Muslim proclivities, epitomised the divide-and-rule policy of the imperial government.

Marudhu Pandian's proclamation in Tiruchirappalli in 1801, made before he was hanged, pointedly referred to this exploitative policy of the British, whom he called 'wretches'.[50] Here, the patriotic call, though through feudal channels, is patently evident. The same anti-alien consciousness is noticed in people of all classes who

---

[50] Marudhu Pandian, Address, 1807, ref. GD51/3/129, National Archives, Scotland.

took part in the upheaval, with their political objective being the overthrow of the European government.

According to historian Eric Hobsbawm, resentment against conquerors, rulers and exploiters, recognisable as foreigners by colour, costume and customs, should be considered anti-imperial. Such anti-imperial outrages, in his view, constitute the proto-nationalist phase on which state-aspiring national movements are built.[51]

Transcending regional, religious, linguistic and caste barriers, the participants in the Vellore Revolt, whether they fit Hobsbawm's characterisation or not, were certainly roused by patriotic feelings. The 1806 uprising, albeit confined to cantonments in the south, in its origin and progress, was certainly a forerunner of the geographically widespread Great Rebellion of 1857 and deserves to be included in the mainstream narrative of history, and to be etched in the memory of the people.

---

[51] Eric J. Hobsbawm, *Nations and Nationalism since 1780: Programme, Myth, Reality*, 2nd ed. (Cambridge: Cambridge University Press, 1997), 47–49.

Appendix 1

Table A1.1 Actions initiated against the two rebel battalions, based on
Colonel Gillespie's report

	No. of Native Officers	No. of Non-Commissioned Rank and File
First Battalion, First Regiment of the Native Infantry		
At Chandragiri and Chittoor; exempted from guilt.	8	401
At Vellore; imprisoned for taking part in the mutiny.	5	152
At Vellore; not arrested but considered generally implicated in the misconduct of the corps.	6	340
At Vellore; considered innocent.	2	1
Missing since 10 July, of whom many were killed or taken prisoner in various parts of the country.	2	240
Total strength	23	1,134
Second Battalion, Twenty-Third Regiment of the Native Infantry		
At Vellore; imprisoned for taking part in the mutiny.	9	223
At Vellore; not arrested but considered generally implicated in the misconduct of the corps.	9	176
Missing since the 10 July, of whom many were killed or taken prisoner (about 150) in various parts of the country.	2	639
Declared innocent.	2	7
Total strength	22	1,045

Source: Secret Department Sundries, vol. 3B, 1567–68.

Appendix 2

Table A2.1 Persons who swore to stand united in resisting the new hat

	Name	Rank
	First Battalion, First Regiment	
1.	Sheik Dawan	Jamedar, Fifth Company
2.	Sheik Kasim	Jamedar
3.	Sheik Nutter	Havildar
4.	Syed Dowd	Havildar
5.	Abdul Kader	Lance Naik
6.	Mohammed Saib	Lance Naik
7.	Sheik Nutter	Grenadier
8.	Reymond Sait	Sepoy, Light Company
9.	Sheik Jaffer	Grenadier
10.	Jaffer Beg	Sepoy
11.	Mohammed Khan	Jamedar
12.	Sheik Sikkathar	Havildar, First Company
13.	Sheik Natten	Sepoy
14.	Sheik Imam	Lance Naik
15.	Khader Saib	Havildar, Light Company
16.	Sheik Madar	Sepoy
17.	Hunji Beg	Havildar
18.	Khadar Beg	Havildar
19.	Syed Mohammed	Sepoy
20.	Khan Saib	Lance Naik
21.	Yusuf Khan	Lance Naik

(Contd)

Table A2.1 (Contd)

	Name	Rank
22.	Mohammed Ali	Grenadier
23.	Abdul Nabi	Sepoy
24.	–	Honcho

Note: Designation-wise: Sepoy, 6; Grenadier, 3; Lance Naik, 5; Havildar, 6; Jamedar, 3; Honcho, 1—all drawn from the First Battalion, First Regiment. No subedar's name is mentioned. In the final list released by the government (see Appendix 3), the names of Sheik Jaffer, Reymond Sait, Jaffer Beg, Mohammed Khan, Sheik Natten, Khader Saib, Sheik Madar, Khan Saib, Mohammed Ali and the honcho are missing. Presumably, these ten persons became approvers. This would have facilitated inclusion of more persons in the list of accused.

Source: *Secret Department Sundries*, vol. 1B, 310–13.

Appendix 3

Table A3.1 Muslim soldiers and officers implicated by the military court in the Vellore Revolt

	Name	Rank and Remarks
First Battalion, First Regiment		
1.	Sheikh Dawan	Jamedar
2.	Sheikh Kasim	Jamedar
3.	Sheikh Nutter	Havildar; different from Sheik Nutter, Sepoy Grenadier
4.	Side Dowd (Syed Dawood)	Havildar
5.	Sheikh Modeen (Sheik Mohideen)	Havildar
6.	Dowd Cawn (Dawood Khan)	Havildar; one of the first to take the oath to resist the imposition of the new hat.
7.	Sheikh Secunder (Sheik Sikkandar)	Havildar; first to take the oath to resist the imposition of the new hat.
8.	Syed Esaph (Syed Yusuf)	Naik
9.	Sheikh Meeran	Naik
10.	Mohummed Ally (Mohammed Ali)	Naik
11.	Sheikh Midar (Sheik Madar)	Naik
12.	Mohommed Saib	Lance Naik
13.	Sheikh Adam	Lance Naik
14.	Sheikh Imam	Lance Naik; in charge of a party posted at the main guard with orders to fire upon every European they came across.

(Contd)

Table A3.1 (Contd)

	Name	Rank and Remarks
15.	Abdul Cawder (Abdul Khadar)	Lance Naik
16.	Sheikh Nutter	Sepoy Grenadier; formerly an errand boy to officers, then promoted to sepoy. Born in Madras, he was one of the principal conspirators.
17.	Emam Cawn (Imam Khan)	Sepoy; from Mysore. Had access to the palace through a fakir. After the cavalry arrived in the fort, he was found at the palace of Moiz-ud-Deen.
18.	Sheikh Rumjermce	Sepoy
19.	Side Homed (Syed Hamid)	Sepoy
20.	Mohammed Hussain	Sepoy
21.	Meer Hussain (Mir Hussein)	Sepoy
22.	Sheikh Midar (Sheik Madhar)	Sepoy
23.	Side Mohummad (Syed Mohammed)	Sepoy
24.	Side Modeen (Syed Mohideen)	Sepoy
25.	Abdul Nubby (Abdul Nabi)	Sepoy
26.	Meer Hussain (Mir Hussein)	Sepoy
27.	Sheikh Hurrjennce	Sepoy
28.	Jamal-ud-Din	Foster brother of Moiz-ud-Deen. Attended private meetings and consultations held in Imam Khan's house.
29.	Cawder Saib (Khadar Sahib)	Havildar; volunteered to shoot Lieutenant Colonel Forbes.
30.	Mohammed	Sepoy; shot Lieutenant Colonel McKerras.
31.	Sheikh Email (Sheik Ismail)	Shot the paymaster, Mr Smith.

(Contd)

Table A3.1 (Contd)

	Name	Rank and Remarks
32.	Sheikh Email (Sheik Ismail)	Principal accused; shot Lieutenant Jolly.
33.	Hunje Beg	Hoisted the Mysore flag.
34.	Khadar Beg	Hoisted the Mysore flag.
35.	Mohammed Ally (Mohammed Ali)	Worked the guns.
	Second Battalion, Twenty-Third Regiment	
36.	Sheikh-ud-Deen	Subedar
37.	Sheikh Umad	Subedar
38.	Sheikh Hussain	Jamedar
39.	Fakeer Mohammed	Havildar

Note: Comparing the list with the one provided by Sheik Ahmed (Appendix 2), there are 10 names missing, while 24 new names were added to the list above.

Source: *Secret Department Sundries*, vol. 7B, 3700–04.

Appendix 4

Table A4.1 Persons on duty accused of indulging in murder or plunder during the revolt

Name, Rank and Company	Charges
First Battalion, First Regiment	
1. Shaik Chan Havildar, Fourth Company	On duty at the main guard. He was active in getting the men together at 2 a.m. when the mutiny commenced, and was seen in arms at Moiz-ud-Deen's palace at 6 a.m.
2. Shaik Nutter Sepoy, Grenadier	On duty at the barracks. He admitted that he was one of the sworn and very active in the mutiny. His evidence before the court martial brought some of the principal offenders to conviction.
3. Meer Hussain Sepoy, Grenadier	On duty at the main guard. He abandoned his post and deserted, but was seen by Lieutenant Colonel Forbes conversing with one of the princes during the mutiny.
4. Ramasamy Sepoy, Grenadier	On duty at the barracks. He deserted and returned. Plundered articles were found in his possession.
5. Venkatachalam Sepoy, Third Company	On duty at the north-west bastion of the fort. Seen in arms near the post office by Havildar Ramudu, and was also seen in arms by Appah Swamy, *dubash* (translator or interpreter) to Dr Prichard, in whose presence he admitted that he himself had killed four Europeans.
6. Nureessoo (Narasu) Sepoy, Third Company	On duty as orderly to the officer of the day outside the fort. He joined the mutineers and was found with a plunder of 135 pagodas.

(Contd)

Table A4.1 (Contd)

	Name, Rank and Company	Charges
7.	Permalloo (Perumalu) Sepoy, Fourth Company	On duty at the barracks. He deserted but was apprehended by the police with plundered goods.
8.	Subramoneyah (Subramanian) Sepoy, Fourth Company	On duty at the outer gate guard, but came into the fort by climbing the walls. Apprehended by the police with plundered goods.
9.	Veerapha Sepoy, Twentieth Company	On duty at the outer gate guard, but came into the fort climbing the walls. He deserted, but was found with a bag of money when arrested.
10.	Sidu Ally (Sidhu Ali) Sepoy, Fourth Company	On duty at the main guard. Brought ball cartridges and handed them out to mutineers. Evidence: Mootyah (Muthiah).
11.	Rustom Khan Sepoy, Fourth Company	On duty at the main guard. Took an active part in the mutiny and assisted in the murder of Captain David Willison. Evidence: Jamedars Perumalu and Setchnnyah (in confinement).
12.	Rangapah Sepoy, Fourth Company	On duty in the picket. Confessed that he deserted his duty and fled with plundered articles. Arrested by the police.
13.	Syed Ally (Syed Ali) Sepoy, Fourth Company	On duty at the main guard. Confessed that he was present at the main guard in the crowd of sepoys who fired at the Europeans. He received a wound on his temple and was found among the wounded and sent to prison.
14.	Nella Tomby (Nalla Thambi) Sepoy, Fourth Company	On duty at the outer gate guard. Abandoned his post, entered the fort and plundered it. He was apprehended by the police and found to be in possession of a small bundle of rupees.
15.	Mahomed Saib Sepoy, Fourth Company	On duty at the barracks. Confessed that Abdul Khader filled his pouch with ball cartridges, and that he received orders to kill as many Europeans as he could.

(Contd)

Table A4.1 (Contd)

Name, Rank and Company	Charges
16. Futty Mahomed (Fateh Mohammed) Sepoy, Fourth Company	On duty at the main guard. Confessed that he fled with others into the western zamindaries. He was charged for bringing out a gun from the arsenal. Evidence: Mootyen (Muthayan).
17. Mooneapah (Muniappah) Sepoy, Fifth Company	On duty at the general stores guard at the arsenal. Left his post without leave. He had with him a telescope and two swords, of which one belonged to a European officer.
18. Syed Hussein Sepoy, Fifth Company	On duty as orderly to the European adjutant. He shot at a European officer. Evidence: Mootyah (Muthiah) and Mannaru.
19. Letchamanah (Latchumana) Sepoy, Fifth Company	On duty at the inner gate guard. Deserted, but was apprehended by the magistrate at Chittoor. Found in possession of a new table knife, which had been plundered.
20. Chennatomby (Chinnathambi) Sepoy, Fifth Company	On duty at the outer gate guard. Major de Sylva testified that he had plundered a bundle of cloth and a bottle of liquor, and that his bayonet was covered with blood. The sepoy's firelock was loaded and had the appearance of having been discharged several times.
21. Colundavalen (Kolandaivelan) Sepoy, Fifth Company	On duty at the arrack godown. He was seen bringing plundered goods from an officer's house. Evidence: Chennatomby (Chinnathambi).
22. Ramah (Rama) Sepoy, Fifth Company	On duty at the outer gate. Admitted that he scaled the walls and came into the fort. He brought out a bundle of plundered property (allegedly money) from the fort. Evidence: Sepoy Mootyah (Muthiah).
23. Balloo (Balu) Sepoy, Eighth Company	On duty at the general hospital. He was proved to have killed a European soldier. Evidence: Sepoys Kolandaivelan, Perumalu and Muthu.

(Contd)

Table A4.1 (Contd)

	Name, Rank and Company	Charges
24.	Syed Homed (Syed Hamid) Sepoy, Eighth Company	Forbes and Lieutenant Coombs testified that this man was one of the sworn. When the firing commenced at the main guard, he was the sentry at Colonel Fancourt's house from where a musket fired killed a European sentry. This shot was allegedly fired by him. Evidence: Havildar Murty and Mustafa Beg.
25.	Venctachellam (Venkatachalam) Sepoy, Light Company	On duty at the barracks in the picket line and was very active in the mutiny. He remained inside the fort till the cavalry entered, and afterwards took refuge in the pagoda and was arrested.
26.	Shaik Madar Sepoy, Light Company	On duty at the main guard. Seen in arms near the palace on the morning of 10 July. According to Forbes and Coombs, he was one of the sworn and was active in the mutiny.
27.	Hussein Khan Sepoy, Light Company	On duty at the main guard. Confessed that he fired at the Europeans, and that afterwards, went to the palace and deserted the next morning. He was proved to have killed a sergeant. Evidence: Sepoys Mootiah (Muthiah) and Rangappa, and Munnaroo (Mannaru) (imprisoned).
28.	Venkataraman Sepoy, Light Company	On duty at the outer gate. Came into the fort and proved to have been very active in plunder; was seen in arms and with plundered property. Evidence: Sepoys Moniapah (Muniappah) and Murty, and Havildar Murty.
29.	Punzem Sing Sepoy, Light Company	On duty at the main guard. He was seen in arms at the palace the next morning. Evidence: Havildar Murty (in service) and Kolandaivelu (imprisoned).

(Contd)

Table A4.1 (Contd)

	Name, Rank and Company	Charges
30.	Mooteen (Muthian) Sepoy, Light Company	On duty at the main guard. Admitted that he loaded his musket. Evidence: Sepoys Tondamurty and Ramaswamy and Havildar Ramdoss.
31.	Allavadeen (Alla-ud-Deen) Sepoy, Fifth Company	On duty at the weekly guard, at the commanding officer's bungalow. Abandoned his guard, forced open a godown, took out arms and was seen in arms near the palace. Evidence: Jamedar Soobaray (Subbarayan) and Havildar Murty.
32.	Mootooveerah (Muthuveeran) Sepoy, Eighth Company	On duty at the eastern bastion. Charged with pointing out to the mutineers where some Europeans were hiding, due to which the Europeans lost their lives. Evidence: Mootooverah (Muthuveeran) (imprisoned).
Second Battalion, Twenty-Third Regiment		
33.	Venkatram Sepoy, Fifth Company	On duty in the fort as orderly to the adjutant. Forbes and Coombs accused him of being active in the mutiny and was seen in arms.

Note: In this list of persons actively involved in the insurrection, excepting Shaik Chan, who was a havildar, all others were sepoys. One cannot miss the fact that Hindu sepoys (19) outnumbered Muslim sepoys (14). Significantly, Venkatachalam, sepoy, Third Company, First Battalion, First Regiment, claimed that he himself killed four Europeans, while another sepoy, Balloo, of the Fifth Company of same battalion and regiment, admitted that he had killed a European soldier. Syed Homed killed a European sentry.

Source: *Secret Department Sundries*, vol. 10B, 1458–1552.

Appendix 5

Table A5.1 Persons on duty in the sepoy barracks accused of
taking an active part in the revolt

	Name, Rank and Company	Charges
	First Battalion, First Regiment	
1.	Syed Karim Sepoy, Third Company	Killed a European soldier. Witness: Mootooveren (Muthuveeran).
2.	Shaik Moodeen (Sheik Moideen) Sepoy, Third Company	In the fort on 9 July and was active in the mutiny and plunder. Evidence: A servant of the adjutant, Lieutenant Ewing.
	Second Battalion, Twenty-Third Regiment	
3.	Syed Abseb Havildar, Fourth Company	Accused of having served ammunition to the men of his company during the mutiny. Evidence: Sepoy Cunniah (Kannaiah) (in confinement at Madras).
4.	Nuddeen Saib Havildar, Fourth Company	Seen on the ramparts in arms and in a party that fired at three Europeans. Evidence: Havildar Ramudu.
5.	Kondamal Naik Havildar, Seventh Company	Confessed that he knew of Rs 200 being plundered and brought into the pettai, but did not inform his commanding officer.
6.	Fackerah (Fakirah) Havildar, Eighth Company	Assisted in preparing his men with arms and thereby facilitating the massacre of European officers. Evidence: Sepoy Mootean (Muthian).
7.	Mootookurpen (Muthu Karuppan) Naik, Grenadier	Claimed that he remained passive and deserted, but there was no one to support his implication in the revolt. Forbes and Coombs accused him of active involvement in the mutiny.

(Contd)

Table A5.1 (Contd)

Name, Rank and Company	Charges
8. Gopaulloo (Gopalu) Naik, Fifth Company	Charged with leading a band of sepoys, who thrust their bayonets into the bodies of Europeans who were hiding in the bath. Evidence: Sepoy Canniah (Kanniah) (in confinement at Madras).
9. Jaganadan Sepoy, Fifth Company	Claimed that he fled and deserted. But Forbes and Coombs asserted that he was active in the mutiny.
10. Muthuswamy Sepoy, Eighth Company	Accused of distributing ball cartridges to the men. Evidence: Muthaiyan (Eighth Company).
11. Anthony Sepoy, Grenadier	Deserted, and was found with Rs 70 of looted money.
12. Shaik Moodeen (Sheik Mohideen) Sepoy, Eighth Company	Actively connected with Subedar Sheik Adam in all plans of the conspiracy. Forbes and Coombs stated he was found with 88 pagodas of looted money.
13. Permalloo (Perumalu) Sepoy, Eighth Company	Deserted, and was apprehended by the police with a lot of money in his possession.
14. Modeen Cawn (Mohideen Khan) Sepoy, Eighth Company	He claimed that he remained passive and deserted. Forbes and Coombs however stated that Rs 60 was found upon this person.
15. Lingapun (Lingappan) Sepoy, Eighth Company	Deserted, but was apprehended by police with Rs 30 in his possession, which he claimed was his own. The court deemed it plundered money.
16. Shaik Hoosain (Sheik Hussein) Naik, Grenadier	Killed the European sentry guarding the magazine. He deserted, but was arrested at Cuddalore. Evidence: Mohideen (in confinement).
17. Ramasamy Sepoy, First Company	Deserted but was apprehended by the police with plundered money in his possession.

Note: Sepoy Jaganadan and Muthuswamy were accused of distributing cartridges, indicating that Hindu soldiers too were actively engaged in the revolt. Syed Karim killed a European soldier, while Sheik Hussein stood charged with killing a European sentry. Syed Abseb and Nuddeen Saib were found serving ammunition to the mutineers.

Source: *Secret Department Sundries*, vol. 10B, 1458–1552.

Appendix 6

Table A6.1 Persons who returned to the fort after deserting their place of duty

Name, Rank and Company	
First Battalion, First Regiment	

1. Sheik Ismail
   Havildar, Fifth Company

2. Shaik Madar
   Naik, Grenadier Company

3. Syed Meer (released)
   Naik, Grenadier Company

4. Michael (released)
   Drummer, Grenadier Company

5. Veerabadra (released)
   Sepoy, Grenadier Company

6. Tondavarayah (Thandavarayan)
   (released)
   Sepoy, Grenadier Company

7. Cawder Cawn (Khadar Khan)
   (released)
   Sepoy, Grenadier Company

8. Sheik Imam (released)
   Sepoy, Grenadier Company

9. Mootiah (Muthiah) (released)
   Sepoy, Grenadier Company

10. Sheik Hussein (released)
    Sepoy, Grenadier Company

11. Sheik R. Najimi (released)
    Sepoy, Grenadier Company

12. Mullock Mahomed (released)
    Sepoy, Grenadier Company

13. Soobah Naick (Subba Naickan)
    (released)
    Sepoy, Grenadier Company

14. Sheik Imraun (released)
    Sepoy, Grenadier Company

15. Syed Hamid (released)
    Sepoy, Grenadier Company

16. Mahomed Usman (released)
    Sepoy, Grenadier Company

17. Ramasamy (released)
    Sepoy, Grenadier Company

18. Noor Khan (released)
    Sepoy, Grenadier Company

19. Shasanig (released)
    Sepoy, Third Company

20. Rangarau (Ranga Rao)
    (released)
    Sepoy, Third Company

(Contd)

Table A6.1 (Contd)

Name, Rank and Company

21.	Mahomed Cassim (released) Sepoy, Third Company	22.	Sunjeevee (Sanjivi) (released) Sepoy, Third Company
23.	Ramah (released) Sepoy, Third Company	24.	Mootoo (Muthu) (released) Sepoy, Third Company
25.	Veerapah (released) Sepoy, Third Company	26.	Nene Beg (released) Sepoy, Fourth Company
27.	Adum Cawn (Adam Khan) (released) Sepoy, Fourth Company	28.	Bungros (released) Sepoy, Fourth Company
29.	Budder Deen (released) Sepoy, Fourth Company	30.	Narayanah (released) Sepoy, Fourth Company
31.	Sheik Budden (released) Sepoy, Fourth Company	32.	Chinnoo (released) Sepoy, Fifth Company
33.	Chinnathamby (released) Sepoy, Fifth Company	34.	Mustopha Khan (released) Sepoy, Fifth Company
35.	Chinnathambi (released) Sepoy, Fifth Company	36.	Sai Mitter (released) Sepoy, Fifth Company
37.	Sankaralingam (released) Sepoy, Fifth Company	38.	Mootoo (Muthu) (released) Sepoy, Fifth Company
39.	Ramasamy (released), Sepoy, Fifth Company	40.	Ramasamy (released) Sepoy, Fifth Company
41.	Madar Khan (released) Sepoy, Fifth Company	42.	Pitchamoottoo (Pitchamuthu) (released) Sepoy, Light Company
43.	Syde Hussein (released) Sepoy, Light Company	44.	Mootoo (Muthu) (released) Sepoy, Light Company
45.	Kistnamah (released) Sepoy, Light Company	46.	Veerapah (released) Sepoy, Light Company
47.	Mootoo (Muthu) (released) Sepoy, Light Company	48.	Sheik Ali Sepoy, Light Company
49.	Syed Ameen (released) Havildar, Second Company	50.	Abdul Khadar (released) Havildar, Eighth Company

Second Battalion, Twenty-Third Regiment

51.	Mahomed Hussein Havildar, First Company	52.	Muthaian Havildar, Second Company

(Contd)

Table A6.1 (Contd)

Name, Rank and Company	
53. Sheik Settar Havildar, Second Company	54. Mahomed Saib Havildar, Second Company
55. Sheik Baddon Havildar, Third Company	56. Chinnoo Havildar, Sixth Company
57. Sheik Hussein Havildar, Seventh Company	58. Syed Husman Havildar, First Company
59. Sheik Yusuf Naik, Grenadier Company	60. Syed Noor Naik, First Company
61. Francis Fifer, Second Company	62. Chodalaymootoo (Sudalaimuthu) Sepoy, Grenadier Company
63. Alagiri Sepoy, Grenadier Company	64. Mootoo (Muthu) Sepoy, Grenadier Company
65. Kistnapah Sepoy, Grenadier Company	66. Subramanyan Sepoy, Grenadier Company
67. Chellaperumal Sepoy, Grenadier Company	68. Shanbogum (Shenbagam) Sepoy, Grenadier Company
69. Mootoo Kurpen (Muthu Karuppan) Sepoy, Grenadier Company	70. Faudden Sepoy, Second Company
71. Ramsing Sepoy, Third Company	72. Venkataraman Sepoy, Third Company
73. Sasoonaik Sepoy, Third Company	74. Cheeinain (Chinnayan) Sepoy, Third Company
75. Subramanyan Sepoy, Fifth Company	76. Alwar Sepoy, Fifth Company
77. Ramalingam Sepoy, Fifth Company	78. Letchumana Sepoy, Fifth Company
79. Mawden (Madan) Sepoy, Fifth Company	80. Mootnnah (Muthanna) Sepoy, Sixth Company
81. Perumalu Sepoy, Seventh Company	82. Bavah Saib Sepoy, Seventh Company
83. Munnaroo (Mannaru) Sepoy, Seventh Company	84. Anthony Sepoy, Seventh Company

(Contd)

Table A6.1 (Contd)

Name, Rank and Company	
85. Sillah Buteawn Sepoy, Seventh Company	86. Venkatasamy Sepoy, Seventh Company
87. Tirumalayan Sepoy, Seventh Company	88. Muthuswamy Sepoy, Eighth Company
89. Munnaroo (Mannaru) Sepoy, Third Company	90. Ramasamy Sepoy, Grenadier Company

Note: Of the 90 deponents, 50 in the First Battalion, First Regiment, and 40 in the Second Battalion, Twenty-Third Regiment, though on duty at different places, they all made the same statement—that they remained passive throughout the revolt. They swore that they had left and returned to the fort only after hearing the tom-tom. Excepting Sheik Ismail, havildar, and Sheik Madar, naik, both of the First Battalion, First Regiment, all others were released. In the Second Battalion, Twenty-Third Regiment, none of those detained (40) was released.

Source: *Secret Department Sundries*, vol. 10B, 1458–1552.

APPENDIX 7

TABLE A7.1 Persons who were captured and imprisoned after the mutiny

Name, Rank and Company			
First Battalion, First Regiment			

1. Syed Hussein
   Subedar, Fourth Company

2. Ramasamy
   Subedar, Fourth Company

3. Rangapah (released)
   Sepoy, Grenadier Company

4. Abdul Naby (released)
   Sepoy, Grenadier Company

5. Mohammed Usmon (released)
   Sepoy, Grenadier Company

6. Sheik Imam (released)
   Sepoy, Grenadier Company

7. Syed Fakeerah (released)
   Sepoy, Third Company

8. Futty Khan (Fateh Khan)
   (released)
   Sepoy, Fourth Company

9. Racapah (Rakkappah)
   (released)
   Sepoy, Fourth Company

10. Shaik Currim (released)
    Sepoy, Fifth Company

11. Pupiah (Papaiah) (released)
    Sepoy, Fifth Company

12. Sheik Hussein (released)
    Sepoy, Fifth Company

13. Ramasamy (released)
    Sepoy, Fifth Company

14. Perumalu (released)
    Sepoy, Fifth Company

15. Abdul Khadar (released)
    Havildar, Eighth Company

Second Battalion, Twenty-Third Regiment

16. Vellian (released)
    Sepoy, Fifth Company

17. Kondapah
    Naik, First Company

18. Fatharoo
    Drummer, First Company

19. Megale (Michael)
    Drummer, Fifth Company

20. Narrayadoo
    Sepoy, Grenadier Company

21. Peersaib
    Sepoy, Grenadier Company

(Contd)

Table A7.1 (Contd)

Name, Rank and Company

22.	Rangan Sepoy, Grenadier Company	23.	Shaik Emam Sepoy, Grenadier Company
24.	Raman Sepoy, Grenadier Company	25.	Chinnatambi Sepoy, Grenadier Company
26.	Alwar Sepoy, Grenadier Company	27.	Durmadass (Dharmadas) Sepoy, Third Company
28.	Kooroopen (Karuppan) Sepoy, Third Company	29.	Ramalingum Sepoy, Third Company
30.	Daraveyam (Diravium) Sepoy, Fifth Company	31.	Veerapan Sepoy, Sixth Company
32.	Mootoosawmy (Muthuswamy) Sepoy, Sixth Company	33.	Aroomogum (Arumugam) Sepoy, Sixth Company
34.	Ramasamy Sepoy, Seventh Company	35.	Mootoo (Muthu) Sepoy, Eighth Company
36.	Letchumanan Sepoy, Grenadier Company	37.	Raman Sepoy, Sixth Company
38.	Mootain (Muthian) Sepoy, Second Company	39.	Palavesam Sepoy, Second Company
40.	Sheik Hussein Sepoy, Grenadier Company	41.	Shaik Hussein Sepoy, Second Company
42.	Mootoo Sawmy (Muthusamy) Sepoy, Eighth Company	43.	Rangan Sepoy, Eighth Company
44.	Eukoo (released) Sepoy, Light Company	45.	Veerapah (released) Sepoy, Light Company

Note: Of the 15 persons belonging to the First Battalion, First Regiment, 13 were released. Two Subedars of the Fourth Company, Syed Hussain and Ramasamy, continued to be kept in confinement. With regard to the Second Battalion, Twenty-Third Regiment, except for one sepoy (Vellian), all others (35) languished in jail. The government ordered the release of those detained because they had convinced the enquiry commission that they had obeyed the orders of their English officers. As a matter of fact, they played the role of quislings, helping their masters in identifying active rebel sepoys and officers. The fate of these people in detention is not known—these names are not in Appendix 10, which contains a list of persons who convinced the English of their innocence and were released.

Source: *Secret Department Sundries*, vol. 10B, 1458–1552

APPENDIX 8

Table A8.1 Persons who entered the fort from outside during the revolt

Name, Rank and Company	Charge
Second Battalion, Twenty-Third Regiment	
1. Perumalu Naik, First Company	Entered the fort, took up arms and stayed till the cavalry appeared. Received three sword wounds and absconded.
2. Shaik Meyan Sepoy, First Company	Wounded. Deserted and came in after the beating of the tom-tom.
3. Arngherry (Arunagiri) Sepoy, Second Company	Deserted and came in after the beating of the tom-tom.
4. Ramasamy Sepoy, Second Company	Entered the fort and was wounded in 13 places. Deserted but came in after the beating of the tom-tom.
5. Allagoo (Alagu) Sepoy, Third Company	Entered the fort and plundered. He was seized with plundered goods.
6. Shaik Hussein Sepoy, Eighth Company	Joined the mutineers and remained within the fort till 9 a.m. Confessed that he deserted with a bundle of money, which was found upon his person when he was arrested by the police.
7. Mooroogah (Murugan) (released) Sepoy, Third Company	Came into the fort over the walls and actively participated in the mutiny. Dr Prichard's dubash, Appah Swamy, testified that he saw him at the doctor's house in arms. Mustapha Beg also stated that he was active in the mutiny. Evidence: Sepoy Madurai Muthu.

(Contd)

Table A8.1 (Contd)

Name, Rank and Company	Charge
8. Side Audum (Syed Adam) (released) Sepoy, Third Company	Came into the fort through the sally port to see his father, Subedar Hussein.
9. Shaik Homed (Sheik Hamid) (released) Sepoy, Eighth Company	Confessed that he came into the fort and then fled. He concealed himself for a short time in the hills and then returned.
10. Side Dewan (Seyed Diwan) (released) Sepoy, First Company	Sick in hospital. Came into the fort and then deserted. He returned on hearing the tom-tom.
11. Chowry Mootoo (Savarimuthu) Sepoy, First Company	Sick in hospital. Came into the fort over the walls, was active in the mutiny and was seen in possession of plundered goods. Evidence: Ramasamy and Chinnoo.
12. Veerapah (released) Sepoy, First Company	Sick in hospital outside. Came into the fort and was seen in arms by Sepoys Mannaru and Muthiah, who were later confined. He deserted but was apprehended.
13. Venkataraman Sepoy, Eighth Company	Outside the fort. Deserted, came in and served for a short time but deserted again. Lieutenant Colonel Forbes and Lieutenant Coombs remarked that he was apprehended with plundered goods.
14. Jangum Jamedar, Seventh Company	Outside the fort. He was the native adjutant of the Second Battalion, Twenty-Third Regiment. Forbes and Coombs remarked that he was aware of the plan to mutiny and had attended a conference at the palace. Evidence: Havildar Yusuf Khan (in confinement).
15. Muthusamy Havildar, Fifth Company	Outside the fort, but was proved to have come into the fort and killed a sergeant's wife. Evidence: Sepoys Muthayan and Mannaru (in confinement).

(Contd)

Table A8.1 (Contd)

	Name, Rank and Company	Charge
16.	Mootoo (Muthu) (released) Sepoy, Third Company	This man was outside the fort but went in to look for his brother. He left the fort as soon as the cavalry arrived and ran away to the hills but returned after hearing the tom-tom.
17.	Hassim Khan (released) Sepoy, Third Company	This man was outside the fort, but Forbes and Coombs observed that he was closely connected with Subedar Sheik Adam in planning the mutiny. Evidence: Rama, a sepoy at Madras.
18.	Andy Sepoy, Fifth Company	This man remained outside the fort but was apprehended by the police with Rs 100 and could not satisfactorily state how he obtained this money. There is a strong presumption that he came into the fort and engaged in plundering.
19.	Velludum (released) Sepoy, Eighth Company	Outside the fort, off duty, but came in to seek his brother. Moreover, he stated in his declaration that he assisted in saving two Europeans. Evidence: Sepoy Muthu, according to whom this man left the fort on the approach of cavalry, but was apprehended.
20.	Chodalay Mootoo (Sudalai Muthu) Sepoy, Eighth Company	Remained outside the fort but was caught with Rs 123, hence there was a strong suspicion that he went into the fort and engaged in plundering.
21.	Peermaulloo (Perumalu) (released) Naik, Fifth Company	Commanded the guard at the hospital outside the fort. Forbes and Coombs remarked that this man entered the fort and took part in the mutiny.

Note: As in Appendix 7, Hindu soldiers outnumber their Muslim colleagues. Of those imprisoned, 12 persons' detention was confirmed. Of them, 8 were Hindus and 4 were Muslims. Of those found guiltless and released, 4 were Muslims and only 1 person was a Hindu.

Source: *Secret Department Sundries*, vol. 10B, 1458–1552.

APPENDIX 9

TABLE A9.1 Quislings who resisted or helped suppress the revolt

Name, Rank and Company	Role Played in the Mutiny
Fifth Battalion, Seventeenth Regiment	
1. Veerappa Sepoy, Third Company	On duty at the nawab's battery. Naik Venkatram stated that this man belonged to his guard and obeyed his orders.
2. Mootoveerah (Muthuveeran) Sepoy, Third Company	On duty at the north-east bastion. He obeyed his havildar's orders and also gave evidence against Sepoy Syed Karim.
3. Abdul Nabi Sepoy, Third Company	On duty at the old Ambur gate and the nawab's battery. Naik Venkatram stated that he obeyed his orders. He received a wound outside the fort.
4. Sheik Hussein Sepoy, Third Company	On duty at the old Ambur gate and the nawab's battery. Venkatram Naik stated that they obeyed his orders.
5. Khader Saib Sepoy, Third Company	On duty at the old Ambur gate and the nawab's battery. Venkatram Naik stated that he obeyed his orders.
6. Veeragoo (Viraragu) Sepoy, Third Company	On duty at the north-west bastion. James Alexander, a European invalid, spoke favourably of his conduct during the mutiny.
7. Mootiah (Muthiah) Sepoy, Fourth Company	On duty at the main guard. By his evidence, Sepoy Syed Hussein was convicted of the murder of an officer. He also gave evidence against Sepoys Veerapan, Hussain Cawn, Raman, Fateh Mahomed and Syed Ali, and Havildar Muthusamy.

(Contd)

Table A9.1 (Contd)

Name, Rank and Company	Role Played in the Mutiny
8. Narynah (Narayana) Sepoy, Fourth Company	On duty at the main guard. This man informed the committee that he had assisted in saving Mrs Fancourt and her children. He had no evidence to prove the fact. Yet he pointed out correctly to Lieutenant Colonels Lang and Maclean, fort adjutant, the exact spot where she and her children hid.

Fifth Battalion, Eighth Regiment

9. Mucundoo (Mukundu) Sepoy, Fourth Company	On duty at the garrison treasury. Lieutenant Colonel Forbes and Lieutenant Coombs certified that he did his duty as a good soldier and did not quit his post as sentry. This man gave evidence against the Sheik Ismail, who killed the garrison's paymaster, Mr Smith.
10. Sappermal Sepoy, Fourth Company	On duty at the arrack godown. Jamedar Perumal spoke favourably of this man's conduct. He assisted in preserving the life of two soldiers. This man gave evidence against sepoy, Alagappan.
11. Mootoo (Muthu) Sepoy, Fourth Company	On duty at the general stores in the fort. The jamedar spoke favourably of this man's conduct, stating that he joined his guard and remained with him till 9 a.m. the next morning.
12. Nunny Cawn Sepoy, Fifth Company	On duty at the arrack godown. Jamedar Perumalu testified that he was present when two Europeans were concealed in the arrack godown and that he remained obedient till 6:30 a.m. the next day. He later deserted and hence was arrested.
13. Venkatachalam Sepoy, Light Company	On duty at the main guard. This man received two wounds from the mutineers because he refused to bring ball cartridges when ordered. Forbes and Coombs recommended that he be released.

Note: It seems apart from the First Battalion, First Regiment and the Second Battalion, Twenty-Third Regiment, there were also two other regiments present at Vellore Fort, the Fifth Battalion, Seventeenth Regiment and the Fifth Battalion, Eighth Regiment. They had moved into the fort to strengthen the European forces in their task of retaining control over the fort immediately after the suppression of revolt. The determination and solidarity of the former two battalions is revealed by their uniting for the common cause of resisting English rule. At the same time, the English used the 13 men belonging to these two battalions to identify the 'rebels'.

Source: *Secret Department Sundries*, vol. 10B, 1458–1552.

Appendix 10

Table A10.1 Persons who, according to Forbes and Coombs, satisfactorily proved to the enquiry committee that they did not take part in the revolt, and were hence ordered to be released

Name	Rank	Company
First Battalion, First Regiment		
1. Khadar Saib	Havildar	First
2. Sheik Madar	Havildar	Fifth
3. Shaik Ebram (Sheik Ibrahim)	Naik	Fifth
4. Narasu	Sepoy	Grenadier
5. Shaik Abbas	Sepoy	Grenadier
6. Perumalu	Sepoy	Grenadier
7. Venkatachalam	Sepoy	Grenadier
8. Elloo	Sepoy	Grenadier
9. Abdul Cawder	Sepoy	Grenadier
10. Shaik Modeen (Sheik Moideen)	Sepoy	Grenadier
11. Esmal Khan (Ismail Khan)	Subedar	First
Second Battalion Twenty-Third Regiment		
12. Shiekh Madar	Subedar	Second
13. Trumille Naig (Tirumalai Naicken)	Subedar	Fourth
14. Venketah	Jamedar	Sixth
15. Hullian Sing	Jamedar	Third
16. Ram Sing	Jamedar	Second
17. Venkatachalam	Sepoy	First
18. Sheekh Sulliman (Sheik Sulaiman)	Sepoy	First
19. Grovapun (Guruvappan)	Sepoy	First

(Contd)

Table A10.1 (Contd)

Name	Rank	Company
20. Letchumanan	Sepoy	First
21. Rangan	Sepoy	First
22. Mootoo	Sepoy	First
23. Veerapah Naig (Veerappan Naicken)	Sepoy	First
24. Ebram Cawn (Ibrahim Khan)	Sepoy	First
25. Allegharry (Alagiri)	Sepoy	First
26. Aunundan (Anandan)	Sepoy	First
27. Pitcha Mootoo (Pitcha Muthu)	Sepoy	First
28. Ramasamy	Sepoy	First
29. Veerabadran	Sepoy	First
30. Ramasamy	Sepoy	First
31. Megall	Sepoy	First
32. Pylnaundy (Palaniandi)	Sepoy	First
33. Sheik Bheilum	Havildar	First
34. Mitty Shah	Havildar	Fourth
35. Imam Sheriff	Havildar	Eighth
36. Abdul Khader	Havildar	Eighth
37. Sheikh Emam	Naik	First
38. Sheikh Ibrahim	Sepoy	Fifth
39. Chach Perumal	Sepoy	Fifth
40. Subramanyan	Sepoy	Fifth
41. Sheikh Abdullah	Sepoy	Fifth
42. Ramasamy	Sepoy	Sixth
43. Muthusamy	Sepoy	Sixth
44. Venketepuddy (Venkatapathy)	Sepoy	Sixth
45. Perumalu	Naik	Third
46. Ali Khan	Sepoy	Grenadier
47. Poovalingam	Sepoy	Grenadier
48. Sheikh Ibrahim	Sepoy	Grenadier
49. Ramsamy	Sepoy	Grenadier

(Contd)

Table A10.1 (Contd)

Name	Rank	Company
50. Venkatachellum	Sepoy	Grenadier
51. Perumalu	Sepoy	First
52. Viraghu	Sepoy	First
53. Iyah Kunnoo (Ayyakannu)	Sepoy	First
54. Sungarun (Sankaran)	Sepoy	First
55. Raman	Sepoy	First
56. Ramasamy	Sepoy	First
57. Veerabadran	Sepoy	First
58. Muthu Samy	Sepoy	First
59. Subrayan	Sepoy	Fourth
60. Soobrayamanyan (Subramanian)	Sepoy	Fourth
61. Sankiralingam	Sepoy	Fourth
62. Ramasamy	Sepoy	Fourth
63. Perumalu	Sepoy	Fifth
64. Muthu Karuppan	Sepoy	Fifth
65. Perumalu	Sepoy	Fifth
66. Raman	Sepoy	Fifth
67. Sooben (Subban)	Sepoy	Fifth
68. Mootoo Naig (Muthu Naicken)	Sepoy	Fifth
69. Rama Samy	Sepoy	Fifth
70. Muthu Samy	Sepoy	Fifth
71. Kustoree (Kasturi)	Sepoy	Fifth
72. Soobroymain (Subramanian)	Sepoy	Fifth
73. Shaikh Bahawder	Sepoy	Fifth
74. Tondaroyan (Thandavarayan)	Sepoy	Fifth
75. Allagree (Alagiri)	Sepoy	First
76. Rangan	Sepoy	First
77. Viraghu	Sepoy	First
78. Subbah Naiken	Sepoy	First
79. Sheikh Mohiddeen	Sepoy	Seventh

(Contd)

Table A10.1 (Contd)

Name	Rank	Company
80. Sheikh Imam	Sepoy	Seventh
81. Ramasamy	Sepoy	Seventh
82. Mahamed Cassim	Sepoy	Seventh
83. Muthusamy	Sepoy	Seventh
84. Ramasamy	Sepoy	Eighth
85. Yakub Khan	Sepoy	Eighth
86. Perumalu	Sepoy	Eighth
87. Angappan	Sepoy	Eighth
88. Jungamyah	Sepoy	Seventh
89. Goowah (Koovai)	Sepoy	Seventh
90. Syed Hussein	Sepoy	Eighth
91. Viragu Naicken	Sepoy	Eighth
92. Perumalu	Sepoy	Eighth
93. Mootoo (Muthu)	Sepoy	Eighth
94. Chettumbarum (Chithambaram)	Sepoy	Eighth
95. Nullay Kunnoo (Nalla Kannu)	Sepoy	Eighth
96. Ramasamy	Sepoy	Eighth
97. Pylney (Palani)	Sepoy	Eighth
98. Muthu Karuppan	Sepoy	Eighth
99. Rungun	Sepoy	Eighth
100. Iyah Sawmy (Ayyasamy)	Sepoy	Eighth
101. Sheik Hamid	Sepoy	Eighth
102. Mahomed Ghabi	Naik	Eighth
103. Sheik Adam	Sepoy	Fifth
104. Samy	Sepoy	Fifth
105. Coopun (Kuppan)	Sepoy	Sixth
106. Isuph Cawn (Yusuf Khan)	Havildar	Seventh
107. Mootoo Ramalingum (Muthu Ramalingam)	Sepoy	First
108. Venkatasamy	Sepoy	Light
109. Nubby Cawn (Nabi Khan)	Sepoy	Eighth

(Contd)

Table A10.1 (Contd)

Name	Rank	Company
110. Ramasamy	Sepoy	Eighth
111. Syed Mahomed	Sepoy	Eighth
112. Perumalu	Sepoy	Eighth
113. Mylaroom Peermal (Mylerum Perumal)	Sepoy	Eighth
114. Sheik Dawood	Sepoy	Eighth
115. Alagiri	Sepoy	Eighth
116. Samy	Sepoy	Eighth
117. Shaik Farid	Sepoy	Eighth
118. Perumalu	Sepoy	Eighth
119. Perumalu	Sepoy	Eighth
120. Poodyaven (Puthiyavan)	Sepoy	Eighth
121. Ramasamy	Sepoy	Eighth
122. Mootuswamy (Muthusamy)	Sepoy	Eighth

Note: As the British realised the impracticability of bringing white men from England to serve the British army in India in view of the cost involved and the hostile weather, they decided to reconcile themselves with the aggrieved men of the Indian army. The latter, too, devoid of any other source of livelihood and prompted by survival instinct, had no other option but to accept the humiliating terms dictated by their crafty masters. Of those released, presumably under general admonition, a vast majority belonged to the rank of sepoy in the Second Battalion, Twenty-Third Regiment, recruited from south Tamil Nadu. It is to be noted that earlier, the rank and file of this regiment was detained, while many in the First Battalion, First Regiment had been released.

Source: *Secret Department Sundries*, vol. 10B, 1458–1552.

Appendix 11

Table A11.1 List of Mysore's princes and their relatives, and the number of attendants who were shifted to Calcutta

Name	No. of Servants
Fateh Hyder	7
Abdul Khalick	4
Sultan Mohi-ud-Deen	4
Sultan Moiz-ud-Deen	3
Yassin Sheik Jamal-ud-Deen Muneer-ud-Deen	8
Subhan Sahib	2
Shakirullah Sahib	3
Swarur-ud-Deen	3
Karim Sahib (Tipu's brother)	3
Hyder Hussein Khan (Tipu's nephew)	3
Total servants	**40**
Princes	12
Total	**52**

Note: This list was signed off on 20 August 1806 in Vellore by Captain Charles Marriott, assistant paymaster of stipends.

Source: Secret Department Sundries, vol. 3A, 1252.

Appendix 12

Table A12.1 Prisoners in the St Thome Lunettes, Madras

Name of Prisoner	Rank, Corps / Company	Caste	Place of Birth / Domicile
First Battalion, First Regiment			
1. Bura Khan	Naik, Eighth Corps	Pathan	Gwalior
2. Veerapah	Sepoy, Eighth Corps	Parayar	Madurai
3. Venkatachalam	Sepoy, First Grenadier	Agamudayar	Pudukottai
4. Venketaram	Sepoy, First Grenadier	Balija Naidu	Tiruchi
5. Coopaunpandy (Kuppan Pandi)	Sepoy, First Grenadier	Pillai (Saiva Vellalar)	Tirunelveli
6. Gulam Moideen	Sepoy, First Grenadier	Sheikh	Tiruchi
7. Mootoocarpen (Muthu Karuppan)	Sepoy, Fourth Grenadier	Agamudayar	Pudukottai
8. Mohammed Usman	Sepoy, Fourth Grenadier	Sheikh	Thanjavur
9. Sheik Manullah	Sepoy, Fourth Grenadier	Sheikh	Guntur
10. Mauyandy (Mayandi)	Sepoy, Fourth Grenadier	Pillai	Srivaikundam
11. Sheik Ismail	Sepoy, Fifth Grenadier	Sheikh	Palghat
12. Soondarum (Sundaram)	Sepoy, Seventh Grenadier	Pillai	Tirunelveli

(Contd)

Table A12.1 (Contd)

Name of Prisoner	Rank, Corps / Company	Caste	Place of Birth / Domicile
13. Mootoo Veeran	Sepoy, Third Grenadier	Parayar	Palayamkottai
14. Munnauroo (Mannaru)	Sepoy, Fourth Corps	Pillai	Nagoor
15. Moottien (Muthian)	Sepoy, Fourth Corps	Pillai	Thanjavur
16. Mahomed Hussein	Sepoy, Fourth Corps	Sheikh	Cuddapah
17. Letchoomen	Sepoy, Fifth Corps	Maratha	Numil
18. Sheik Karim	Sepoy, Fifth Corps	Sheikh	Tiruchi
19. Venkatasamy	Sepoy, First Corps	Balija Naidu	Kalastry
20. Maurymootoo (Marimuthu)	Sepoy, Fourth Corps	Pillai	Chidambaram
21. Narayan	Sepoy, First Corps	Pallar	Wandavasi
Second Battalion, Twenty-Third Regiment			
22. Narayan Naidu	Havildar, First Grenadier	Balija Naidu	Srivilliputhur
23. Mootoo (Muthu)	Drummer, First Grenadier	Parayar	Madurai
24. Mootooswammy (Muthuswamy)	Sepoy, First Grenadier	Balija Naidu	Srivilliputhur
25. Veerapah Naidoo	Sepoy, First Grenadier	Balija Naidu	Srivilliputhur
26. Shaik Emaum (Sheik Imam)	Sepoy, First Grenadier	Sheikh	Srirangapatnam
27. Baulagooroo (Balaguru)	Sepoy, First Grenadier	Balija Naidu	Erode
28. Runga Sammy (Rangasamy)	Sepoy, First Grenadier	Balija Naidu	Tirunelveli
29. Mootoo Caroopen (Muthu Karuppan)	Sepoy, First Grenadier	Pallar	Tiruchi

(Contd)

Table A12.1 (Contd)

Name of Prisoner	Rank, Corps / Company	Caste	Place of Birth / Domicile
30. Ramasamy	Sepoy, First Grenadier	Balija Naidu	Madurai
31. Polly Naidoo	Sepoy, First Grenadier	Balija Naidu	Dindigul
32. Sodalai Mootoo (Sudalai Muthu)	Sepoy, First Grenadier	Pillai	Sankaran Kovil
33. Raman	Sepoy, First Grenadier	Pallar	Thanjavur
34. Candiah (Kanthiah)	Sepoy, First Grenadier	Balija Naidu	Vathlagund
35. Seeny	Sepoy, First Grenadier	Parayar	Tirunelveli
36. Mootoo Samy	Sepoy, First Grenadier	Parayar	Tiruchi
37. Mootoo (Muthu)	Sepoy, First Grenadier	Pallar	Madurai
38. Ramasamy	Havildar, First Grenadier	Balija Naidu	Tiruchi
39. Shaik Hussan Ally (Sheik Hussein Ali)	Naik, First Grenadier	Sheikh	Madurai
40. Permauloo (Perumalu)	Naik, First Grenadier	Pallar	Madurai
41. Bauggyam (Bagyam)	Fifer, First Grenadier	Parayar	Palayamkottai
42. Sungara Lingum (Sanakaralingam)	Sepoy, First Grenadier	Maravar	Madurai
43. Sheik Mullick	Sepoy, First Grenadier	Sheikh	Tirunelveli
44. Permauloo	Sepoy, First Corps	Balija Naidu	Mannar Kovil, Thanjavur
45. Veeraragoo (Veera Raghu)	Sepoy, First Corps	Telugu Jungun	Madurai
46. Chaury Mootoo (Saveri Muthu)	Sepoy, First Corps	Parayar	Dindigul

(Contd)

Table A12.1 (Contd)

Name of Prisoner	Rank, Corps / Company	Caste	Place of Birth / Domicile
47. Shaik Careem (Sheik Karim)	Sepoy, First Corps	Sheikh	Madurai
48. Mootoo	Sepoy, First Corps	Pallar	Samayanallur
49. Peddoo (Pethu)	Sepoy, First Corps	Balija Naidu	Tirunelveli
50. Veerapah	Sepoy, First Corps	Balija Naidu	Kallupatti
51. Mootoo (Muthu)	Sepoy, First Corps	Pallar	Vilangudi, Madurai
52. Rungun (Rangan)	Sepoy, First Corps	Pallar	Thanjavur
53. Veeruppen	Sepoy, First Corps	Agamudayar	Madurai
54. Mootoo	Sepoy, First Corps	Pallar	Thanjavur
55. Sungely Caroopen (Sangli Karuppan)	Sepoy, First Corps	Pillai	Madurai
56. Palany	Sepoy, First Corps	Pillai	Palayamkottai
57. Mootoo Sammy (Muthu)	Sepoy, First Corps	Pillai	Melur, Madurai
58. Moorthy	Sepoy, First Corps	Balija Naidu	Solavandan
59. Arunachalam	Naik, First Corps	Vanniar	Madras
60. Syed Moiden Saib	Naik, First Corps	Syed	Tiruchi
61. Comauren (Kumaran)	Drummer, Second Corps	Parayar	Tirunelveli
62. Allagun (Alagan)	Sepoy, First Corps	Pallar	Ammapatti
63. Veerabadran	Sepoy, First Corps	Agamudayar	Ramanathapuram
64. Narayanan	Sepoy, First Corps	Maravar	Kamanaickanoor

(Contd)

Table A12.1 (Contd)

Name of Prisoner	Rank, Corps / Company	Caste	Place of Birth / Domicile
65. Mootoo Sammy (Muthusamy)	Sepoy, First Corps	Koravar	Kulasekara Mangalam
66. Aurmogum (Arumugam)	Sepoy, First Corps	Pillai	Tirunelveli
67. Soobra Manean (Subramanian)	Sepoy, First Corps	Pillai	Tirunelveli
68. Vellyen (Vellaian)	Sepoy, First Corps	Pillai	Tirunelveli
69. Mootoo Samy (Muthusamy)	Sepoy, First Corps	Pillai	Madurai
70. Allaguppen (Alagappan)	Sepoy, First Corps	Pallar	Madurai
71. Hussein Saib	Sepoy, Third Corps	Sheikh	Krishnagiri
72. Raman	Sepoy, Third Corps	Parayar	Srivilliputhur
73. Veerappan	Sepoy, Third Corps	Pillai	Poovakulam
74. Mootoo (Muthu)	Sepoy, Third Corps	Parayar	Srivilliputhur
75. Mootoo (Muthu)	Sepoy, Third Corps	Parayar	Periyakulam
76. Mooto Sawmy (Muthusamy)	Sepoy, Third Corps	Parayar	Srivilliputhur
77. Caroopen (Karuppan)	Sepoy, Third Corps	Parayar	Tirunelveli
78. Madurai Veeren	Sepoy, Third Corps	Pallar	Solavandan
79. Choken	Sepoy, Third Corps	Pillai	Thanjavur
80. Ali Khan	Sepoy, Third Corps	Pathan	Chidambaram
81. Sheik Ibrahim	Sepoy, Third Grenadier	Lubbai	Ramanathapuram

(Contd)

Table A12.1 (Contd)

Name of Prisoner	Rank, Corps / Company	Caste	Place of Birth / Domicile
82. Bawah Sahib	Sepoy, Third Grenadier	Pathan	Tirunelveli
83. Sankarlingam	Sepoy, Third Grenadier	Naickar	Palayamkottai
84. Mahamed Sherif	Havildar, Fourth Corps	Syed	Tiruchi
85. Aggylandum (Akilandam)	Havildar, Fourth Corps	Chetty	Iyempettai, Thanjavur
86. Abdul Osmaun (Usman)	Naik, Fourth Grenadier	Sheikh	Thanjavur
87. Mootoo (Muthu)	Drummer, Fourth Grenadier	Parayar	Palayamkottai
88. Maigole (Michael)	Fifer, Fourth Grenadier	Parayar	Ramanathapuram
89. Maigole (Michael)	Fifer, Fourth Grenadier	Parayar	Palayamkottai
90. Mootoo Sammy (Muthusamy)	Sepoy, Fourth Grenadier	Balija Naidu	Tirunelveli
91. Shaik Emaum (Sheik Imam)	Sepoy, Fourth Grenadier	Lubbai	Kottur, Tirunelveli
92. Veeraragoo (Veeraragu)	Sepoy, Fourth Grenadier	Balija Naidu	Srivilliputhur
93. Periya Karuppan	Sepoy, Fourth Grenadier	Pallar	Solavandan
94. Mootoo Sammy (Muthusamy)	Sepoy, Fourth Grenadier	Balija Naidu	Tirunelveli
95. Ramasamy	Sepoy, Fourth Grenadier	Balija Naidu	Veeragavanallur
96. Solay	Sepoy, Fourth Grenadier	Parayar	Madurai
97. Ramasamy	Sepoy, Fourth Grenadier	Agamudayar	Ramanathapuram
98. Perumal Naik	Sepoy, Fourth Grenadier	Balija Naidu	Tiruchi

(Contd)

Table A12.1 (Contd)

Name of Prisoner	Rank, Corps / Company	Caste	Place of Birth / Domicile
99. Cunniah (Kanniah)	Sepoy, Fourth Grenadier	Balija Naidu	Madurai
100. Gopauloo (Gopalu)	Sepoy, Fourth Grenadier	Balija Naidu	Senkottai
101. Ramasamy	Sepoy, Fourth Grenadier	Balija Naidu	Sankagiridurg
102. Rama Samy	Sepoy, Fourth Grenadier	Parayar	Kalakadu
103. Cunnavady	Sepoy, Fourth Grenadier	Mutharayar	Thanjavur
104. Peer Mahamed	Sepoy, Fourth Grenadier	Sheikh	Kottur
105. Komaura Sawmy (Kumaraswamy)	Sepoy, Fourth Grenadier	Maravar	Madathur, Tirunelveli
106. Rama Samy	Havildar, Fifth Corps	Balija Naidu	Tiruchi
107. Yaukiah Kahn (Yahiah Khan)	Havildar, Fifth Corps	Pathan	Madurai
108. Nauga Lingum (Nagalingam)	Sepoy, Fifth Corps	Agamudayar	Ramanathapuram
109. Mootoo Veran (Muthu Veeran)	Sepoy, Fifth Corps	Pallar	Dindigul
110. Abdullah Khan	Sepoy, Fifth Corps	Lubbai	Madurai
111. Maugole (Michael)	Sepoy, Fifth Corps	Pallar	Ottankudi, Tiruchi
112. Caunoo Mohomed (Kanu Mohammed)	Sepoy, Fifth Corps	Sheikh	Palayamkottai
113. Rammen (Raman)	Sepoy, Fifth Grenadier	Pallar	Madurai
114. Moodon Naidu (Muthan Naidu)	Sepoy, Fifth Grenadier	Balija Naidu	Tirunelveli
115. Yaguppen (Yagappan)	Sepoy, Fifth Grenadier	Aasaari (Goldsmith)	Palayamkottai

(Contd)

Table A12.1 (Contd)

Name of Prisoner	Rank, Corps / Company	Caste	Place of Birth / Domicile
116. Shaik Emaum (Sheik Imam)	Sepoy, Fifth Grenadier	Sheikh	Tirunelveli
117. Vunna Mootoo (Vanna Muthu)	Naik, Sixth Corps	Pillai	Palayamkottai
118. Permalloo (Perumalu)	Sepoy, Sixth Corps	Balija Naidu	Srivilliputhur
119. Sunjevy (Sanjivi)	Sepoy, Sixth Corps	Parayar	Madurai
120. Mootoo (Muthu)	Sepoy, Sixth Corps	Parayar	Palayamkottai
121. Paupadoo	Sepoy, Sixth Corps	Parayar	Madurai
122. Mootoo Sawmy (Muthusamy)	Sepoy, Sixth Corps	Balija Naidu	Palayamkottai
123. Soobra Manian (Subramanian)	Sepoy, Sixth Corps	Parayar	Tirunelveli
124. Mootoo Caumatchy (Muthu Kamatchy)	Sepoy, Sixth Corps	Agamudayar	Sivagangai
125. Mootoo Sawmy	Sepoy, Sixth Corps	Maravar	Nagalapurum
126. Comara Sawmy (Kumarasam)	Sepoy, Sixth Corps	Maravar	Nagalapurum
127. Mootoo Carpen (Muthu Karuppan)	Sepoy, Sixth Corps	Pillai	Tirupathur, Madurai
128. Mootoo Sawmy (Muthusamy)	Sepoy, Sixth Corps	Maravar	Madathupatti, Tirunelveli
129. Rungapah (Rangappa)	Sepoy, Sixth Corps	Balija Naidu	Karur
130. Permalloo (Perumalu)	Sepoy, Sixth Corps	Vanniar	Madurai
131. Ramasamy	Sepoy, Sixth Corps	Pillai	Nagalapurum
132. Permalloo (Perumalu)	Sepoy, Sixth Corps	Pallar	Ottankudi

(Contd)

Table A12.1 (Contd)

Name of Prisoner	Rank, Corps / Company	Caste	Place of Birth / Domicile
133. Soobra Manian (Subramanian)	Sepoy, Sixth Corps	Pillai	Madurai
134. Shaik Mahomed	Sepoy, Sixth Corps	Sheikh	Cuddalore
135. Curpunnen (Karupannan)	Sepoy, Sixth Corps	Agamudayar	Ramanathapuram
136. Shaik Abdul Cawder	Havildar, Seventh Grenadier	Sheikh	Tiruchi
137. Coopoo Naik (Kuppu Naikar)	Naik, Seventh Grenadier	Balija Naidu	Srivilliputhur
138. Joseph	Fifer, Seventh Grenadier	Parayar	Palayamkottai
139. Ramasamy	Sepoy, Seventh Grenadier	Maravar	Ramanathapuram
140. Jagananden (Jeganandan)	Sepoy, Seventh Grenadier	Parayar	Thanjavur
141. Sunthoshy (Santhoshi)	Sepoy, Seventh Grenadier	Parayar	Madurai
142. Parennen (Periannan)	Sepoy, Seventh Grenadier	Pallar	Anupanadi, Madurai
143. Ramasamy	Sepoy, Seventh Grenadier	Balija Naidu	Solavandan
144. Mootoo Samy (Muthusamy)	Sepoy, Seventh Grenadier	Balija Naidu	Tirunelveli
145. Singappah Naik	Sepoy, Seventh Grenadier	Balija Naidu	Edayankottai, Dindigul
146. Veerappen	Sepoy, Seventh Grenadier	Pallar	Thanjavur
147. Cylausem (Kailasam)	Sepoy, Seventh Grenadier	Pillai	Pudur, Tirunelveli
148. Baurah Saib	Sepoy, Seventh Grenadier	Lubbai	Madurai
149. Shaik Hussain	Sepoy, Seventh Grenadier	Sheikh	Palghat

(Contd)

Table A12.1 (Contd)

Name of Prisoner	Rank, Corps / Company	Caste	Place of Birth / Domicile
150. Permalloo (Perumalu)	Trumpeter, Seventh Grenadier	Parayar	Kalakadu
151. Palanyady (Palaniyandi)	Naik, Eighth Corps Grenadier	Pillai	Thanjavur
152. Letch Manen	Sepoy, Eighth Corps Grenadier	Pillai	Thenkanji
153. Vellien (Vellayan)	Sepoy, Eighth Corps Grenadier	Pillai	Tirunelveli
154. Ramasamy	Sepoy, Eighth Corps Grenadier	Balija Naidu	Madurai
155. Mootiah (Muthiah)	Sepoy, Eighth Corps Grenadier	Pillai	Thanjavur
156. Mootoo Sawmy (Muthusamy)	Sepoy, Eighth Corps Grenadier	Pillai	Pudur
157. Maunica Vausagum (Manikka Vasagam)	Sepoy, Eighth Corps Grenadier	Pillai	Senkottai
158. Motoo Sawmy	Sepoy, Eighth Corps Grenadier	Agamudayar	Thanjavur
159. Abdul Cauder (Khadar)	Havildar, Eighth Corps Grenadier	Sheikh	
160. Rungiah (Rangiah)	Sepoy, Eighth Corps Grenadier	Balija Naidu	Srivilliputhur
161. Ramasamy	Sepoy, Eighth Corps Grenadier	Balija Naidu	Srivilliputhur
162. Cooroou Apen (Kuruvappan)	Sepoy, Eighth Corps Grenadier	Balija Naidu	Srivilliputhur
163. Cundun (Kanthan)	Sepoy, Light Grenadier	Parayar	Madurai
164. Shaik Abdul	Sepoy, Light Grenadier	Sheikh	Salem
165. Shaik Meyam	Sepoy, Light Grenadier	Sheikh	Kalakadu
166. Vencata Sawmy (Venkatasamy)	Sepoy, Light Grenadier	Balija Naidu	Karur

(Contd)

Table A12.1 (Contd)

Name of Prisoner	Rank, Corps / Company	Caste	Place of Birth / Domicile
167. Mootooloo (Muthulu)	Sepoy, Light Grenadier	Balija Naidu	Karur
168. Mootoo Sawmy (Muthusamy)	Sepoy, Light Grenadier	Maravar	Tirunelveli.
169. Ramasawmy	Sepoy, Light Grenadier	Edayar	Madurai
170. Sheik Hussein	Sepoy, Light Grenadier	Sheikh	Tiruchi
171. Comawarvale (Kumaravel)	Sepoy, Light Grenadier	Pillai	Dindigul
172. Syed Mahomed	Sepoy, Light Grenadier	Syed	Madurai

Note: This list was prepared by R. Barclay, town major, Fort St George, and sent to the governor-in-council on 9 November 1807. Here, we get a caste-wise representation of the Vellore Revolt of 10 July 1806. The presence of Parayars, nearly equal to the number of Pillais (Saiva Vellalars), is striking. They, 27 in number, together with 17 Pallars, seem to have constituted the largest contingent that participated in the revolt. Land-owning communities like the Tirunelveli Saiva Vellalars and Balija Naidus forming a major part of the native army (28 and 38 from this list alone) is surprising and is illustrative of the acute agrarian distress in the region that forced them to opt for a military career. There is also a significant presence of the Mukulathor people in this list of prisoners (16), with the Agamudayars outnumbering the other two, the Kallars and Maravars.

Source: *Secret Department Sundries*, vol. 11, 1628–1705.

APPENDIX 13

TABLE A13.1 Madras domiciled soldiers detained in Madras for trial

Name	Age	Caste / Religion
Ramsamy	44	Hindu
Syed Imam	29	Muslim
Jandriah	30	Barber
Ramasamy	28	Hindu
Muthiah	29	Parayar
Sheik Ibrahim	26	Muslim
Sunjeve (Sanjivi)	32	Parayar
Narroo (Naaru)	30	Hindu
Ramah	27	Parayar
Narrain	20	Parayar
Futty Khan (Fateh Khan)	35	Muslim
Adeemkhan	27	Muslim
Mukundoo	27	Malabar (Tamil)
Ramasamy	20	Parayar
Ramasamy	20	Malabar (Tamil)
Sheik Imam	22	Muslim
Mohammed Sahib	18	Muslim
Fateh Mahomed	35	Muslim
Mustapha Khan	27	Muslim
Chinnatambi	30	Parayar
Kasturi	30	Parayar
Muniappa	24	Malabar

(Contd)

Table A13.1 (Contd)

Name	Age	Caste / Religion
Madar Khan	18	Muslim
Kistnamah	30	Muslim
Shaik Madar	30	Muslim
Punjumsing	26	Rajput
Muthu	28	Parayar
Sheik Ali	25	Muslim
Mahomed Hussein	27	Muslim
Sheik Booden	30	Muslim
Nadeem Sahib	25	Muslim
Shaek Yusuf	23	Muslim
Darmadass	17	Rajput
Savarimuthu	25	Parayar
Sheik Dawood	18	Muslim

Note: Strikingly, as in Appendix 12, Parayars are in large numbers (9). Upper caste Tamils are referred to as Hindus, whereas other Tamils of intermediate castes are listed as Malabar (Tamil). Together with Malabars and Rajputs, they are 8 in number. The number of Muslims is 17. The remaining one person belonged to the barber caste.

Source: *Secret Department Sundries*, vol. 12, 32–39.

Appendix 14

Colonel Gillespie's second detailed letter to the commander-in-chief after the retake of the Fort

My Lord,

The fort has remained all night perfectly tranquil, and I am this morning unable to enter into a more detailed account of the transactions which took place here yesterday. On the approach of the advance of my party a great number of the insurgents retired to the south and west ramparts leaving the gateway and one of the cavalries to the north of it in possession of the gallant remains of His Majesty's 69th Regiment who continued to defend themselves with much resolution although, when the advance arrived at the gateway their last round of ammunition was expended.

This position of the 69th left my party but little exposed as it approached and enabled us to dash up at once to the second gateway, which, as stated in my dispatch of yesterday, was opened by some of the 69th who let themselves down from the top of the wall by ropes.

We found on coming up close to the fourth or inner gate, by the repeated discharges of musquetry against it, that the road leading to it was commanded by the mutineers, and having lost several men in attempting to break the lock, I resolved to wait the arrival of the guns of the 19th in order to blow it open.

In the meantime, in order to encourage the brave fellows above the gateway, and who having no ammunition had to trust entirely to the bayonet, I deemed it proper, there being no officer with them, to head them in the charge I intended to make in concert with the cavalry. Accordingly, I ascended the wall by a rope and immediately employed the men in turning the guns on the adjacent battery towards the palace. Whilst thus occupied, the gallopers came up and prevented me from executing a resolution I had just formed of attacking the arsenal when they were very strong with the bayonet. I deem it a fortunate circumstance that I was not reduced to this expedient, which, however necessary for the purpose of obtaining ammunition, would undoubtedly have been attended with considerable loss. I instantly on the arrival of the guns ordered Mr. Blackiston, from whom I have received every support, to proceed in blowing open the gate – my order was most promptly and effectually obeyed and at the first discharge of both guns the gate flew wide open.

During this operation I desired the ramparts with the 69th and with the bayonet alone dispersed the sepoys, who were formed in every direction, in order to clear the way for the charge of a squadron of the Majesty's 19th Dragoons who, ably supported by native cavalry, advanced at full speed into the body of the place headed by Captain Killon, 19th Dragoons. At this moment the enemy kept up an incessant fire and I have to regret the loss of many of the 69th who were destroyed by it. I soon found myself, gallantly and ably supported by the main body of the cavalry under Lieutenant Colonel Kennedy aided by Captain Mason, commanding the details and Captain Doveton commanding the 7th native cavalry. The enemy soon broke and were pursued and cut up in all directions. In about a quarter of an hour the Fort was entirely in our possession.

I cannot omit mentioning in this place how much I feel enabled to the exertions of Captain Young commanding a squadron of His Majesty's 19th Dragoons and to Lieutenant Woodhouse who aided him with a party of the 7th regiment native cavalry. Captain Young had been most actively employed by me all the morning and those two officers acquitted themselves highly to my satisfaction in cutting off the fugitives who were making their escape at the sally port on the south side of the Fort on getting possession of the Fort. I found Lieutenant Colonel Marriott, to whom I gave the most decided orders for securing the princes and posted strong guards over them. I have great satisfaction in informing Your Lordship that none of them have made their escape and they are now in safe custody as I have strong reason for supposing that if not the instigators they were at least abettors of this infernal plot.

Moiz-Ud-Deen in particular, the third son, actually sent his own flag to the insurgents and it was hoisted for several hours on the garrison flagstaff. It is peculiarly gratifying to me to have secured the person of the princes, as Your Lordship is well aware of the destructive consequences which in all probability would have attended their effecting an escape at such a juncture. Ever since the final reduction of the Fort, we have been most busily and incessantly employed in refitting the store and repairing the dooms of the magazine, which were all broke open, and in short in putting the place into the best possible state that circumstance will admit. The whole weight of these exertions has fallen upon the troops, for we have neither lascars, coolies nor public followers to adjust, as most of the inhabitants of the Pettah having fled through fear and the heads of every public department being all destroyed. We are, in consequence, much fatigued and are anxiously awaiting the arrival of a regular garrison.

Lieutenant Colonel Forbes commanding the 1st battalion 1st regiment, whose corps appear not to have been generally disaffected, after making several, vain efforts to get into the Fort early in the morning, very judiciously collected as many of his men as he could and took possession of the target hill fort. His men, having slept in the Pettah, were without arms, but being reinforced by about thirty Europeans who made their escape from the Fort, he resolved to maintain to the last a post that would have been of the greatest consequence had we not happily succeeded in our Camp-de-main. Lieutenant Colonel Forbes was relieved in the evening of the 10th and has been since of the greatest service to me from his local experience and general information.

At this moment a committee are assembled for the purpose of examining most minutely into every circumstance of this most diabolical combination. I have good reason to hope that from the distinct and clear evidence of several native officers, I shall be enabled to trace the whole business to its origin. I shall not fail to make a progressive report on this head to Your Lordship daily.

I should be very remiss in my duty if I have omitted to express how much assistance and ready obedience to my orders I have uniformly found throughout the whole of the officers in every department under my command. I beg leave to recommend in the most particular manner to Your Lordship's notice as highly worthy of reward Sergeant Brady of His Majesty's 69th regiment by whose increasing exertion and genuine bravery the remains of that corps were kept together without an officer and continuance to make the most determined resistance till my arrival – In our sally from the ramparts, this man, My Lord, behaved in the most gallant manner and has since been uncommonly useful in preventing all access on the part of his men to the various liquors thrown in their way.

Vellore   By
July 11, 1806   **Gillespie, Colonel**

Source: Secret Consultations, vol. 19, 830–38.

Content of Marudhu Pandian's Proclamation, 1801

His Highness the Nawab Mahemed Ally Cawn (Mohammed Ali Khan) having foolishly given the Europeans place amongst you, is become like a widow. The Europeans violating their faith have deceitfully made the kingdom of their own, and considering the inhabitants as Dogs accordingly exercise authority over them, there existing no unity of friendship among you the above casts, who not aware of the duplicity of these Europeans, not only calumniated each other, but have absolutely surrendered the kingdom to them. In these countries now governed by these low wretches, the habitants are become poor, and the rice become vellam and although they manifestly suffer, they are still without understanding to discern it. It is certain that a man must die although he may live a thousand years, and it is as certain that his fame will survive him as long as the sun and the moon; therefore it is desired and determined that in future each shall enjoy his hereditary rights viz Arcot Subah, His Highness the Nabob, Carnatic Vesyuhkommarah [Visvakumara], the son of Vesvanatha naik, and their offspring, Tanjore, the first place, all to be given to their rightful sovereigns without any violation of faith and national customs. Then we shall enjoy, as in the service of the Nabob, constant happiness without tears, as the authority of the Europeans will be destroyed. It is therefore recommended that every man in his place and pallam fly to arms and unite together in order to make even the name of low wretches cease. Then all the poor and needy will get sustenance; but should there be any who, like Dogs, enjoy their ease, and obey the Commands of these low wretches such should be cut off to the foetus in the womb, as all know with what subtlety these low wretches, always in unity with each other, have subdued this country. Therefore, you Birmahs, Chitterahs, Soodras and Mussalmen all who whiskers whether civil or military serving in the field or elsewhere, and you subedars, jemedars, havildars, naigues and sepoys in the service of the low wretches and all capable of bearing arms, let them in the first instance display their bravery, that is to say, wherever you find any of the low wretches destroy them-whoever serves the low wretches will never enjoy eternal bliss after death.

Know this, consider and deliberate on it and he who does not subscribe to this; may his whisker be like the hair of my secret part and his food be tasteless without nourishment and may his wife and children belong to another and be considered as the offspring of the low wretches to whom he has prostituted her. Therefore all whose blood is not contaminated by Europeans will begin to unite, whoever reads this or hears of its contents let him make it as public as possible, by writing it and sending it to his friends who in like manner must publish it to theirs. Everyone who shall not write it and circulate it, as before mentioned, let him be held as guilty of the enormous crime of having killed a Black cow on the banks of the Ganges and suffer all the various punishments of Hell. The Mussalman who does not conform to this, let him be considered having (eat) drank the blood of a pig.

Whoever takes this of the wall where it is posted, let him he held as guilty of five greatest sins. Let everyone read and take a copy of this address.

This Maroodah Paundayan, the servant of the Great Rajahs, but the implacable enemy of the European low wretches.

To all living at Sereengam (Srirangam), the priests and great people, Muroodah Pandayan prostrates himself at their feet. The sovereigns of the south made and kept forts and bastions, churches and chapals, the above great Rajahs' descendants polygars and other Rajahs and people, by the injustice of the low wretches are now reduced to poverty.

To great a people as you are reduced to this state, grant me your blessing.

Maroodah Paundayan

Source: National Archives, Scotland, file no. GD51/3/129.

BIBLIOGRAPHY

PRIMARY SOURCES

Tamil Nadu Archives, Chennai

Military Department

Military Department Consultation (1806 and 1807), vols 354–64.
Military Department Miscellaneous (1806 and 1807), vols 75–77.
Military Department Despatches to England (1806 and 1807), vols 37–40.
Military Department Despatches from England (1806) vols 32–34.

Secret Department

Secret Department Sundries (1806 and 1807), 12 vols.
Secret Department Consultation (1806 and 1807), vols 13–25.

Political Department

Political Department Consultation (1806 and 1807), vols 23–26.

Public Department

Public Department Consultation (1806 and 1807), vols 306–35.

Judicial Department

Judicial Department Consultation (1806 and 1807), vols 17–21.

Revenue Department

Revenue Department Consultation (1806), vols 150–53.
Board of Revenue Proceedings (1806), vols 428–30.
Guide to the Records of North Arcot District (1806), vol. 39.

National Records of Scotland & National Library of Scotland, Edinburgh

An Account of the Origin, Progress and Consequences of the Late Discontents of the Army of the Madras Establishment. London: Cadell & Davies, 1810.

Captain Homes to the Court of Directors. Memorial, contains memorandum on the causes of mutiny of the sepoys at Vellore, ref. GD51/3/429.

Colonel James Brunton. Letters (copies), connected with the Vellore disturbance and its causes. 28 June 1806, ref. FD1/1153/3(2).

Colonel John Malcolm to Robert Dundas. Memorandum, on the native army of Madras. ref. GD363/1/1195.

Major J. Buchan to his Father. Letter (copy), regarding outbreak of mutiny amongst sepoys at Palamcottah and stating that General Maitland was not on cordial terms with the Madras government. Colombo, 20 November 1806.

Major Joseph Haslewood to Hall Plumer. Letter (copy), as to origin and causes of the mutiny of the Madras sepoys at Vellore. Madras, 2 March 1807, ref. GD51/3/432.

Marudhu Pandian. Address. 1807, ref. GD51/3/129.

Sir George Barlow. Minutes, on the mutiny of officers of the company army at Madras. 14 August 1806, ref. GD51/3/432.

Sir John Anstruther to Robert Dundas. Letter, commenting on state of the government in India, with an enclosed extract of a letter from Madras on the causes and circumstances surrounding the mutiny of sepoys at Vellore. London, April 1807, ref. GD51/3/434/1–2.

Unknown author. Letter, extract enclosed in a communiqué sent to Robert Dundas. 20 October 1806, ref. GD51/3/434/1–2.

William Currie to unknown recipient. Letter. 17 September 1806, ref. GDI/1153/3(2).

India Office Library / British Library, London

Home Miscellaneous Series, vols 504–10.
Madras Secret Proceedings (1806–09).
Madras Political Proceedings (1806–09).
Papers relating to East India Affairs (1805–07).
Lord William Bentinck Papers (1803–07), Portland Collection.
Minto Papers, MSS 11322, 11328 and 11338.

Agnew, P. A. *Letter to the Honourable Court of Directors of the East India Company.* 1808, ref. W 2430(b).
An Account of the Origin, Progress, and Consequences of the Late Discontents of the Army of the Madras Establishment. 1810.
Bentinck, William. *Memorial Addressed to the Honourable Court of Directors Containing an Account of the Mutiny at Vellore.* 7 February 1809, ref. 9055 h5 in V8872.
Call, John. View of the Forts on the Hills of Veloor as Seen from the Pettah. Arcot Fort, 1778, ref. 850.1.17.
Description of Vellore Fort, the Pettahs, the Hills and the Attacks Carried on by the English Army under the Command of John Caillaud.
Documents Connected with the Case of Colonel P. A. Agnew. 1808.
Letters from Indophilus to the editor of the newspaper, *Bengal Hurkara. Mutiny of Vellore: Its Parallelisms and Its Lessons.* 1857.
Pierce, Frederick. Letter to the Honourable Court of Directors of the East India Company. 1808, ref. W 2430(c).

SECONDARY SOURCES

Aiyangar, Krishnaswami, S. *South India and Her Muhammadan Invaders.* Madras: University of Madras, 1921.
Aiyar, Kumaraswami T. S. *Velapuri, or A Peep into the Past of Vellore.* Vellore: V. N. Press, 1900.
Ali, A. Yusuf. *The Making of India.* London: A & C Black, 1925.
Anonymous. *Memorandum of the Fort of Vellore and Others in its Neighbourhood as Recorded in 1815.*
Bayly, C. A. *The New Cambridge History of India: India's Society and the Making of the British Empire.* New Delhi: Orient Longman, 1988.
——. *Imperial Meridian: The British Empire and the World, 1780–1830.* London: Longman, 1989.

Bayly, Susan. *Caste, Society, and Politics in India from the Eighteenth Century to the Modern Age.* Cambridge: Cambridge University Press, 2001.

Berger, Theodore Mark. *From Commerce to Conquest: The Dynamics of Early British Imperial Expansion into Bengal.* Vancouver: University of British Colombia, 1983.

Bhatia, H. S., ed. *Military History of British India, 1607–1947.* New Delhi: Deep & Deep Publications, 1977.

Blakiston, John. *Twelve Years' Military Adventure,* 2 vols. London: Henry Colburn, 1829.

Boulger, Demetrius C. *Lord William Bentinck* (Rulers of India), ed. W. W. Hunter. Oxford: Clarendon Press, 1897.

Buchanan, Francis. *A Journey from Madras Through the Countries of Mysore, Canara and Malabar,* vol. 3. New Delhi: Asian Educational Services, 1988. First published 1807 by T. Cadell & W. Davies (London).

Butler, William Francis. *A Narrative of the Historical Events Connected with the Sixty-Ninth Regiment.* London: W. Mitchell, 1870.

Callahan, Raymond. *The East India Company and Army Reform, 1783–1798.* Cambridge: Harvard University Press, 1972.

Cameron, A. D. 'The Vellore Mutiny'. PhD thesis, University of Edinburgh, 1984.

Cardew, Alexander. *The White Mutiny: A Forgotten Episode in the History of the Indian Army.* London: Constable, 1929.

Carson, Penelope. *The East India Company and Religion, 1698–1858.* Woodbridge: The Boydell Press, 2012.

Chatterjee, Partha. *The Black Hole of Empire: History of a Global Practice of Power.* Princeton: Princeton University Press, 2012.

Chaudhuri, Haripado. 'The Vellore Mutiny: A Reappraisal'. *Modern Review* 98 (August 1955): 125–28.

Chaudhuri, K. N. *The English East India Company: The Study of an Early Joint-Stock Company, 1600–1640.* London: Frank Cass, 1965.

——, ed. *The Economic Development of India under the East India Company, 1814–58.* Cambridge: Cambridge University Press, 1971.

Chick, N. A., comp., and David Hutchinson, ed. *Annals of the Indian Rebellion, 1857–58.* London: Charles Knight, 1974.

Chinnayan, P. *The Vellore Mutiny, 1806.* Madras: 1982.

Cohen, Stephen P. *The Indian Army: Its Contribution to the Development of a Nation.* Berkeley: University of California Press, 1971.

Cox, Arthur F. *A Manual of the North Arcot District in the Presidency of Madras*. Madras: Government Press, 1881.

Dasgupta, Sabyasachi. *In Defence of Honour and Justice: Sepoy Rebellions in the Nineteenth Century*. Delhi: Primus Books, 2015.

Dirks, Nicholas B. *Castes of Mind: Colonialism and the Making of Modern India*. New Delhi: Permanent Black, 2002.

Dodwell, H. H. *Report on the Madras Records, 1670–1856*. Madras: Government Press, 1934.

———, ed. *The Cambridge History of India*, vol. 5. New Delhi: S. Chand, 1963. First published 1929 by Cambridge University Press (Cambridge).

Dow, Alexander. *The History of Hindostan*, vol. 1. London: J. Walker, 1812. First published 1772 by T. Becket and P. A. de Hondt (London).

Dutta, Manas. 'The Army as a Tool for Social Uplift: The Experience of the Paraiyans in the Madras Presidency Army, 1770–1895'. *Social Scientist* 44, no. 3/4 (March–April 2016): 57–71.

Embree, Ainslee T., ed. *1857 in India: Mutiny or War of Independence?* (Problems in Asian Civilisations). Boston: D. C. Heath, 1963.

English, Barbara. *John Company's Last War*. London: Collins, 1971.

Firminger, W. K., ed. *Affairs of the East India Company*, 3 vols. Delhi: Neeraj Publishing House, 1985. First published 1812 by R. Cambray (Calcutta).

Fisher, Michael H. *Indirect Rule in India: Residents and the Residency System, 1764–1857*. Delhi: Oxford University Press, 1991.

Francis, W. *Gazetteer of South India*. New Delhi: Mittal Publications, 1988.

Forrest, Denys. *Tiger of Mysore: The Life and Death of Tipu Sultan*. Bombay: Allied Publishers, 1970.

Frykenberg, R. E. 'New Light on the Vellore Mutiny'. In *East India Company Studies: Papers Presented to Professor Sir Cyril Philips*, ed. Kenneth Ballhatchet and John Harrison, 207–31. Hong Kong: Asian Research Service, 1986.

Furnell, S. S. *The Mutiny of Vellore*. Publication details not available at the Tamil Nadu Archives. According to A. D. Cameron, it was published in Madras in 1840. Only thirty-five pages are available.

Gleig, G. R. *The Life of Major-General Sir Thomas Munro*, vol. 1. London: Henry Colburn & Richard Bentley, 1830.

Gupta, Maya, 'Vellore Mutiny, July 1806'. In *Defying Death: Struggles Against Imperialism and Feudalism*, ed. Maya Gupta and Amit Kumar Gupta, 18–38. New Delhi: Tulika, 2001.

Hamilton, Walter. *The East-India Gazetteer*, vol. 2. London: W. H. Allen, 1828.

Heathcote, T. A. *The Military in British India: The Development of British Land Forces in South Asia, 1600–1947*. Manchester: Manchester University Press, 1995.

Heideman, Eugene P. *From Mission to Church: The Reformed Church in America Mission to India*. Grand Rapids, MI: Wm. B. Eerdmans Publishing, 2001.

Hobsbawm, Eric J. *Nations and Nationalism since 1780: Programme, Myth, Reality*, 2nd ed. Cambridge: Cambridge University Press, 1997.

Holland, William L., ed. *Asian Nationalism and the West*. New York: Macmillan, 1952.

Hoover, James W. *Men Without Hats: Dialogue, Discipline and Discontent in the Madras Army, 1806–1807*. New Delhi: Manohar, 2007.

Kaye, John William. *The Administration of the East India Company: A History of Indian Progress*. London: R. Bentley, 1853.

_____. *Christianity in India: A Historical Narrative*. London: Smith, Elder, 1859.

_____. *Lives of Indian Officers*, vol. 1. London: A. Strahan, 1867.

_____. *The Sepoy Army in India*, vol. 2. London: W. H. Allen, 1880.

_____. *A History of the Sepoy War in India, 1857–1858*. London: W. H. Allen, 1881.

Kaye, John William. *History of the Indian Mutiny of 1857–8*, vol. 1, ed. G. B. Malleson. London: Longmans, Green, 1914.

Keene, H. G. *History of India: From the Earliest Times to the End of the Nineteenth Century*, vol. 1. Edinburgh: John Grant, 1906.

Khan, Shafaat Ahmad. *The East India in the XVIIth Century: In its Political and Economic Aspects*. London: Oxford University Press, 1923.

Kincaid, Dennis. *British Social Life in India, 1608–1937*. 2nd ed. London: Routledge & Kegan Paul, 1973.

Kirby, Charles F. *The Adventures of an Arcot Rupee*, 2 vols. London: Saunders, Otley, 1867.

Lawson, Philip. *The East India Company: A History*. London: Longman, 1993.

Maclean, C. D. *Manual of the Administration of the Madras Presidency*, vol. 3. New Delhi: Asian Educational Services, 1982. First published 1893 by Government Press (Madras).

Majumdar, R. C., ed. *History and Culture of the Indian People*, vol. 9. Bombay: Bharatiya Vidya Bhavan, 1963.

Malcolm, John. *The Political History of British India*. Delhi: Discovery Publishing House, 1986. First published in 1811.

Mani, R. *History of Vellore Fort*. Vellore: Poongavanam Ramasamy Illam, 2004.

Marshman, John Clark. *The History of India: From Earliest Period to the Close of Lord Dalhousie's Administration*, vol. 2. London: Longmans, Green, Reader & Dyer, 1867.

Mason, Philip. *A Matter of Honour: An Account of the Indian Army, its Officers and Men*. London: Ebenezer Baylis & Son, 1974.

———. *The Men Who Ruled India*. New Delhi: Rupa, 1974.

Menezes, S. L. *Fidelity and Honour: The Indian Army from the Seventeenth to the Twenty First Century*. New Delhi: Oxford University Press, 1999.

Mill, James and H. H. Wilson. *The History of British India, from 1805 to 1835*, vol. 7. London: James Madden, 1840.

Moodley, Devadas. 'Vellore 1806: The Meanings of Mutiny'. Paper presented at a seminar at Ohio University, 1998.

———. 'Vellore 1806: The Meanings of Mutiny'. In *Rebellion, Repression, Reinvention: Mutiny in Comparative Perspective*, ed. Jane Hathaway, 87–102. Westport, CT: Praeger, 2001.

Mount, Ferdinand. *The Tears of the Rajas: Mutiny, Money and Marriage in India, 1805–1905*. London: Simon & Schuster, 2015.

Mukherjee, Sipra. *Indian Administration of Lord William Bentinck*. Calcutta: K. P. Bagchi, 1994.

Nair, Janaki. 'Tipu Sultan, History Painting and the Battle for "Perspective"'. *Studies in History* 22, no.1 (February 2006): 97–143.

Neill, Stephen. *A History of Christianity in India, 1707–1858*. Cambridge: Cambridge University Press, 2002.

O'Malley, L. S. S., ed. *Modern India and the West: A Study of the Interaction of their Civilisation*. London: Oxford University Press, 1968.

Oswell, G. D. *Sketches of Rulers of India: The Company's Governors*, vols 2–3. Oxford: Clarendon Press, 1908.

Pakkianathan, Samuelraj. 'The Mutiny at Vellore and Related Agitations, 1806–1807'. PhD thesis, University of Saskatchewan, 1971.

Philips, C. H. *East India Company, 1784–1834*. Manchester: Manchester University Press, 1940.

Phythian-Adams, E. G. *The Madras Soldier, 1746–1946*. Madras: Government Press, 1948.

Pillay, K. K. 'The Causes of the Vellore Mutiny'. *Proceedings of the Indian History Congress* 20 (1957): 306–311.

Raghavaiyangar, S. Srinivasa. *Memorandum on the Progress of the Madras Presidency during the Last Forty Years of British Administration.* Madras: Government Press, 1893.

Rajayyan, K. *South Indian Rebellion: The First War of Independence 1800–1801.* Mysore: Rao & Raghavan, 1971.

———. *History of Madurai, 1736–1801.* Madurai: Madurai University, 1974.

Raju, A. Sarada. *Economic Conditions in the Madras Presidency, 1800–1850.* Madras: University of Madras, 1941.

Ramachandran, C. *East India Company and South Indian Economy.* Madras: New Era Publications, 1980.

Reddy, D. Subramanyam. 'The Ryotwari Land Revenue Settlements and Peasant Resistance in the "Northern Division of Arcot" of the Madras Presidency during Early British Rule'. *Social Scientist* 16, no. 6/7 (1988): 35–50.

Regani, Sarojini. *Nizam-British Relations, 1724–1857.* New Delhi: Concept Publishing, 1988.

Rosselli, John. *Lord William Bentinck: The Making of a Liberal Imperialist, 1774–1839.* Berkeley: University of California Press, 1974.

Roy, Kaushik, ed. *War and Society in Colonial India, 1807–1945.* New Delhi: Oxford University Press, 2006.

Roy, Tapti. *Sepoy Mutiny and the Uprising of 1857 in Bundelkhand.* Calcutta: Centre for Studies in Social Sciences, 1991.

———. *The Politics of Popular Uprising: Bundelkhand in 1857.* Delhi: Oxford University Press, 1994.

Russell, William Howard. *My Indian Mutiny Diary*, ed. Michael Edwardes. London: Cassell, 1957.

Sanjeevi, N. *Velur Puratchi* [Tamil]. Chennai: Parry Nilayam, 1956.

Saravanan, K. *Vellore Fort: Historical Significance and Architectural Marvel* [Tamil]. Vellore: Department of Museums, 2005.

Sathianathaier, R. *A Political and Cultural History of India*, vol. 1. Madras: S. Viswanathan, 1972.

Sen, Surendra Nath. *Eighteen Fifty-seven.* Calcutta: Publications Division, Government of India, 1957.

Seshadri, A. K. *Vellore Fort and the Temple through the Ages.* Vellore: Sri Jalakandeswarar Dharma Sthapanam, 2006.

Sinha, R. M., and A. Avasthi, eds. *Elphinstone Correspondence, 1804–1808.* Nagpur: Nagpur University Historical Society, 1961.

Smith, Adam. *An Inquiry into the Nature and Causes of the Wealth of Nations.* London: T. Nelson & Sons, 1852.

Srinivasachari, C. S. *A History of Gingee and its Rulers*. Annamalainagar: Annamalai University, 1943.

———. 'The Vellore Mutiny of 1806: A New Study of Its Origin.' *Proceedings of the Indian History Congress* 11 (1948).

Stein, Burton. *Thomas Munro: The Origins of the Colonial State and His Vision of Empire*. New York: Oxford University Press, 1989.

———. *A History of India*. New Delhi: Oxford University Press, 2004.

Stokes, Eric and C. A. Bayly, eds. *The Peasant Armed: The Indian Revolt of 1857*. Oxford: Clarendon Press, 1986.

Thorn, William. *A Memoir of Major-General Sir R. R. Gillespie*. London: T. Egerton, 1816.

Vibart, Henry Meredith. *The Military History of the Madras Engineers and Pioneers, from 1743 up to the Present Time*, vol. 1. London: W. H. Allen, 1881.

Welsh, James. *A Memorial Addressed to the Court of Directors of the Honorable the East India Company*. London: Smith, Elder, 1830.

———. *Military Reminiscences*, 2 vols. London: Smith, Elder, 1830.

Wilks, Mark. *History of Mysore*, 2 vols. New Delhi: Asian Educational Services, 1989.

Wilson, W. J. *History of the Madras Army*, vol. 3. Madras: Government Press, 1882.

Wright, Julia M. *Ireland, India and Nationalism in Nineteenth-Century Literature*. Cambridge: Cambridge University Press, 2007.

INDEX